New Perspectives on the Rock Art and Prehistoric Settlement Organization of Tumamoc Hill, Tucson, Arizona

edited by
Gayle Harrison Hartmann
and
Peter C. Boyle

contributions by
Suzanne K. Fish
Paul R. Fish
Todd Pitezel
Gary Christopherson
James T. Watson
Phillip O. Leckman
Janine Hernbrode
Katherine M. Cerino
John Fountain

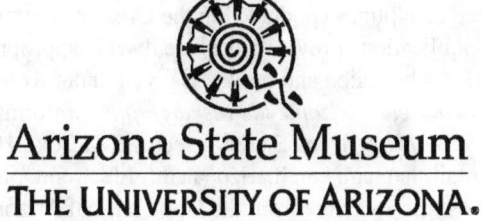

Arizona State Museum
THE UNIVERSITY OF ARIZONA.

<figure>In Collaboration with the
Arizona Archaeological and Historical Society
Tucson

Arizona State Museum Archaeological Series 208</figure>

Arizona State Museum
The University of Arizona
Tucson, Arizona 85721-0026

ISBN (paper): 978-1-889747-93-4
Library of Congress Control Number: 2013949950

ARIZONA STATE MUSEUM ARCHAEOLOGICAL SERIES

General Editor: Richard C. Lange
Technical Editor: Alicia M. Vega

The *Archaeological Series* of the Arizona State Museum, The University of Arizona, publishes the results of research in archaeology and related disciplines conducted in the Greater Southwest. Original, monograph-length manuscripts are considered for publication, provided they deal with appropriate subject matter. Information regarding procedures on manuscript submission and review is given under Research Publications on the Arizona State Museum website: *www.statemuseum.arizona.edu/research/pubs*. Information may be also obtained from the General Editor, *Archaeological Series*, Arizona State Museum, P.O. Box 210026, The University of Arizona, Tucson, Arizona, 85721-0026; Email: langer@email.arizona.edu. Electronic publications and previous volumes in the Arizona State Museum Library or available from the University of Arizona Press are listed on the website noted above. Print-on-demand versions of the latest Arizona State Museum Archaeological Series may be obtained from several booksellers on-line.

Publication of this report was financed by the Arizona Archaeological and Historical Society; we are most grateful for their support.

Cover: Curvilinear abstract (TH-F4349) that may belong to the Western Archaic Tradition (Figure II.21c)
Back: Top, Cienega phase floor plan of community structure (Figure I.5, top). Bottom, Glyph at summer solstice (Figure III.7, right).

Contents

Figures

Tables

Preface

Tumamoc Hill, the prominent, flat-topped, black volcanic hill just west of the Santa Cruz River near downtown Tucson, Arizona, has been revealing its secrets for decades. This hill, the most prominent of the *cerros de trincheras* in the Tucson Basin, continues to teach us about the long temporal range and complexity of prehistoric life in the Tucson area. A *cerro de trincheras* is generally defined as a hill with linear stone walls, usually near the summit, as well as other stone features such as bedrock mortars, stone-ringed structures, trails, and frequently rock art. The three papers published here present new data on Cienega-phase and Tortolita-phase village organization in a hilltop community, the universe of rock art found on the hill, and petroglyphs that seem likely to be functioning as solar markers. The research on which the first paper is based began in the 1980s and continued through the excavation of the community structure in 2008. The rock art recording effort was conducted between 2006 and 2009. The solar marker research grew out of the rock art recording project.

More specifically, research was conducted on the hill by University of Arizona Archaeological Field Schools in 1999, 2004, 2005, 2006, and 2007. The field schools were directed by Paul R. Fish, Suzanne K. Fish, and Gary Christopherson as a joint effort of the School of Anthropology, Arizona State Museum, and Center for Applied Spatial Technology. Arizona Antiquities Permit 1999-80ps to Paul Fish, Suzanne Fish, and Gary Christopherson covered the field school research and the Arizona Archaeological and Historical Society rock art recording project.

The preparation of a management plan and a National Register nomination was under the direction of John Madsen, Arizona State Museum, and Susan Bartlett, University of Arizona Facilities Management, and was funded by a grant from the Arizona Lottery administered by the Arizona Parks Board. Field school mapping in 2006 and 2007 was supported in part by this grant. The maps that resulted from the field school research and the rock art recording project were part of the National Register nomination. The Tumamoc Hill Archaeological District was placed on the National Register of Historic Places at a National Level of Significance on 5 April 2010.

The nomination of the Archaeological District expanded upon previous designations that underscored the place of the hill in American scientific history. On 21 December 1965 the Desert Laboratory was designated a National Historic landmark and on 15 October 1966 it was placed on the National Register of Historic Places. In 1976, the Desert Laboratory and Tumamoc Hill were designated a National Environmental Study Area by the U.S. Department of the Interior and in 1981 a State Scientific and Educational Natural Area. These designations were the culmination of several decades of research on desert ecosystems that began in 1903 with the establishment of the Desert Laboratory on Tumamoc Hill by the Carnegie Institution of Washington, D.C. (Madsen et al. 2008:1).

The first paper in this report, by Suzanne K. Fish, Paul R. Fish, Todd Pitezel, Gary Christopherson, James T. Watson and Phillip O. Leckman, focuses on the cultural and temporal affiliation of the walls, terraces and pit structures on the summit of the hill. Their work provides evidence that the earliest construction episode on the hill dates to the Early Agricultural period (ca. 800 B.C. to A.D. 150) while a second episode dates to the Early Pioneer period (ca. A.D. 475 to 700). We learn about the spatial organization of this early hilltop community and the presence of one of the earliest communal-scale construction efforts in the Southwest.

The second paper, by Gayle Harrison Hartmann and Peter C. Boyle, updates rock art research on the hill—research begun by archaeologist Alan Ferg in 1979. This recording effort adds substantially to the known rock art universe on the hill and attempts to place the glyphs in a cultural and temporal framework. Some glyphs, which the authors believe belong to the Western Archaic Tradition, may be contemporary with the construction activities of the Early Agricultural-Early Pioneer periods as discussed in "Emerging Settlement Differentiation in Preceramic and Early Hohokam Villages on Tumamoc Hill." However, most of the rock art clearly belongs to the Hohokam (Gila) style and very likely dates to the Colonial-Sedentary periods, later than the two villages discussed in Part I. Two glyphs suggest that the hill was used by indigenous peoples after the Classic period (late prehistoric times) and possibly into historic times. Historic graffiti are, unfortunately, quite common and have been recorded to provide a baseline for future research; management recommendations for the rock art are presented.

The final paper, by John Fountain and Janine Hernbrode, is the first research that supports the probability of petroglyphs acting as solar markers on Tumamoc Hill. Seven proposed solar markers were observed with interactions occurring at equinox and both solstices, but not occurring on cross-quarter days.

All records and photographs related to these Tumamoc Hill archaeological projects are curated at Arizona State Museum as part of ASM Accession No. AP-2013-437: Tumamoc Hill Mapping and Excavation Project. Photographs of all rock art associated with Part II of this volume are available on the ASM website: www.statemuseum.arizona.edu/research/pubs/archseries/companion_materials.

Many scientific books and reports conclude with the following statement: "more remains to be learned." In fact, this statement is so common it has become trite. Nonetheless, it is valid here. In spite of the fact that considerable archaeological research has been conducted on the hill over a period of 40 years, and considerable modern disturbance has reduced the potential for some kinds of research, the more archaeological research we do on Tumamoc Hill, the more we learn about hilltop sites and the roles they played in the lives of the early inhabitants of the Tucson Basin.

•　　•　　•　　•　　•

All the authors wish to thank Richard Lange, general editor, and Alicia M. Vega, technical editor, for seeing this volume through to fruition.

Part I

Emerging Settlement Differentiation in Preceramic and Early Hohokam Villages on Tumamoc Hill

Suzanne K. Fish, Paul R. Fish, Todd Pitezel, Gary Christopherson, James T. Watson, and Phillip O. Leckman

A prominent Tucson landmark, Tumamoc Hill has an extensive complex of stone trincheras features that reflect a preceramic village and a subsequent early Hohokam village. It is the only such hill site in southern Arizona with substantial, well-documented occupations dating to the Early Agricultural period (500 to 300 B.C. during the Cienega phase) and the Pioneer period beginnings of the Hohokam sequence (A.D. 475 to 700 during the Tortolita phase). Massive walls and terraces encircling the hilltop residential area by the Cienega phase represent the earliest communal-scale construction other than canals in the U.S. Southwest. Precise mapping of Tortolita phase stone house foundations reveals a village layout that precedes the typical arrangement of Hohokam courtyard groups. A remodeled community room that served both the Cienega and later Tortolita phase residents and a Tortolita phase central plaza represent integrative features with civic and ritual implications. Unique in Tucson Basin setting and residential structure, the Tumamoc Hill villages reveal emergent expressions of differentiation in regional settlement pattern marked by distinctive elevated location, scale of communal labor, ritual practice, and diversified exchange networks.

Suzanne K. Fish School of Anthropology and Arizona State Museum, University of Arizona (sfish@email.arizona.edu)

Paul R. Fish School of Anthropology and Arizona State Museum, University of Arizona (pfish@email.arizona.edu)

Todd Pitezel Arizona State Museum, University of Arizona (pitezel@email.arizona.edu)

Gary Christopherson Center for Applied Spatial Analysis, University of Arizona (garych@casa.arizona.edu)

James T. Watson School of Anthropology and Arizona State Museum, University of Arizona (watsonjt@email.arizona.edu)

Phillip O. Leckman Statistical Research, Inc. (phil@email.arizona.edu)

Tumamoc Hill (AZ AA:16:6 [ASM]) is an iconic, flat-topped peak that affords an unsurpassed view to the east encompassing the Tucson Basin (Figure I.1), north as far as Picacho Peak, west to the Baboquivari Mountains, and south halfway to the Mexican border. A prominent dark volcanic mass rising 228 m (700 ft) above the Santa Cruz River in today's downtown Tucson (Figure I.2), Tumamoc must have been a defining element of the Tucson Basin landscape in the past as well. Archaeological remains dating from at least the Middle Archaic period to the present mark the hill's enduring significance for a continuing succession of visitors and residents. It is the only hilltop location of villages in southern Arizona with substantial, well-documented occupations that date to the Cienega phase of the Early Agricultural period and the Tortolita phase of the Early Ceramic period, which is also considered to be the initial phase (Wallace et al. 1995; Wallace and Lindeman 2003) of the Hohokam sequence.

Tumamoc Hill exemplifies a specialized site type that occurs mainly on volcanic hills throughout the U.S.-Mexico borderlands. Termed "*cerros de trincheras*" or "trincheras sites," these sites are further defined by the presence of walls, terraces, and other features built of stone (Downum et al. 1994; Fish et al. 2007). Tumamoc possesses one of the most extensive and diverse complexes of trincheras features in southern Arizona (Figures I.3 and I.4). Massive walls and terraces surround the hill summit, where a wide array of additional features includes pit houses and other structures, residential walls and terraces, numerous bedrock mortars and cupules, extensive rock art, and an elaborate trail system. The massive walls and terraces encircling the hilltop that date to the Cienega phase (ca. 800 B.C. to A.D. 150) represent one of the earliest communal-scale constructions or "public architecture" in the U.S. Southwest. Using advanced mapping techniques augmented by excavations, recent University of Arizona investigations have generated data that allow an organizational assessment of Tumamoc's Tortolita phase (A.D. 475-700) village and insights into its place in regional settlement at the beginning of the Hohokam sequence.

RESEARCH BACKGROUND

The archaeology of Tumamoc Hill was systematically recorded by an Arizona Archaeological and Historical Society survey and mapping project, published in a 1979 special issue of *The Kiva* with an introduction by David Wilcox and Stephen Larson (1979). Project members mapped the layout of massive upper walls and terraces (Wilcox 1979), trails (Hartmann and Hartmann 1979), rock art (Ferg 1979), and ground bedrock features (Larson 1979), and they identified more than 100 rounded outlines or enclosures made of local stone (Larson 1979). In the absence of excavation, the predominantly circular cobble enclosures were interpreted as "sleeping circles," the result of clearing the dense surface rocks to provide spaces for limited domestic activities and possibly ephemeral brush structures (Larson 1979:71-76; Wilcox et al. 1979:188-189). Study conclusions emphasized a defensive function for the massive walls and terraces around the summit (Wilcox 1979). The 1970s study attributed the trincheras features to the Hohokam of the late Sedentary or early Classic periods (Wilcox 1979:29) and possibly the Rillito or Rincon phases (Hartmann and Hartmann 1979:53-56). This interpretation was based on a surface collection of only 25 decorated sherds widely dispersed over the entire hill (Hartmann and Hartmann 1979:53). It was also noted, however, that there was an abundance of plain wares concentrated on the summit; plain ware densities were as high as 40 sherds per square meter (Larson 1979:76).

In 1985, a University of Arizona archaeological field school taught by Paul Fish and

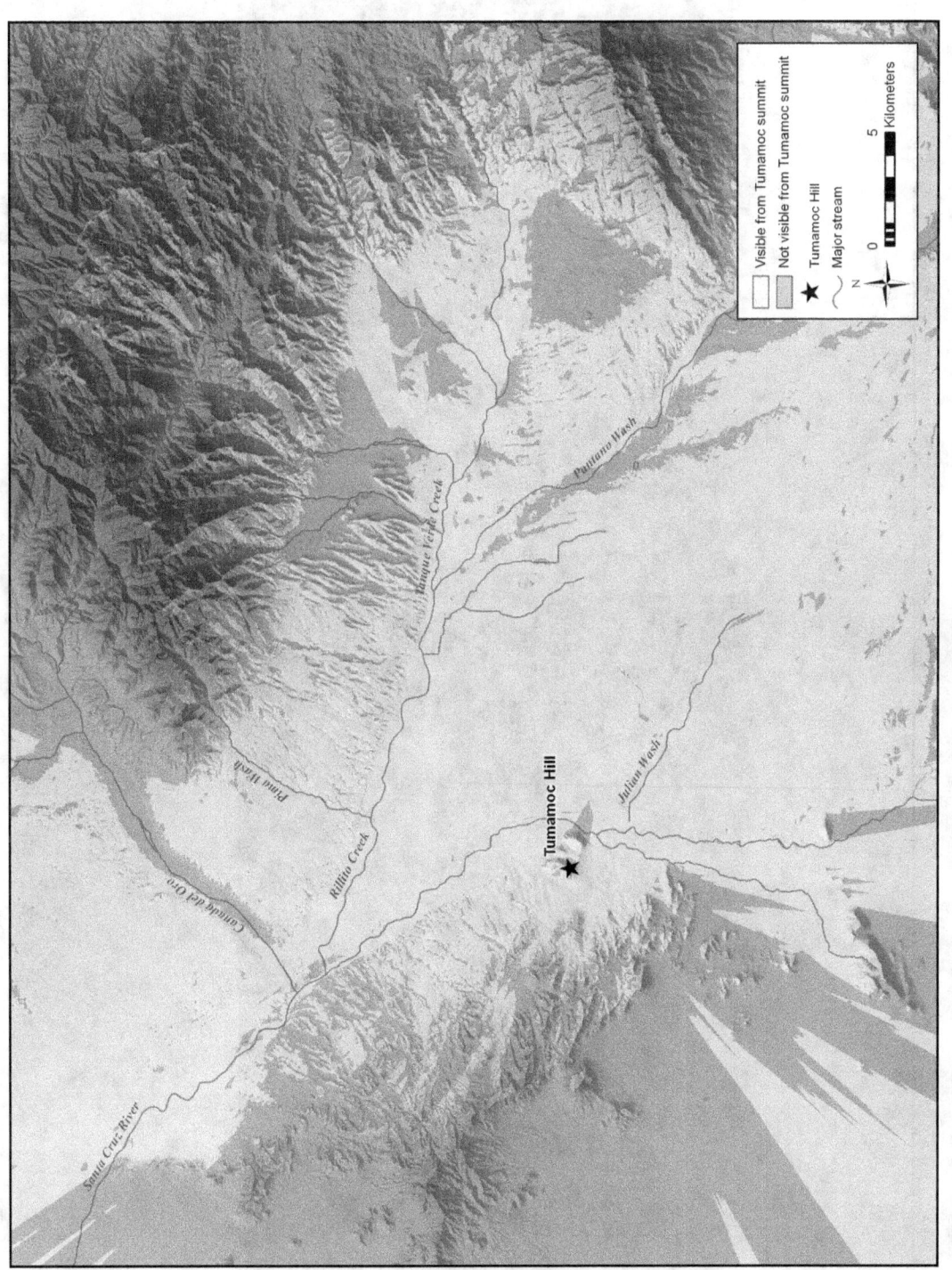

Figure I.1. A digital elevation model documents Tumamoc Hill's viewshed prominence over the Tucson Basin. The digital elevation models (DEMs) were obtained from the U.S. Geological Survey's National Elevation Dataset. The ArcGIS-based viewshed calculated intervisibility between the site and each 10-meter-resolution DEM cell within the area illustrated.

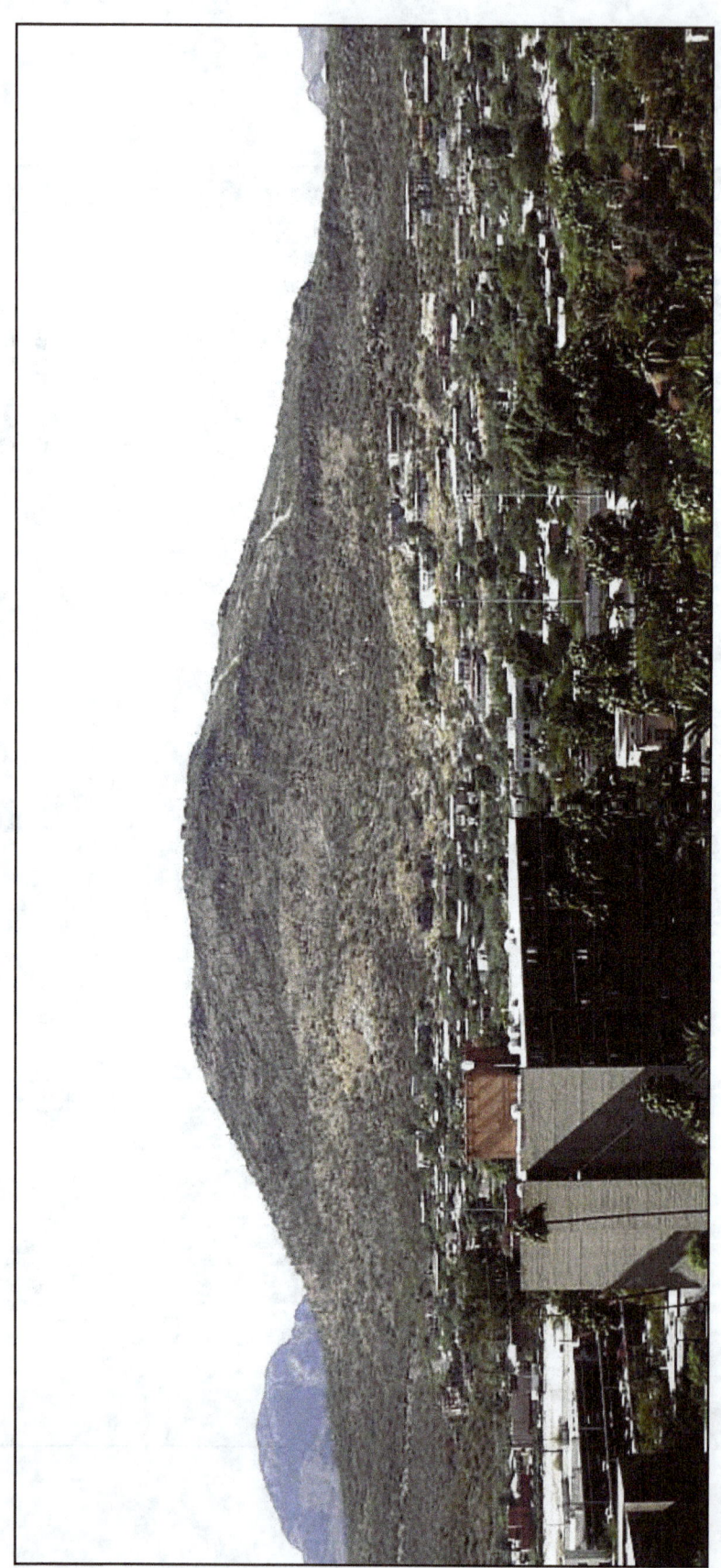

Figure I.2. Tumamoc Hill from downtown Tucson, Arizona.

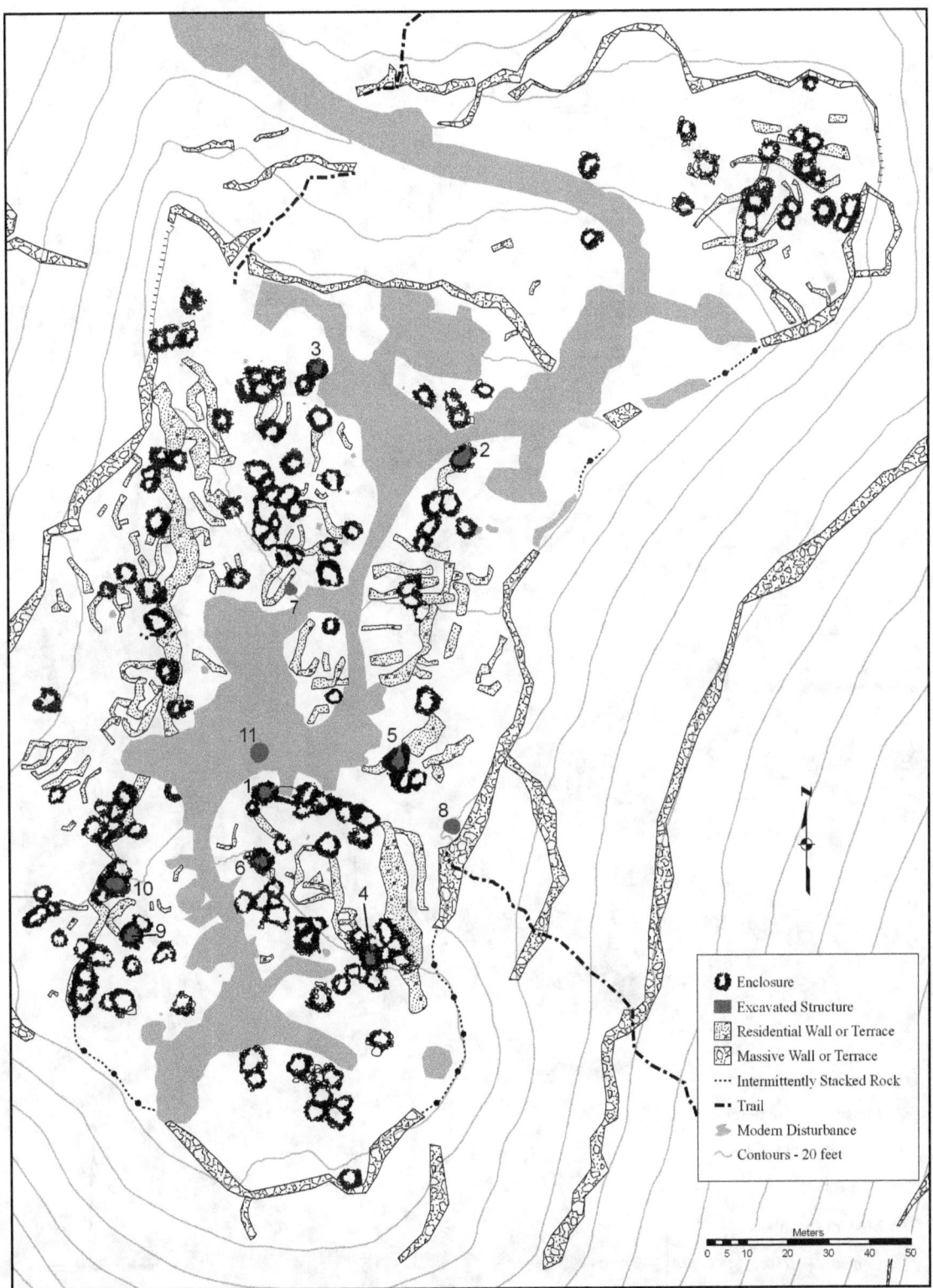

Figure I.3. Excavated Tumamoc structures. Round enclosures (Structures 1-7), rectangular enclosures (Structures 9 and 10), Cienega/Tortolita phase pithouse (Structure 8), and Cienega/Tortolita phase community structure (Structure 11).

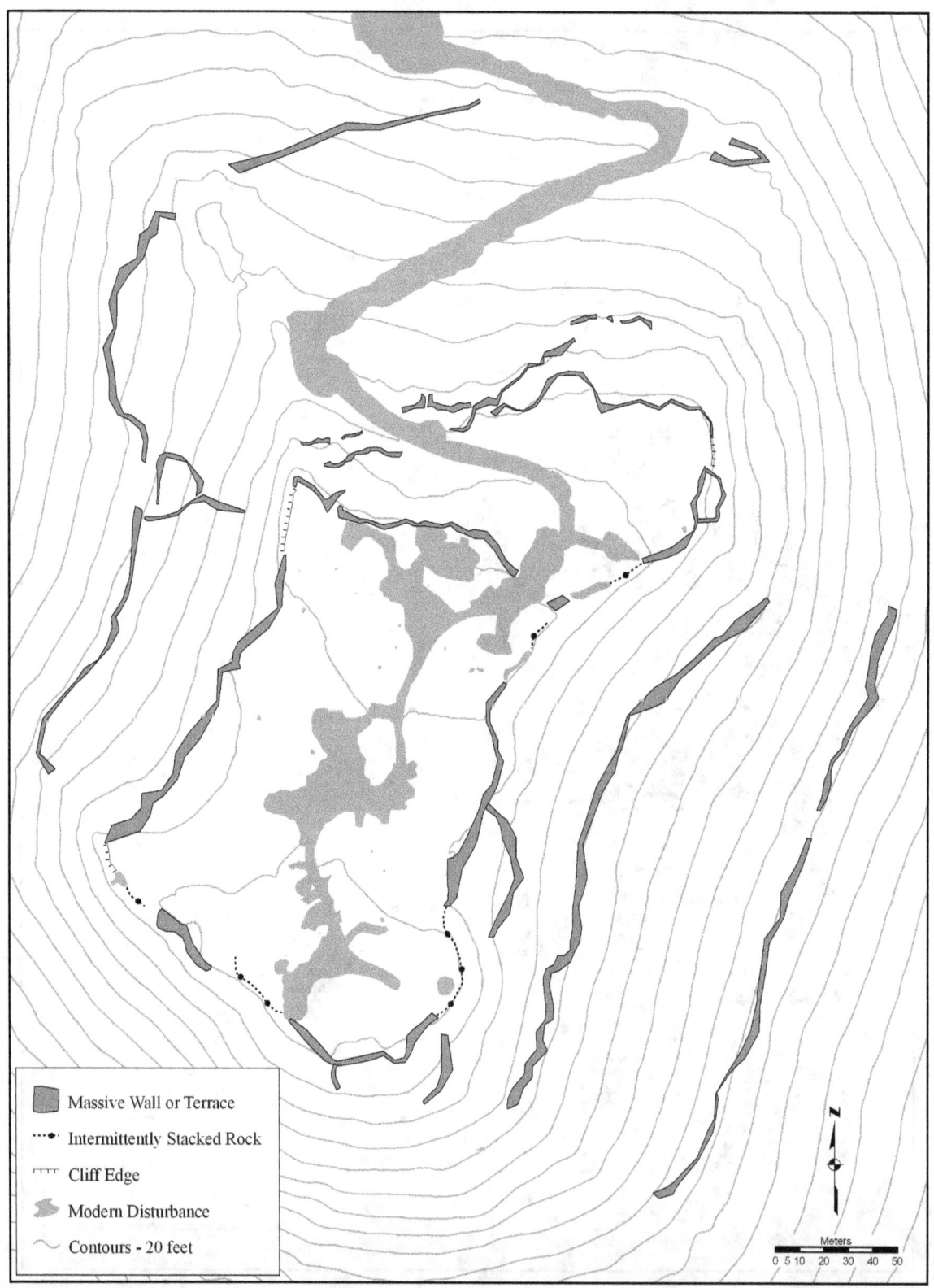

Figure I.4. Massive walls and terraces encircling the Tumamoc summit.

Suzanne Fish placed a single trench perpendicular to the wall of what was presumed to be a massive Hohokam terrace along the eastern summit edge to investigate the method of its construction and nature of the fill (Fish et al. 1986). A wholly unanticipated outcome was the recovery and direct dating of corn substantially older than the advent of ceramics in conjunction with Late Archaic period projectile points and burned daub. These materials were interpreted at the time as stratigraphically underlying the Hohokam terrace that contained plain ware ceramics in its fill. Contrary to the then-current belief that corn and pottery appeared in the Southwest at roughly the same time (e.g., LeBlanc 1982; Plog 1980), the earliest Tumamoc Hill occupants clearly were farmers well before the everyday use of ceramic vessels. A Hohokam date for the major trincheras features, however, stood essentially unchallenged until the same researchers returned in 1998 as part of a subsequent field school.

The 1998 expansion of the 1985 trench revealed that, rather than underlying the massive terrace, the early corn and projectile points came from a small pithouse without ceramics (Structure 8 in Figure I.3) that was cut down from the terrace surface after the terrace was built. The pithouse depression had been reused during a subsequent occupation associated with plain wares and a few red-slipped ceramics. Previously radiocarbon-dated material collected from the 1985 trench (Fish et al. 1986:569, Table 5) inadvertently had been drawn from both the original and secondary pithouse occupations.

The 1998 field school also excavated or tested seven of the cobble outlines or enclosures that are visible on the surface of the hilltop. This work confirmed that most rounded outlines marked the basal stone walls of pithouses. These structures yielded plain wares, minor amounts of red wares, and small, contracting-stem points that appear in the Tortolita phase, along with a mixture of larger and generally earlier point types (Wallace et al. 2007:57-63).

By 1998 at the time of the second field school, a series of Tucson-area investigations had defined a long agricultural sequence preceding the appearance of Hohokam decorated pottery types (e.g., Huckell 1995, 1996; Mabry et al. 1996). According to this sequence, the small pithouse (typical of chronologically equivalent counterparts in Early Agricultural period settlements along the Santa Cruz River) was cut into the massive Tumamoc terrace during the middle-to-late interval of the Cienega phase (ca. 500 to 300 B.C.) at the end of the Early Agricultural period. Together, the pottery, points, and radiocarbon dates from the later re-use of the terrace pithouse and from the other excavated cobble-outlined pithouses across the Tumamoc summit placed them in the Tortolita phase (ca. A.D. 475 to 700) at the interface of the Early Ceramic period and the ensuing Hohokam Pioneer period (Wallace et al. 2007:58-59). The advent of low percentage of red wares (< 5 percent) differentiates Tortolita phase assemblages from the solely plain ware assemblages of the preceding Agua Caliente phase (ca. A.D. 150 to 475) of the Early Ceramic period.

Archaeological investigations in southern Arizona and adjacent northwest Mexico during the late 1990s provided a regional framework for the realigned Tumamoc chronology. Massive terraces resembling those at Tumamoc Hill were described on Cerro Juanaqueña and other hills in northwest Chihuahua (Hard and Roney 1998). They proved to be the work of early agriculturalists who had not yet adopted pottery, and their construction had begun even earlier than the Cienega phase dates from Tumamoc Hill (Roney and Hard 2002). Following the 1998 field school, other trincheras occupations dating to an early era of plain ware ceramics were reported in southwest New Mexico (Roney 1999) and encountered during survey in northwest Sonora (Fish and Fish 2004:56).

University of Arizona field schools in 2005 and 2007 further confirmed the Tortolita phase affiliation of cobble-outlined pithouses throughout the Tumamoc summit. Investigations in 2007 included testing of two more structures, selected for their rectangular shape and large size. The 2005 and 2007 field schools conducted high resolution re-mapping of the massive encircling walls, trails, cobble outlines, and other hill features such as bedrock mortars, cupules, and grinding slicks; a preliminary inventory of rock art was incorporated into the more focused and comprehensive Arizona Archaeological and Historical Society project described in Part II of this volume. Field school efforts also documented for the first time the considerable extent of residential walls and terraces that modified the summit topography to facilitate village life. Guided by Gary Christopherson of the Center for Applied Spatial Analysis, field school participants achieved these objectives through the use of geospatial technology, namely advanced global positioning system (GPS) receivers and total stations for the collection of data, and the development of a geographic information system (GIS) for data management and analysis (Christopherson et al. 2005). Results provide the basis for the quantified estimates of construction effort and an analysis of Tortolita phase settlement structure discussed below.

CIENEGA PHASE VILLAGE: TUCSON'S FIRST PUBLIC ARCHITECTURE

The eastern terrace containing the small Cienega phase pithouse forms a segment of the massive linear features of roughly stacked volcanic boulders and cobbles that encircle the Tumamoc summit and the upper hill in variable tiers (Figure I.4). For significant stretches, the term terrace is appropriate because the rock

walls or berms hold sufficient rock and soil fill to create a level surface. In some of these stretches, the terrace fill also has sufficient width and depth to accommodate the dimensions of a pithouse. In other stretches, massive walls support little fill, and segments of both massive walls and terraces are sometimes connected by smaller walls or even single-boulder alignments. Walls and terraces are often wider than they are tall, with an average width of 2.4 m and a maximum width of 9 m. The standing heights of walls above ground surface almost never exceed 40 cm.

A very preliminary assessment of the effort invested in constructing these features is based on measurements of length and estimated volume of stone. Total length of all massive walls exceeds 1.9 km, and the total volume, calculated from regularly spaced measurements of wall cross-section, approximates 3,200 cubic meters. The larger boulders in the walls would have necessitated multiple persons for transport. Using Hard et al.'s (1999:139) labor figure of 1.9 person-hours per cubic meter of rock for the walls at Cerro Juanaqueña, the stonework of Tumamoc's massive walls would have absorbed 1,013 person/days of labor at six hours per day, or the work of 100 persons for a little more than ten days. In experimental terrace constructions at Cerro Juanaqueña, labor for the rock walls represents only about 40 percent of the total effort, which also entailed clearing the terrace area, laying it out, reinforcing the base, and filling it with stones and earth (Hard et al. 1999:136-138).

Although it is a rough estimate, the magnitude of effort associated with Tumamoc Hill's huge stone features strongly implies the coordinated work of many builders, especially if construction took place within a limited interval. The Cienega phase pithouse directly establishes an early construction date only for the eastern terrace segment on which it sat, although the size of this segment alone implies an appreciable degree of cooperative labor. Given the uneven topography of the hill, however, the encircling layout of the massive hilltop terraces and walls reflects a relatively uniform and continuous plan (Figure I.4), suggesting their overall design and construction was a generally unified effort within the Cienega phase. Furthermore, this encircling pattern occurs only at Tumamoc Hill and not at any of the other Tucson area trincheras sites with later Hohokam occupations. A similar encircling layout at Cerro Juanaqueña is also firmly dated to an early agricultural era before the advent of common domestic pottery.

Tumamoc's eastern summit terrace at a minimum, and likely the massive linear features as a whole, constitute the earliest known "public" architecture in southern Arizona and possibly in the U.S. Southwest, in the sense that their construction was a sustained and coordinated enterprise entailing a communal-level investment of labor. Up to that time, Early Agricultural period farmers in Tucson had only come together at a comparable scale of effort to construct irrigation canals.

Lacking any surface indications, the single Early Agricultural period pithouse (Structure 8 in Figure I.3) was purely a chance encounter while trenching the eastern terrace; cobble outlines visible on the surface have all yielded Tortolita phase ceramic assemblages. Because no additional preceramic structures had been identified, our initial understanding of the potential extent of the Cienega phase residential component at the site was based on the fact that the massive walls encircle the 6.4 ha (16 acres) summit area occupied by the later Tortolita village and that Early Agricultural period projectile point styles are scattered across the hilltop. In an associated investigation the year following the 2007 University of Arizona Archaeological Field School, however, James Watson's Indiana University-Purdue University, Indianapolis field school excavated a second Cienega phase pithouse, a large, specialized structure in a central part of the summit (Figure I.5). Like the small pithouse in the massive terrace, this community structure was first occupied during the Cienega phase and later reused during Tortolita times.

The Cienega phase structure excavated in 2008 is similar to others designated as "community structures" in Early Agricultural period villages along the Santa Cruz floodplain (e.g., Freeman 1998; Halbirt and Henderson 1993; Mabry et al. 1996; Thiel and Mabry 2006). Moreover, its central location on the Tumamoc summit adds substance to the inference that additional village houses would have surrounded it. Given that both of the hill's identified Cienega structures were re-occupied during the Tortolita phase, it is possible that additional pithouses yielding Tortolita ceramics had had earlier occupations as well. This possibility is difficult to assess because Tortolita re-occupants might have removed floor deposits while refurbishing in many instances and diagnostic artifacts of the preceramic Cienega phase are largely limited to projectile points.

As in the case of the small Cienega phase pithouse in the eastern summit terrace, no surface cobble outline indicated the existence of the Cienega community structure (see Structure 11 in Figure I.3). Instead, a modern utility road exposed the edges of its circular outline. It was cut 70 cm into the summit's solid caliche conglomerate substrate, and its ca. 16 m² floor plan recalls those of other Tucson community structures (Figure I.5). The Cienega phase excavation of this structure to such a depth into bedrock represents the expenditure of considerable labor. Floor features include a basin-shaped hearth filled with white ash, 34 perimeter postholes arranged in a double row on the north side and a single row elsewhere, a shallow central pit, and a deeper but smaller subfloor pit.

An unusually long and well-made Cienega phase projectile point with heavily rounded, worn, and polished flake scars (Figure I.6) and three shell beads were found on the community

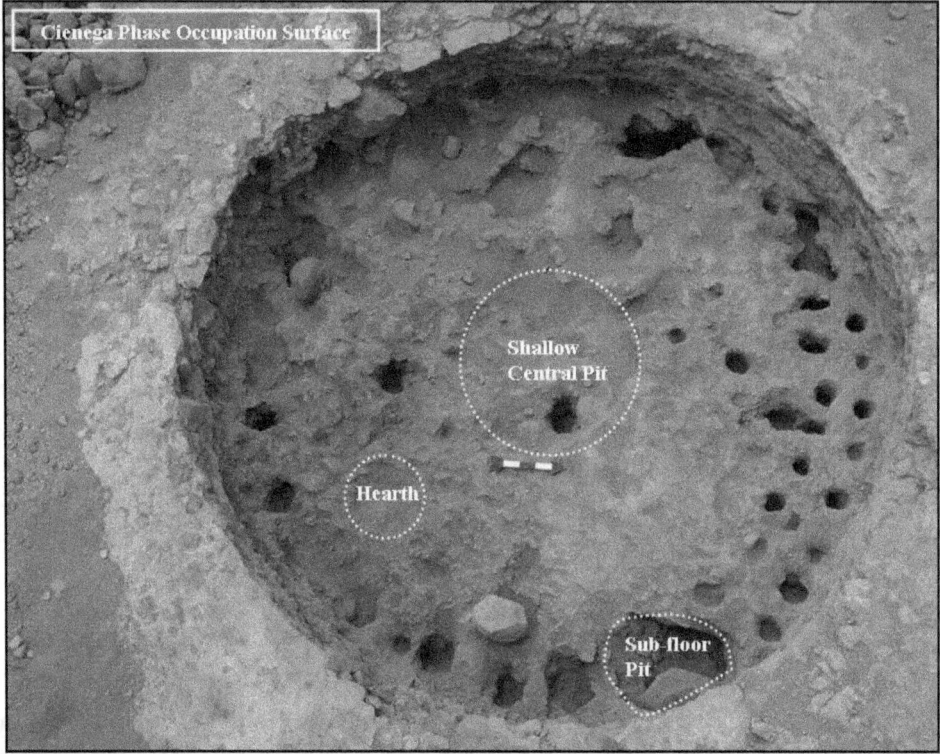

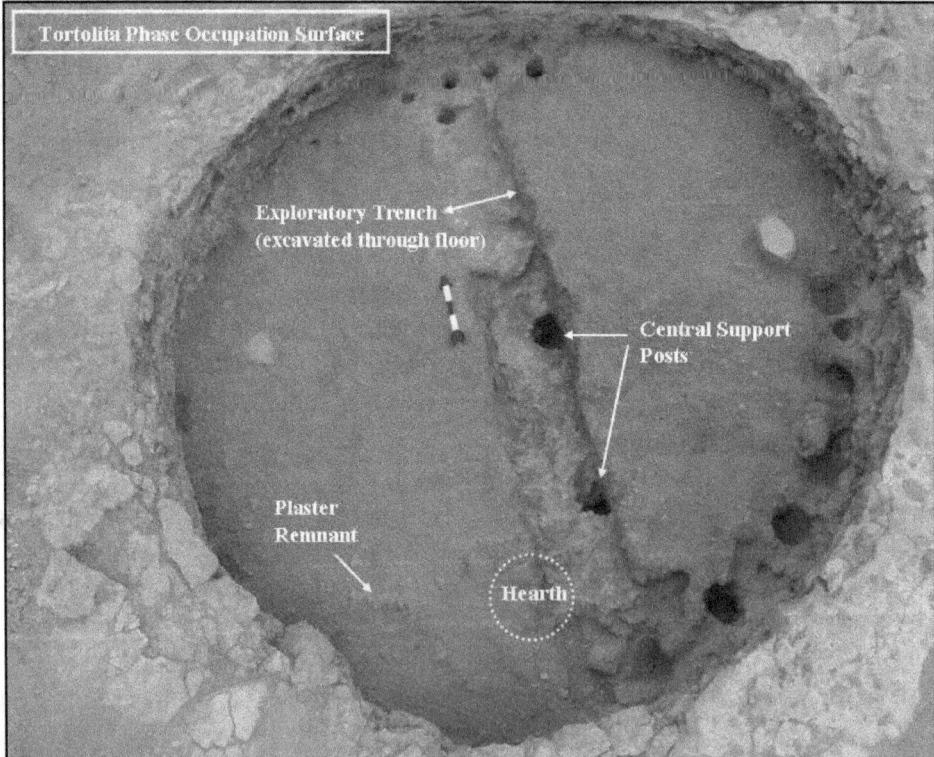

Figure I.5. Cienega phase (above) and Tortolita phase (below) floor plans of the community structure. The elongated boulder protruding through the floors of both earlier and later floors is visible to the left of the sub-floor pit in the Cienega phase floor and near the upper right edge of the Tortolita phase floor.

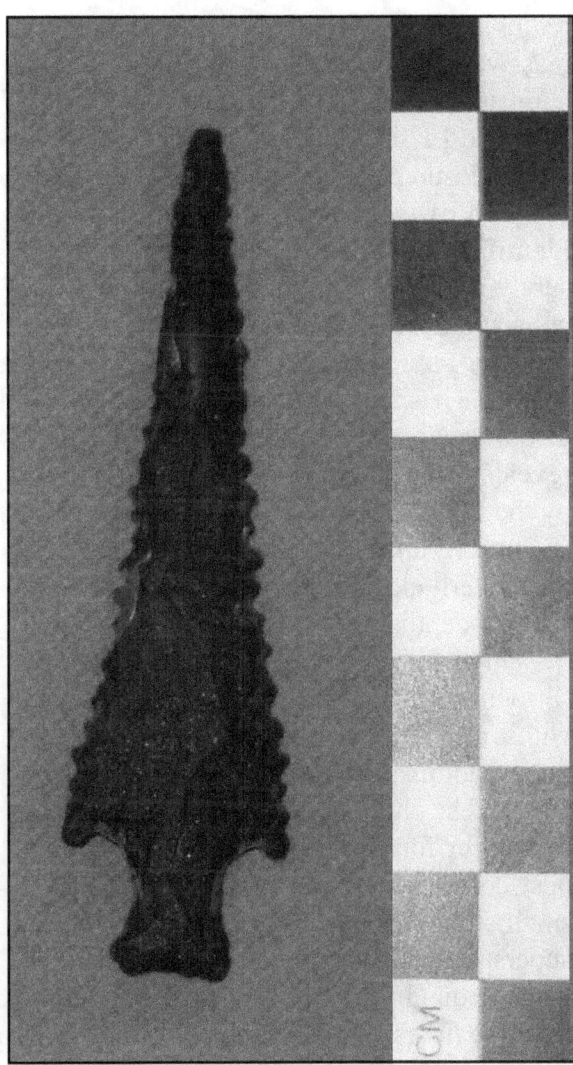

Figure I.6. Unusually large and well-made Cienega phase projectile point recovered from the floor of the earlier community room. Note that flake scars, particularly those near the end of the point, are nearly obliterated through polish from use or handling.

structure floor. An elongated, intentionally shaped rhyolite boulder with a battered upper surface was firmly embedded below the floor and protruded 25 cm above its surface near the western edge of the structure (see Figure I.5), a notable feature duplicated in another recently excavated Cienega phase community structure at the Clearwater site (AZ BB:13:481) on the river floodplain at the base of Tumamoc Hill (Thiel and Diehl 2013). When tapped with hard

wood or stone, the Tumamoc upright boulder produces a distinctive ringing sound similar to boulders with recorded tonal properties at some Hohokam rock art sites (e.g. Waller 2002) and other instances broadly distributed in the western U.S. and elsewhere in the world (e.g. Fagg 1956; Hedges 1990, 1993; Knight 1979). In addition to containing these unusual, upright and elongated stones, the Tumamoc and Clearwater site community rooms are almost mirror images in attributes such as size, feature numbers and placement, and estimated age.

We characterize the Cienega phase occupation of Tumamoc Hill as a "village" with due caution, because it is based on direct information from only three confirmed Cienega phase features: the massive eastern terrace which almost certainly was built by multiple cooperating households, the small domestic pithouse cut into that terrace surface, and the centrally located larger community structure. Botanical remains from the terrace pithouse span multiple seasons, consistent with an occupation of prolonged annual duration (Fish et al. 1986:565-566). The Tumamoc settlement overlooked a relatively dense contemporary occupation on the floodplain immediately below that also included additional community structures smaller houses, and multiple canals (Thiel and Mabry 2006; Thiel and Diehl 2013), but an exclusive role for Tumamoc Hill in Cienega phase settlement pattern is signaled by its unique hilltop location.

TORTOLITA PHASE VILLAGE: STRUCTURE AND ORGANIZATION

An early twentieth century perception of the Tortolita phase village, visibly demarcated by the cobble enclosures and as yet undisturbed by modern buildings and roads, is recounted in a newspaper article about the archaeological remains atop Tumamoc Hill. Archaeologists Byron Cummings and Robert Guilder

(Anonymous 1919) insightfully reported, "The houses were probably one room affairs and were erected about a central plaza, streets radiating from the central point like the spokes of a wheel." They also provided an estimate of 250 structures. Their estimate is a potential maximum number of structures that has been reduced to an unknown degree in the following decades by extensive disturbance over nearly 20 percent of the central summit (Figure I.3).

To capture the full range of residential infrastructure and to record the previously located stone enclosures in greater detail, the 2005 and 2007 fieldwork emphasized total station mapping and the use of overhead photography. Residential retaining walls and terraces were mapped for the first time. Cross-sectional measurements of all these features afford a means to estimate volume and effort. Overhead cameras on booms produced images of enclosures that could be corrected for distortion with total station controls and combined into photographic mosaics to encompass adjacent or conjoined features. Plan views digitized from the photographs accurately portray the attributes of each enclosure, register the size of enclosed areas, and identify entryways more reliably than field observations (Figure I.7). A new view of the Tortolita phase village on Tumamoc Hill emerges from the refined summit maps.

In addition to pithouses, villagers constructed a complex array of residential retaining walls and terraces to create level space for these houses, for possible ancillary structures such as ramadas or storage facilities, for outdoor activities, and to facilitate movement throughout the village (Figures I.3 and I.8). A few of the largest residential walls were built to ameliorate uneven summit topography at major changes in slope. The positioning of some residential terraces to intercept and retain surface runoff suggests their construction for dooryard gardens. In total, the effort invested in residential walls and terraces would have required about one-fourth of the labor for the massive encircling features (ca. 800 m^3 of stone compared to 3,200 m^3).

The 1970s project identified and mapped 125 enclosures (Larson 1979:79). The mapping program of the 2005 and 2007 field schools identified 152. This discrepancy is almost surely attributable in part to the difficulty of consistently discriminating and classifying outlines as enclosures denoting structures amidst a variety of other cobble features. Cobble enclosures excavated in 1998 and 2007 revealed that most were pithouses outlined by the tumbled cobbles of former basal walls (Figures I.9 and I.10). They were cut into rocky soils overlying compact caliche substrates at varying depths up to 60 cm.

Five fully excavated pithouses in 1998 (Structures 1, 2, 3, 7, and 8 in Figure I.3) fell within a smaller-size range for the site and had the predominantly round shape of Tumamoc structures; elongated entries could be confirmed for four. In the absence of discernible post holes in heavily weathered floors, these small structures appear to have had bent-pole superstructures, anchored by poles around the pit at ground level rather than extending up from the floors. Burned daub with impressions implies that they had brush superstructures covered with hardened mud (Figure I.9). Single-trench testing of three additional small round enclosures (Structures 4, 5, and 6 in Figure I.3) failed to define floors and encountered bedrock at relatively shallow depths, although in each case the fill contained abundant sherds and other artifacts. These three enclosures may represent near-surface structures where summit soils were thinnest or bases for ancillary features such as ramadas. Assemblages as a whole included diverse vessel forms, chipped stone of local and exotic materials, formal and informal groundstone, and shell jewelry, as would be expected for a substantial and sustained occupation (Wallace et al. 2007:78-79, Table 3.4).

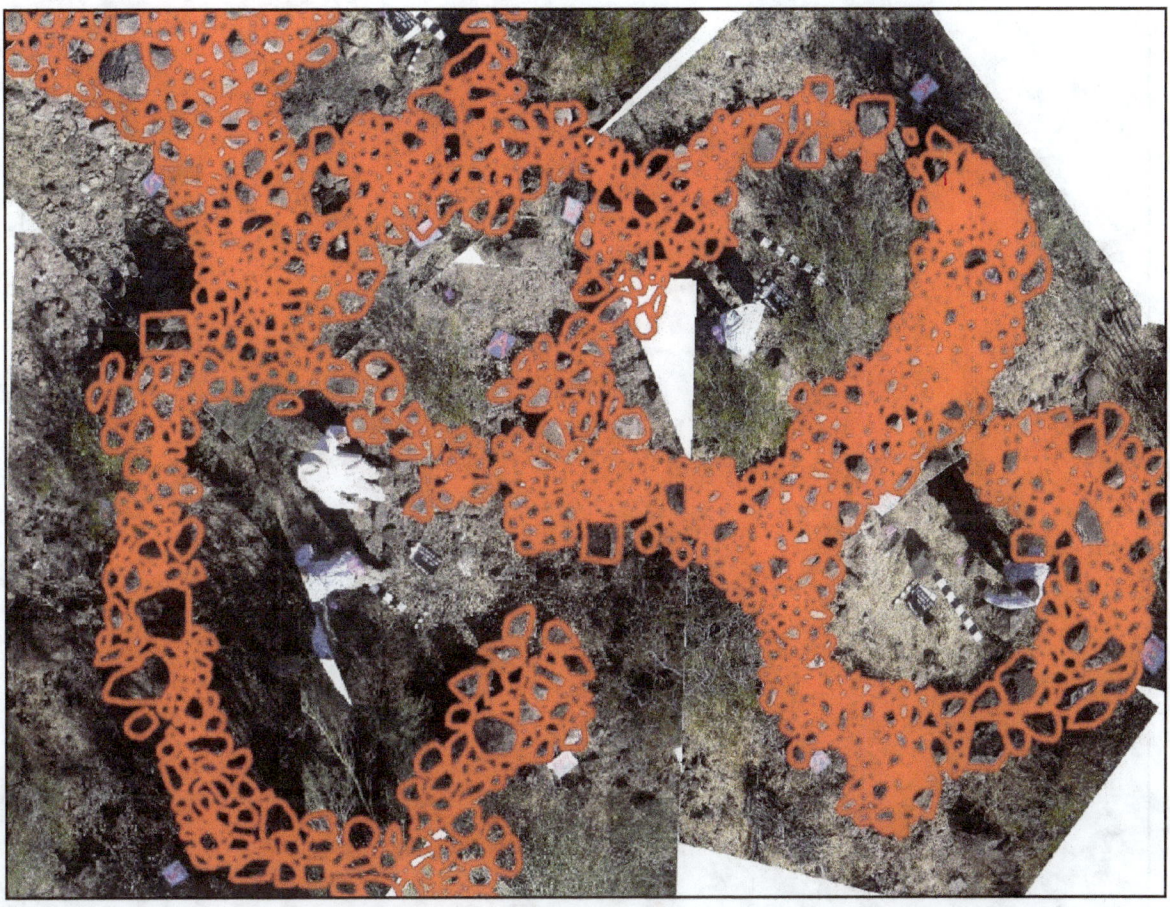

Figure I.7. Digitized photo mosaic of Tumamoc Hill enclosures overlain by digitized maps.

Two larger enclosures distinguished by their rectangular shape were additionally tested in 2007 (Structures 9 and 10 in Figure I.3). Floor exposure in one of these was sufficient to reveal a bowl-shaped hearth and two large postholes, probably part of a four-post roof-support pattern. The community structure (Structure 11 in Figure I.3), first built during the Cienega phase, was a specialized element of the Tortolita phase village as well. A modified floor plan with two central posts marks a stratigraphically higher Tortolita phase floor over intervening fill (see Figure I.5). When use of the Tortolita phase structure ceased, additional deposits accumulated before an apparently intentional effort to further fill the large depression by rolling or pushing cobbles and boulders into it.

Standardized calculations of the areas of enclosures were adjusted based on the exterior of the cobble outline. We adjusted these maximal figures downward to reflect the somewhat smaller corresponding sizes of floor areas in excavated pithouses. Tumamoc structures range from just over 2 m^2 to nearly 22 m^2 (Figures I.8 and I.11). A medium-size range (6 to 15 m^2) of structures with round shapes is most common (n = 135). A small number (n = 6) with round outlines below 6 m^2 may represent a specialized use such as storage. A subset of the largest-size structures (n = 6) also is rounded and covers 16 to 22 m^2. A shape that approaches rectangular distinguishes a fourth class of structures (n = 5). Because the original shape of tumbled basal walls is somewhat conjectural, designation of a

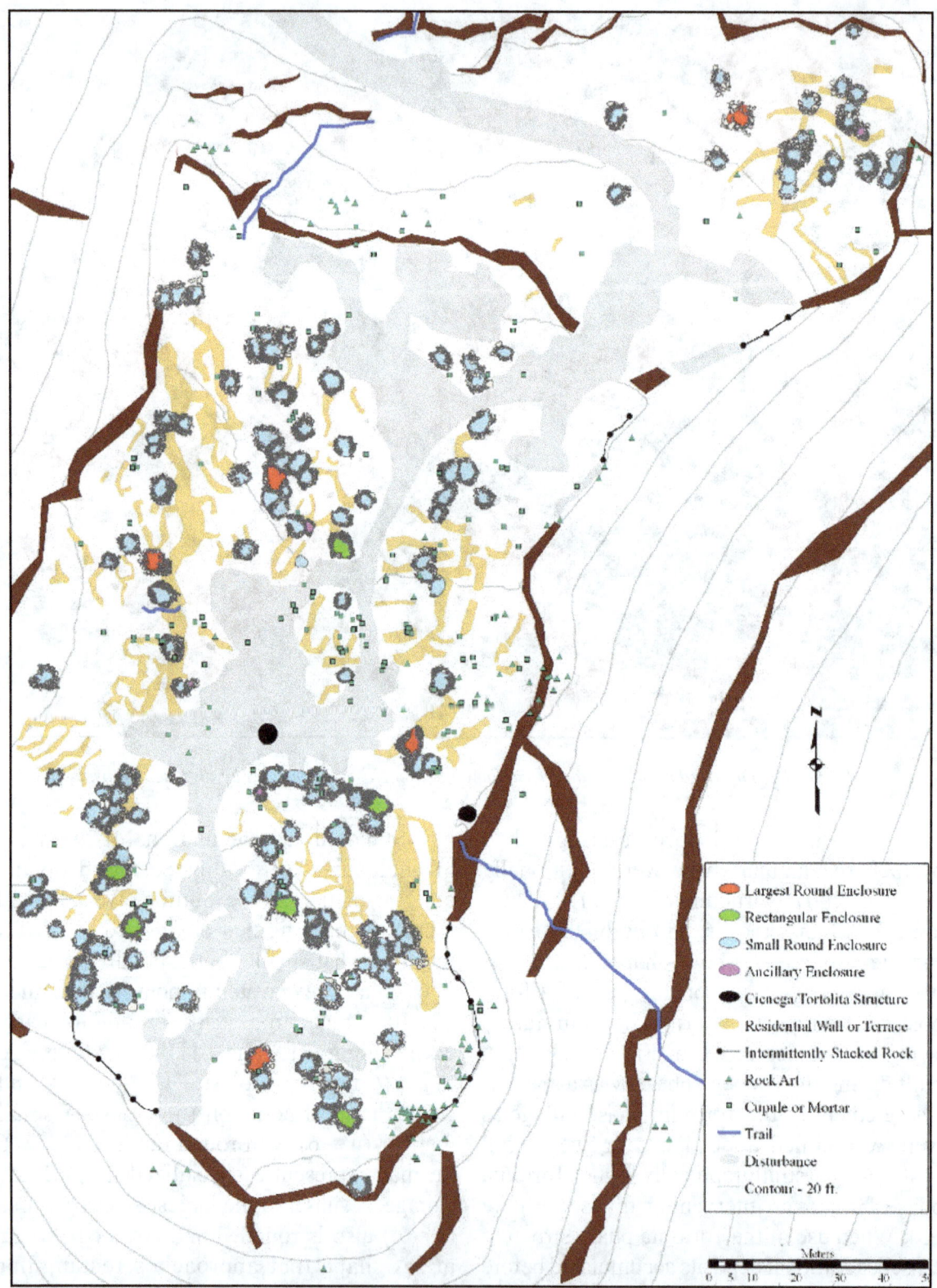

Figure I.8. Tumamoc Hill village plan during the Tortolita phase.

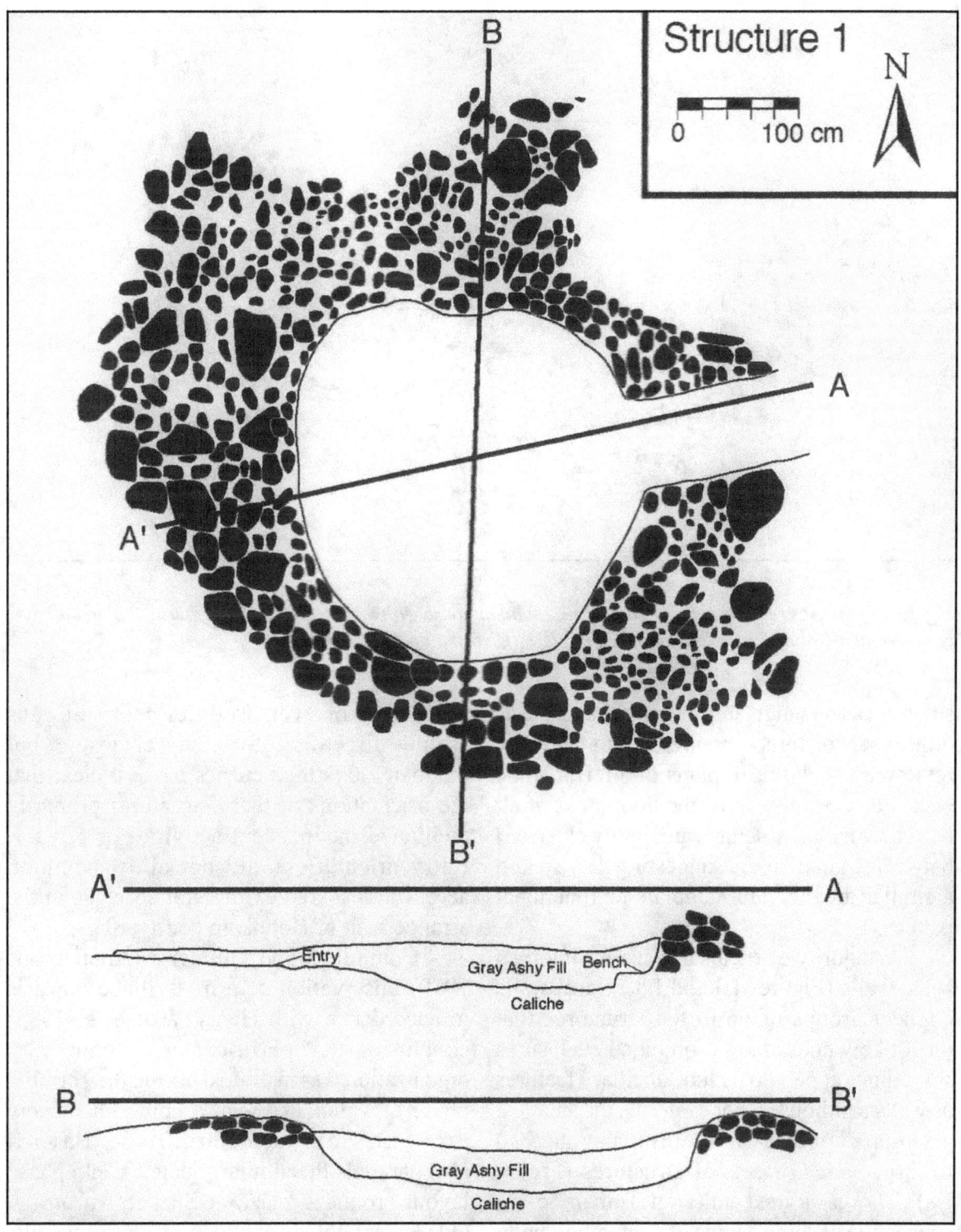

Figure I.9. Plan and cross-section of a typical small, round pithouse with an entryway within a cobble enclosure (Excavated Structure 1 in Figure I.3).

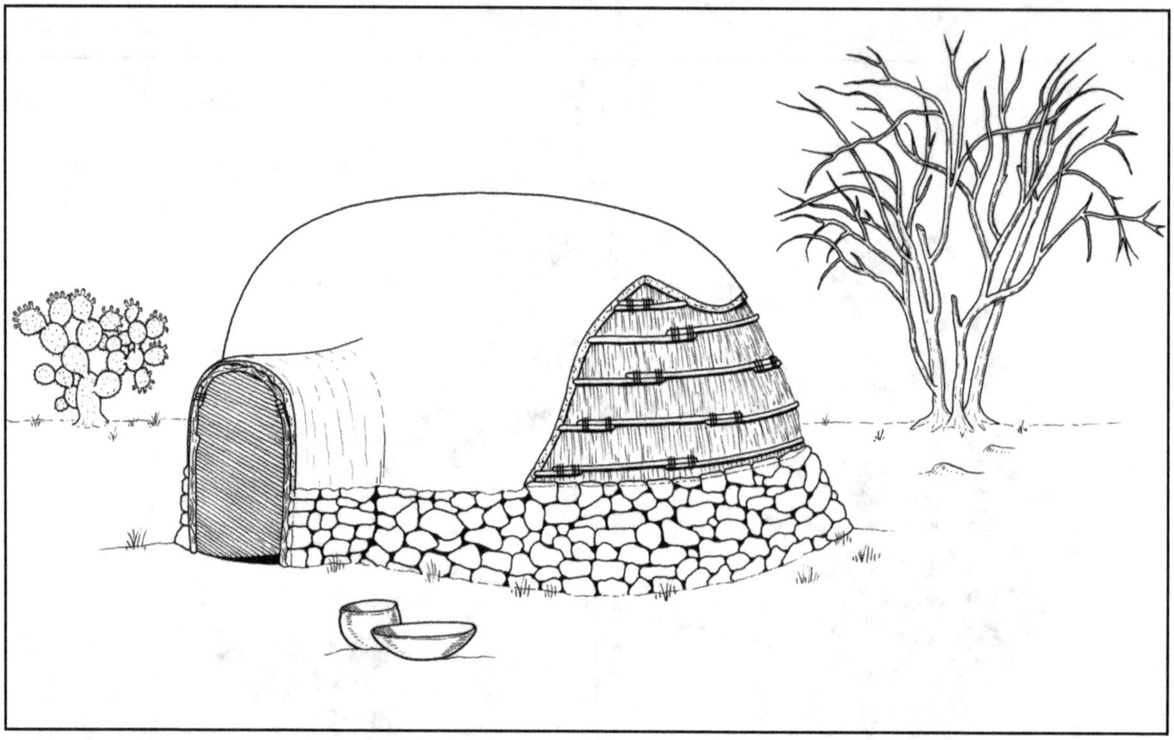

Figure I.10. Artist's reconstruction of the small, round pithouse with an entryway in the Figure I.9 plan and cross-section (Excavated Structure 1 in Figure I.3). (Drawing by Ronald Beckwith)

structure as rectangular necessitated consensus on the part of three observers, who carefully reviewed the digitized plans of all Tumamoc enclosures. Significantly, the floor areas of all five rectangular structures are tightly clustered between 14 and 16 m^2, suggesting they shared a similar architectural template or functional pattern.

A majority of enclosures share conjoined basal walls (Figures I.3 and I.8). Basal walls connect groups of up to ten structures that most likely housed kin. Conjoined enclosures sometimes appear to include ancillary features as well as pithouses. For example, the smallest enclosures less than 6 m^2 are invariably attached to larger ones or sets of structures (Figure I.8). The conjoined units on Tumamoc are suggestive of some degree of contemporaneity and continuity in residence. They are unlike later Hohokam courtyard groups, however, in the spatial relationships among structures.

Entryways or even well-defined wall gaps are not discernible for every enclosure, but the many identified entries make it clear that the orientations of these structures primarily facilitated independent activities or privacy. Entry orientations did not allow common access to a shared extramural space as in the arrangement of Hohokam courtyard groups.

Cummings and Guilder's (Anonymous 1919) observation of a mid-village plaza is in accordance with Henry Wallace's (2003) conclusion that plaza-centered community organization was instituted during the Tortolita phase at Valencia Vieja, a comprehensively excavated site in the southern Tucson Basin. It also parallels the similarly dated Vahki phase layout around a plaza at Snaketown on the Gila River (Wilcox et al. 1981). Unfortunately, the ability to affirm Cummings and Guilder's report of a plaza on Tumamoc Hill has been seriously compromised by the extent of modern disturbance, which is concentrated in the central zone of the site (Figures I.4 and I.8). The most likely location for a plaza lies in the vicinity of bladed roads, parking areas, and buildings. Although the community structure (Figures I.5 and I.8) was in use at some point during the Tortolita phase, its position in the central summit was determined by the original Cienega phase construction. In view of its stratigraphic history, earlier Tortolita residents may have ceased to use the community structure, and then filled it intentionally when an open plaza was subsequently established later in the Tortolita phase.

As with their reference to the plaza, the 1919 description of the site by Cummings and Guilder is auspicious with regard to village structure. They described "streets" radiating out from the plaza, for which we found no convincing evidence. However, our recent mapping efforts documented a pattern that is likely related to this perception. Groups of conjoined and individual enclosures occur in loose, elongated clusters (Figures I.3 and I.8). Although some constituent features are undoubtedly missing due to modern disturbance, these clusters could be construed as predominantly extending outward from a central plaza. If this interpretation is correct, then Cummings and Guilder's "streets" may actually be the open areas between the clusters. In any case, the five rectangular and six largest-sized round enclosures are distributed throughout the clusters, regardless of how they are defined (Figures I.8 and I.11). Probable kin-based groupings of ordinary smaller round houses appear to include one or both of these more specialized structure types.

The organizational unit Wallace (2003:344-363; 2008:17-18) proposed for Tortolita phase Valencia Vieja is structured around an over-sized, square, kin leader's house fronting on the plaza. An associated cluster of smaller residences behind the kin leader's house was arranged around a courtyard and a very small nonresidential structure was placed next to it. This pattern was replicated at least five times around the plaza at Valencia Vieja.

With the exception of Valencia Vieja's largest outliers, the range of structure sizes for Tumamoc Hill and Valencia Vieja overlaps closely (Figure I.11). Tumamoc's village includes only a few structures that are not round, however. In addition, neither its five rectangular enclosures nor its six largest round enclosures front the conjectured plaza, and courtyard groups are notably absent (Figure I.8). One plausible interpretation that would account for the divergence of Tumamoc's organizational configuration from that of Valencia Vieja is a Tumamoc occupation confined to an earlier part of the Tortolita phase, whereas a more extended Valencia Vieja occupation concluded with trends toward later Hohokam modes (Wallace et al. 2003:380-381). This possible sequencing of Tortolita phase occupations at the two sites is supported by available radiocarbon dates (Wallace et al. 2007:58-59, Table 3.1; Wallace 2003:126, Table 4.1). Another equally plausible interpretation is that Tumamoc's distinctive configuration reflects its unique settlement role embodied in a hilltop location.

James Heidke's (Wallace et al. 2007:68-69) examination of ceramic temper demonstrates basin-wide sources for Tumamoc vessels, a striking contrast with largely local pottery elsewhere in the Tucson Basin. At all other analyzed Tortolita phase sites, one predominant local source accounts for over 60 percent of ceramics (see Heidke 2003: Table 5.16; 2011: Table 7:12). Tumamoc residents, however, used ceramics produced in all parts of the basin and no one source area predominates. Such a distribution suggests either that ceramics were carried to the hill through basin-wide participation in Tumamoc events or that Tumamoc residents' exchange relationships took them farther afield in acquiring ceramics than the inhabitants of other contemporary settlements.

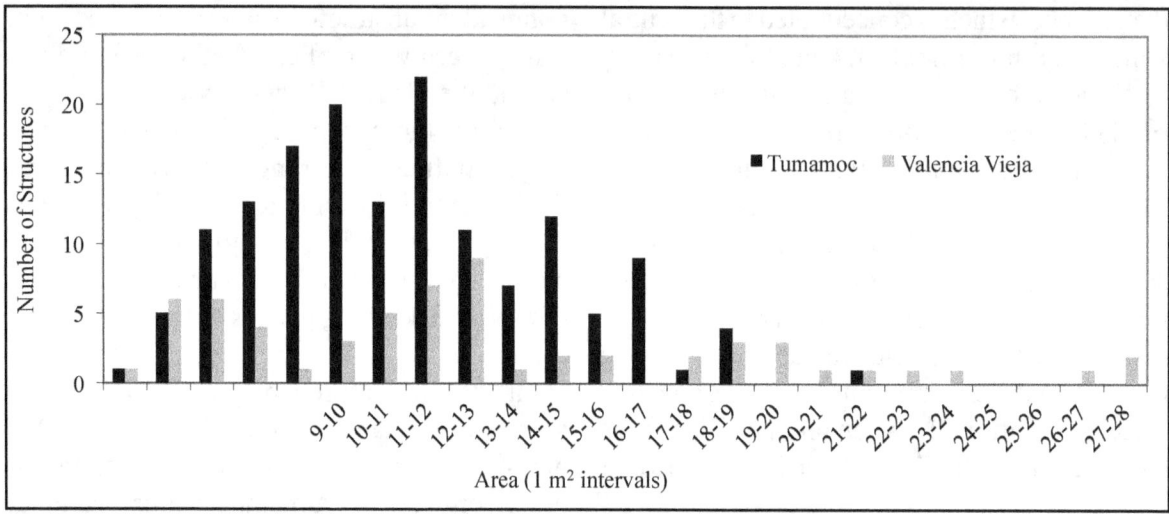

Figure I.11. Tumamoc Hill (n = 152) and Valencia Vieja (n = 62) floor area comparison. Two small Tumamoc cobble outlines (< 4 m) are not included in this graph because they are interpreted as storage features and not structures.

ROCK ART, GRINDING SLICKS, MORTARS, AND CUPULES

Clustering near summit edges (Figure I.8), numerous petroglyphs denote apparent ritual behavior of a concentrated sort that sets apart the Tumamoc summit from village locations on the basin floor below. The imprecision of dating that is possible for rock art elements prohibits an understanding of which subsets of the petroglyphs might be related to the two village occupations. Gayle Hartmann and Peter Boyle (this volume) indicate a minority may be assignable to a Western Archaic Tradition, perhaps overlapping in time with the Cienega phase village. The majority of instances are more compatible with Hohokam styles, with some specific examples likely to be later than the Tortolita village. The Tortolita phase, however, lies at the point of transition to the Hohokam sequence; some unknown fraction of the generally non-elaborate designs found on Tumamoc Hill may have already appeared at the time of the Tortolita occupation.

To the extent that Tumamoc rock art was contemporary with either of the occupations, its creation and use was clustered at the outer perimeters of the summit rather than in the midst of everyday village life (Figure I.8). More occasionally, petroglyphs are located within residential areas of the summit interior, but only rarely on stones in structures or other constructions. Rock art present on the summit prior to and during either of the village occupations undoubtedly made inhabitants and visitors aware of Tumamoc's special nature vis-à-vis contemporary basin settlements. Rock art from a bygone era probably heightened residents' and visitors' awareness of the hilltop's significant occupational history. Ancestral rock art and villages also would have provided the context for continuing ritual enactments that resulted in new rock art and contributed to Tumamoc Hill's status as a persistent landmark.

The distribution of bedrock cupules, mortars, and grinding slicks (Figure I.8) contrasts with that of rock art. These features are more widely scattered throughout the village area although, again, the inability to date them leaves temporal and occupational associations in question. Archaeologists frequently assign functionality to mortars and grinding slicks for plant processing and to a lesser degree for the grinding of other materials. Wallace (1983:176-181) suggests that the relatively small cupules served for making and refurbishing the stone pestles used with the larger mortars; a southwestern and world-wide literature also implicates these enigmatic rounded cavities in ritual and symbolism, often involving fertility. In this vein, for example, Puebloan groups and archaeologists identify cupules, mortars, and grinding slicks of uncertain age (sometimes with gendered associations) as elements of village shrines (e.g. Anschuetz et al. 2001; Duwe 2009; Fowles 2009; Snead 2008). Such shrines may be located in relation to site architecture rather than directly on it (Duwe 2011:333-335), a model for placement that could conceivably apply to Tumamoc rock art as well.

TUMAMOC'S TRINCHERAS VILLAGES

The setting of both villages on Tumamoc Hill is unique among well-studied contemporary occupations in the Tucson Basin. No other Cienega phase settlement has been conclusively identified on a hilltop, surrounded by massive terraces and walls. These huge Cienega phase constructions constitute the earliest community built or "public" architecture in southern Arizona. The later Tortolita phase village, without doubt one of the most populous Tucson settlements of its time, is further distinguished from its neighbors in the valley below. Ceramic temper analysis demonstrates basin-wide sources for Tumamoc vessels (Wallace et al. 2007:68-69), a striking contrast with largely local pottery at all other analyzed Tortolita phase sites (Heidke 2003, 2011). Clustering near summit edges (Figure I.8), numerous petroglyphs denote concentrated ritual behavior of a sort that sets apart Tumamoc Hill from other Tucson Basin village locations. Archaeologists cite unusual aspects of the earlier and later Tumamoc settlements to support both the traditional interpretation that the foremost motive for trincheras occupations must have been defensive (LeBlanc 1999; H. Wallace in Wallace et al. 2007:71-83; Wilcox 1979) and the proposition that elevated landforms of the U.S.-Mexico borderlands were often selected for distinctive types of residential settlement and for specialized ritual practices (P. Fish and S. Fish in Wallace et al. 2007:83-92; Fish and Fish 2008). Of course, these two primary interpretations need not be mutually exclusive.

Wallace (Wallace et al. 2007:82) suggests that both the Early Agricultural and Pioneer period villagers may have appreciated Tumamoc Hill's defensive qualities. Accordingly, the hilltop location in conjunction with the walls and terraces built by the earlier Cienega phase residents would have served a Tortolita phase need for refuge in a time of increasing aggregation and competition for prime agricultural land. S. Fish and P. Fish (Wallace et al. 2007:91-92) observe, on the other hand, that Tumamoc Hill during Tortolita times was a large, prominent village distinguished from neighboring settlements by elevated placement, heightened visibility, imposing communal constructions that may have had ancestral significance, distinctive rituals, and more diversified exchange relations as indicated by pottery. A wide, berm-rimmed trail on the north provides easy access to the summit and could readily accommodate processions. The unique diversity of Tumamoc's Tortolita pottery sources (Wallace et al. 2007:68-69) could reflect periodic congregations on the hill for ritual events, trade, and other social interaction, or the unusually expansive ties of hill residents. Together, recent Tumamoc research provides many new insights into the role of this landmark in Tucson Basin cultural traditions and contributes to the growing realization that many trincheras sites of all periods represent lofty and distinctive villages.

Acknowledgments. The Tumamoc Mapping Project was made possible over the years by talented teaching assistants Margaret Beck, John Chamblee, Chris Downum, Tom Fenn, Emiliano Gallaga, Matt Hill, Ryan Howell, Phil Leckman, Arthur MacWilliams, Jessica Munson, Matt Pailes, Todd Pitezel, and Abby Holeman; and numerous field school students from the University of Arizona and elsewhere. Phil Leckman and Todd Pitezel designed the Tumamoc Hill geodatabase. Gayle Hartmann and Peter Boyle led an Arizona Archaeological and Historical Society team that rigorously recorded the Tumamoc Hill petroglyphs. John Madsen and Susan Bartlett's grant from the Arizona State Historic Preservation Office to support a National Register of Historic Places nomination and management plan helped fund the 2007 mapping program. Finally, we acknowledge critical support from the Arizona State Museum, Center for Applied Spatial Analysis, and School of Anthropology at the University of Arizona throughout our investigations.

References Cited

Anschuetz, Kurt F., Richard H. Wilshusen, and Cherie L. Scheick
2001 An Archaeology of Landscapes: Perspectives and Directions. *Journal of Archaeological Research* 9:157-2011.

Anonymous
1919 Evidence of Ancient Civilization Found West of Tucson. *Arizona Daily Star* 23:1. Tucson.

Christopherson, Gary, Paul R. Fish, Suzanne K. Fish, John Chamblee, and Phillip O. Leckman
2005 Integrating ArcGIS and ArcPad in an Archaeological Field School Track. *ESRI Users Conference Proceedings*, pp. 140-159. ESRI, San Diego.

Downum, Christian E., Paul R. Fish, and Suzanne K. Fish
1994 Refining the Role of Cerros de Trincheras in Southern Arizona Settlement. *The Kiva* 59:271-296.

Duwe, Samuel G.
2011 *The Prehispanic Tewa World: Space, Time, and Becoming in the Pueblo Southwest.* Ph.D. Dissertation, School of Anthropology, University of Arizona, Tucson.

Fagg, B.
1956 The rock gong complex today and in prehistoric times. *Journal of the Historical Society of Nigeria* 1:27-42.

Ferg, Alan
1979 The Petroglyphs of Tumamoc Hill. In "The Tumamoc Hill Survey: An Intensive Study of a *Cerro de Trincheras* in Tucson, Arizona." *The Kiva* 45:(1-2) 95-118.

Fish, Paul R., Suzanne K. Fish, Austin Long, and Charles Miksicek
1986 Early Corn Remains from Tumamoc Hill, Southern Arizona. *American Antiquity* 51:563-572.

Fish, Suzanne K., and Paul R. Fish
2004 In the Trincheras Heartland: Initial Insights from Full-coverage Survey. In *Surveying the Archaeology of Northwest Mexico*, edited by Gillian E. Newell and Emiliano Gallaga, pp. 47-63. University of Utah Press, Salt Lake City.
2008 Una Mirada Desde Las Alturas: Círculos de Piedra, Corrales e Ideológia en Los Cerros de Trincheras. In *Memoria del Seminario de Arqueología del Norte de México*, edited by Elisa Villalpando and Cristina García, pp. 67-86. Instituto Nacional de Antropología e Historia and Museo Nacional de Antropología, Mexico, DF.

Fish, Suzanne K., Paul R. Fish, and M. Elisa Villalpando (editors)
2007 *Trincheras Sites in Time, Space, and Society.* The University of Arizona Press, Tucson.

Fowles, Severin M.
2009 The Enshrined Pueblo: Villagescape and Cosmos in the Northern Rio Grande. *American Antiquity* 74(3):448-466.

Freeman, Andrea K. L. (editor)
1998 *Archaeological Investigations at the Wetlands Site*, AZ AA:12:90 (ASM). Technical Report No. 97-5. Center for Desert Archaeology, Tucson.

Halbirt, Carl D., and T. Kathleen Henderson (editors)
1993 *Archaic Occupation on the Santa Cruz Flats: The Tator Hills Archaeological Project.* Northland Research, Inc., Flagstaff.

Hard, Robert J., and John R. Roney
1998 A Massive Terraced Village Complex in Chihuahua, Mexico, 3000 Years Before Present. *Science* 279:1661-1664.

Hard, Robert J., Jose E. Zapata, Bruce K. Moses, and
    John R. Roney
    1999   Terrace Construction in Northern Chihuahua,
        Mexico: 1150 B.C. and Modern Experiments.
        Journal of Field Archaeology 26:129-146.

Hartmann, Gayle H., and William K. Hartmann
    1979   Prehistoric Trail Systems and Related Fea-
        tures on the Slopes of Tumamoc Hill. In "The
        Tumamoc Hill Survey: An Intensive Study of a
        Cerro de Trincheras in Tucson, Arizona." *The
        Kiva* 45:(1-2) 39-70.

Hedges, Karl
    1990   Petroglyphs in Menifee County. *Rock Art
        Papers* 7:75-83.
    1993   Places to see and places to hear: rock art and
        features of the sacred landscape. In *Time and
        Space: Dating and Spatial Considerations in Rock
        Art Research*, edited by J. Steinbring, A. Watch-
        man, P. Faulstich, and P. Tacon, pp. 121-127 Oc-
        casional AURA Publication No 8. Melbourne.

Heidke, James M.
    2003   Tortolita phase ceramics. In *Roots of Sed-
        entism: Archaeological Excavations at Valencia
        Vieja, a Founding Village in the Tucson Basin of
        Southern Arizona*, edited by Henry D. Wallace, pp.
        145-191. Anthropological Papers No. 29. Center
        for Desert Archaeology, Tucson.
    2011   Prehistoric pottery from Honey Bee Village:
        dating provenance Typology, and Function. In
        *Life in the Valley of Gold, Archaeological In-
        vestigations at Honey Bee Village, A Prehistoric
        Hohokam Ballcourt Village in the Cañada del
        Oro Valley of Southern Arizona*, edited by H. D.
        Wallace. Anthropological Papers No. 48. Center
        for Desert Archaeology, Tucson.

Huckell, Bruce B.
    1995   *Investigations at Milagro: A Late Preceramic
        Site in the Eastern Tucson Basin*. Technical Re-
        port No. 94-5. Center for Desert Archaeology,
        Tucson.
    1996   The Archaic prehistory of the North American
        Southwest. *Journal of World Prehistory* 10:305-
        373.

Knight, L.
    1979   Bell rock and Indian Maze Rock of Orange
        County. *Pacific Coast Archaeological Society
        Quarterly* 15:25-32.

Larson, Stephen M.
    1979   The Material Culture Distribution on the Tum-
        amoc Hill Summit. In "The Tumamoc Hill Survey:
        An Intensive Study of a *Cerro de Trincheras* in
        Tucson, Arizona." *The Kiva* 45:(1-2) 71-82.

LeBlanc, Stephen A.
    1982   Temporal Change in Mogollon Ceramics. In
        Southwestern Ceramics: A Comparative Review,
        edited by A. H. Schroeder. *The Arizona Archaeolo-
        gist* 15:107-128. Phoenix.
    1999   *Prehistoric Warfare in the American South-
        west*. University of Utah Press, Salt Lake City.
        (editor)

Mabry, Jonathan B., Deborah L. Swartz, Helga
    Wocherl, Jeffrey J. Clark, Gavin H. Archer, and
    Michael W. Lindeman
    1996   *Archaeological Investigations of Early Village
        Sites in the Middle Santa Cruz Valley: Descrip-
        tions of the Santa Cruz Bend, Square Hearth, Stone
        Pipe, and Canal Sites*. Anthropological Papers No.
        18. Center for Desert Archaeology, Tucson.

Plog, Fred
    1980   Explaining Culture Change in the Hohokam
        Preclassic. In *Current Issues in Hohokam Prehis-
        tory*, edited by David Doyel and Fred Plog, pp.
        4-22. Anthropological Research Papers No. 23.
        Arizona State University, Tempe.

Roney, John R.
    1999   Canador Peak: An Early Pithouse Period
        Cerro de Trincheras in Southwestern New Mexico.
        In *La Frontera: Papers in Honor of Patrick H.
        Beckett*, edited by Melha S. Duran and David T.
        Kirkpatrick, pp. 173-184. Archaeological Society
        of New Mexico, Albuquerque.

Roney, John R., and Robert J. Hard
    2002   Early Agriculture in Northwestern Chihuahua.
        In *Traditions, Transitions, and Technologies:
        Themes in Southwestern Archaeology*, edited
        by Sarah Schlanger, pp. 160-177. University of
        Colorado Press, Boulder.

Snead, James E.
    2008   *Ancestral Landscapes of the Pueblo World*.
        University of Arizona Press, Tucson.

Thiel, J. Homer, and Michael A. Diehl
    2013   *Archaeological Investigations at the Mission*

and Mission Garden Loci of the Clearwater Site, AZ BB:13:6 (ASM) and the Santa Cruz River Westside Canals, AZ BB481 (ASM), Tucson, Pima County, Arizona. Technical Report 2008-06. Desert Archaeology, Inc., Tucson.

Thiel, J. Homer, and Jonathan B. Mabry (editors)
2006   Rio Nuevo Archaeology, 2000-2003: Investigations at the San Agustin Mission and Mission Gardens, Tucson Presidio, Tucson Pressed Brick Company, and Clearwater Site. Technical Report No. 2004-11. Desert Archaeology, Inc., Tucson.

Wallace, Henry D.
1983   The mortars, petroglyphs, and trincheras on Rillito Peak. The Kiva 48:1-246.
2003   Roots of Sedentism: Archaeological Excavations at Valencia Vieja, a Founding Village in the Tucson Basin of Southern Arizona. Anthropological Papers No. 29. Center for Desert Archaeology, Tucson.
2008   Hohokam beginnings. In The Hohokam Millennium, edited by Suzanne Fish and Paul Fish, pp. 13-22. School for Advanced Research Press, Santa Fe.

Wallace, Henry D., Paul R. Fish, and Suzanne K. Fish
2007   Tumamoc Hill and the Early Pioneer Period Occupation of the Tucson Basin. In Trincheras Sites in Time, Space, and Society, edited by S. K. Fish, P. R. Fish, and M. E. Villalpando, pp. 137-164. The University of Arizona Press, Tucson.

Wallace, Henry D., James M. Heidke, and William H. Doelle
1995   Hohokam Origins. The Kiva 60:575-618.

Wallace, Henry D., and Michael W. Lindeman
2003   Valencia Vieja and the Origins of Hohokam Culture. In Roots of Sedentism: Archaeological Excavations at Valencia Vieja, a Founding Village in the Tucson Basin of Southern Arizona, edited by Henry D. Wallace. Anthropological Papers No. 29. Center for Desert Archaeology, Tucson.

Waller, Steven J.
2002   Rock art acoustics in the past, present, and future. 1999 International Rock Art Conference Proceedings, Volume 2, edited by P. Whitehead, W. Whitehead, and L. Loendorf, pp. 11-20. American Rock Art Research Association, Albuquerque.

Wilcox, David R.
1979   Warfare Implications of Dry-laid Masonry Walls on Tumamoc Hill. In "The Tumamoc Hill Survey: An Intensive Study of a Cerro de Trincheras in Tucson, Arizona." The Kiva 45: (1-2) 15-38.

Wilcox, David R. and Stephen M. Larson
1979   Introduction to the Tumamoc Hill Survey. In "The Tumamoc Hill Survey: An Intensive Study of a Cerro de Trincheras in Tucson, Arizona." The Kiva 45:(1-2) 1-14.

Wilcox, David R., Stephen M. Larson, W. Bruce Masse, Gayle H. Hartmann, and Alan Ferg
1979   A Summary of Conclusions and Recommendations of the Tumamoc Hill Survey. In "The Tumamoc Hill Survey: An Intensive Study of a Cerro de Trincheras in Tucson, Arizona." The Kiva 45:(1-2) 187-195.

Wilcox, David R., Thomas R. McGuire, and Charles Sternberg
1981   Snaketown Revisited: A Partial Cultural Resource Survey, Analysis of Site Structure and an Ethnohistoric Study of the Proposed Hohokam-Pima National Monument. Arizona State Museum Archaeological Series No. 155. University of Arizona, Tucson.

Notes

Part I is closely adapted from Fish et al. 2011:185-196, Two Villages on Tumamoc Hill, *Journal of Arizona Archaeology*, Vol. 1, No. 2.

Part II

Tumamoc Hill Rock Art Revisited: With a Focus on Temporal Affiliation and Management

Gayle Harrison Hartmann and Peter C. Boyle
with contributions by Katherine M. Cerino and Janine Hernbrode

This paper reports on the results of a recent survey of the rock art on Tumamoc Hill, Tucson, Arizona. This survey, conducted under the auspices of the Arizona Archaeological and Historical Society and the Arizona State Museum, took place over three winter seasons from 2006 to 2009. It was occasioned by the writing of both a National Register nomination for the cultural resources of the hill and a management plan for the hill by the Arizona State Museum. The goal of this survey was to re-record all rock art on the hill that had been previously recorded and record rock art that had been overlooked by earlier recorders, as well as all graffiti, thus providing a baseline for future comparisons. Seven hundred thirty-four prehistoric rock art elements (plus six of indeterminate age) were recorded compared with approximately 460 elements previously recorded. In addition, 450 graffiti elements were documented. This paper summarizes previous rock art recording projects on the hill and describes the universe of rock art recorded during the recent survey. Also discussed are possible temporal and cultural affiliations of the prehistoric glyphs, elaborations among anthropomorphs, preferred locations, and the pervasiveness of graffiti including some with historical significance. The presence of probable solar markers among the prehistoric rock art is noted. Finally, recommendations for future management are included.

Tumamoc Hill (AZ AA:16:6 [ASM]) is a *cerro de trincheras* site located just west of the Santa Cruz River near downtown Tucson. The name "Tumamoc," a corruption of "horned toad" in O'odham, was given to the hill by the early staff of the Carnegie Desert Laboratory (Spalding 1909:73). The term "cerro de trincheras," meaning "trenched or walled hill" in Spanish, has been used for many years to designate hilltop archaeological sites with dry-laid- or stacked-rock walls (Sauer and Brand 1931; Hoover 1941). Tumamoc Hill became a botanical research station of the Carnegie Institution of Washington, D.C. in 1903 (Coville and MacDougal 1903). It is now owned by the University of Arizona and is home to the Desert Botanical Laboratory, "a world-renowned center...that attracts leading researchers on desert ecosystems and archaeology" (Madsen 2008:1). The buildings that house the Desert Laboratory are located on a flat spur part way up the north slope of the hill (Figure II.1).

Among a wide variety of cultural resources on the hill including numerous, massive rock walls, more than 152 stone outlines, and a

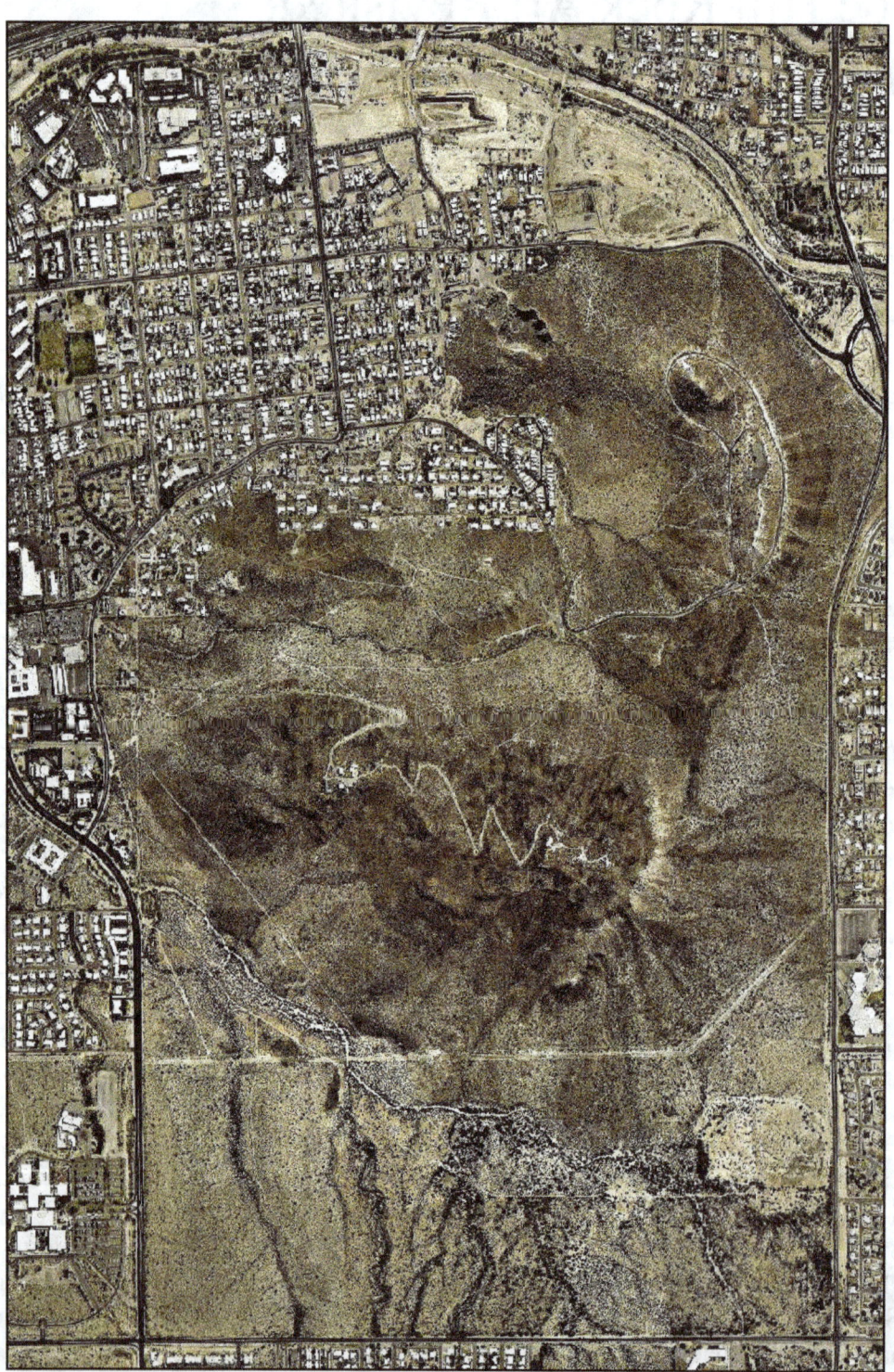

Figure II.1. Aerial photograph of Tumamoc Hill and environs. Tumamoc is in the center of the photo with the modern road clearly visible switchbacking to the summit of the hill (below). The Desert Laboratory buildings can be seen after the first switchback; small buildings on the summit are barely visible. Sentinel Peak (now commonly known as "A" Mountain) is at the lower right. The straight lines (left center) are various modern roads and utility rights-of-way. North is at the top of the photo. Photograph derived from Pima County's Geographic Information System – 2012 Spring Pictometry Color Orthophoto Imagery.

rock-bordered trail on the north slope, there is also extensive rock art, much of which fits within the Gila (Hohokam) petroglyph style. Unfortunately, the proximity of Tumamoc Hill to central Tucson has exposed these cultural resources to ongoing threats. Today the summit is disturbed by a road and parking areas, a number of small buildings, two observatories, and communications towers as well as considerable modern graffiti, some of which deface the prehistoric rock art. The summit of Tumamoc Hill is a very popular walking destination with hundreds of individuals walking up the road on most days.

PREVIOUS RESEARCH

Tumamoc Hill has been the focus of archaeological research since the early 1970s (Larson 1972), and one of the earliest studies of rock art in southern Arizona was conducted there by archaeologist Alan Ferg during the fall of 1974 and spring of 1975. With the assistance of a small number of volunteers and astronomer/photographer Stephen M. Larson, Ferg (1979) produced a pioneering study that described and analyzed the rock art of the hill.

Ferg's study was part of a broader survey of the *cerro de trincheras* under the auspices of the Arizona Archaeological and Historical Society with a goal of publishing a report on the various archaeological features of the hill. This report, "The Tumamoc Hill Survey: An Intensive Study of a *Cerro de Trincheras* in Tucson, Arizona" was published in 1979 as a double issue of *The Kiva* (Wilcox et al. 1979:45[1-2]).

At the time of the 1974-1975 survey, only a modest amount of research had been conducted on hills that exhibit trincheras features, that is, dry-laid masonry walls with soil-filled terraces upslope. Sauer and Brand's

(1931) review of cerros de trincheras in Sonora, and Stacy's (1974) survey of trincheras sites on what was then the Papago Indian Reservation (now Tohono O'odham Nation) are two of the most comprehensive examples. In addition to walls, such hills frequently exhibit rock circles (which, in most cases, are foundations for pithouses), bedrock mortars, one or more trails leading to the summit, and rock art.

The general conclusions reached by Wilcox (1979) in the 1974-1975 survey were that the trincheras walls probably served a defensive purpose and that many *trincheras* belonged to the late Sedentary or early Classic periods (A.D. 1100-1300). In addition, the survey concluded that the large trail on the north slope connected the trincheras to a major Hohokam community at the base of the hill (St. Mary's site, AZ AA:16:26 [ASM]) and that the number and variety of cultural features on the summit suggested that diverse activities occurred there (Wilcox et al. 1979:187-188).

More recently, as a result of work conducted by Paul and Suzanne Fish (Fish et al. 1986; Wallace et al. 2007), the age of the trincheras has been pushed back considerably. Radiocarbon dates on corn found in the terraces fit within the ca. 800 B.C. to A.D. 150 time frame of the Cienega phase of the Early Agricultural period. Excavations within the rock circles on the summit of Tumamoc indicate that many of the features were the foundations of pit structures probably constructed during the Tortolita phase (ca. A.D. 475-700), the initial phase of the Hohokam Pioneer period. An excavation conducted near the center of the summit in 2008 by James Watson (Fish et al. 2011) revealed an exceptionally large pit structure. Watson concluded that it consisted of two occupation layers, the earliest associated with the Cienega phase and the second with the Tortolita phase, thus corroborating the earlier work of Paul and Suzanne Fish. As more work is done on Tumamoc, the hypotheses regarding the prehistoric use of the hill become more complex; at present they include seasonal agriculture, seasonal or permanent residence, ritual activities, and/or defense.

Ferg's (1979) petroglyph study was among the first published in southern Arizona, preceded only by Snyder's (1966) study of the petroglyphs on South Mountain in Phoenix, and the unpublished Senior Honor's Thesis written by University of Arizona undergraduate Cheryl Ann White (1965) on the major petroglyph sites in Saguaro National Monument (now Saguaro National Park). A report on pictographs at the Malapais Hill site near Dudleyville in the lower San Pedro Valley was published by Schaafsma and Vivian in 1975.

Other early work on rock art in the Southwest included Turner's (1963) seminal publication on Glen Canyon and a report by Hayden (1972) on petroglyphs in the Sierra Pinacate in Sonora, Mexico. An additional survey conducted after Ferg's but published prior to the publication of his report was Weaver and Rosenberg's (1978) work on the petroglyphs of the southern Sierra Estrella Mountains, west of Phoenix.

DEFINITIONS

Before proceeding with a brief summary of Ferg's work, we present a few definitions of terms used in this paper. Manipulation of rock surfaces by prehistoric or modern aboriginal humans (excluding the creation of functional mortars and, in this report, cupules) has come to be called "rock art" (Ferg 1979; Schaafsma 1980; and many others) or occasionally "rock imagery" (Wallace 2008). However, as Liz and Peter Welsh (Welsh and Welsh 2004:7) point out in their excellent popular book, *Rock-Art of the Southwest*, "the word *art* can be misleading. In our culture, art is a form of personal expression.... [and] there is no evidence from archaeology, ethnography,

or cross-cultural studies to suggest that prehistoric Southwestern rock-art involved that kind of individual creative expression...." What was intended has been the subject of a considerable amount of printed material ranging from serious discussion and debate, for example, entopic design forms (Vastokas and Vastokas 1973) and shamanic symbolism (Schaafsma 1994; Whitley 2000), to unfounded speculation, for example, "translation" of rock art symbols into words (Martineau 1976). In a recent study of the rock art of South Mountain in Phoenix, archaeologist Todd Bostwick (2002:14) provides the following suggestion for the purpose of the rock art there: "[W]e propose that much of this rock art represents dreams, memories, and signs. The petroglyphs appear to be records of individual dreams or vision quests; memories of important historical or mythological events; and signs relating to local resources and to the heavens." We do not intend to engage in this discussion here, other than to note that we agree that rock art consists of meaningful symbols that are of both cultural and chronological significance.

On Tumamoc Hill all the rock manipulation consists of petroglyphs, defined by Thiel (1995:3) as "an image that has been pecked, scraped, [or] ground onto rock surfaces." Petroglyphs can also be scratched into the rock surface; in fact, the first scratched prehistoric glyphs noted in southern Arizona were defined on Tumamoc Hill by Ferg (1979). On Tumamoc, there are also a few examples of prehistoric glyphs created by incising. We should point out here that, in a few cases, we use the term "abrading," which is the same technique as "grinding," the term used by Thiel (1995:3). Petroglyphs are visible because they almost always cut through a patina, which Thiel (1995:3) defines as "an accretion of manganese, clays, and other minerals that forms on rocks." In the case of Tumamoc nearly all the rock is a moderately vesicular basaltic andesite (Lipman 1993) with a dark, usually shiny, surface patina. When a petroglyph is pecked through that surface it appears as a much lighter design embedded in a dark background. A few petroglyphs are pecked into a tuff or porphyry; in these cases there is no surface patina and the glyphs can be extremely hard to discern. The scratched glyphs, always in the basaltic andesite, often barely penetrated the surface layer and can be very hard to see. We note that the other two principal subclasses of rock art, "pictographs"—"an image painted or drawn on rock surfaces" (Thiel 1995:3)— and "geoglyphs"—"an image produced by scraping, tamping, or clearing areas of desert pavement or by piling gravel or rocks into piles or alignments" (Thiel 1995:3), do not occur on or near Tumamoc Hill. Graffiti are also prevalent on Tumamoc Hill. They can be defined as any unambiguously non-Native American and hence historic-era "rock art." Generally, these are names and/or dates that are scratched or incised into the rock surface.

In our discussion of the field data, we use the term "feature" as the principal organizational unit. We define "feature" as it is generally defined in archaeology: a distinct unit of cultural activity. Thus, a boulder with a single petroglyph is called a feature, as is a boulder with several petroglyphs. Boulders with glyphs on more than one face usually are considered to be a single feature. In some instances, rock images on boulders that are very close together are also defined as a single feature.

In defining the images that he saw, Ferg also recorded them by features as well as by individual glyphs or elements. In current literature, the term "element" has come to be used instead of "petroglyph" or "glyph." Element is defined by Thiel (1995:3) as "a single design or image. . . ." In our discussion of the rock art on Tumamoc we use the term "glyph" and "element" interchangeably. Thus, in our usage, a rock art <u>feature</u> may consist of several <u>glyphs</u> or several <u>elements</u>.

OVERVIEW OF ROCK ART RESEARCH ON TUMAMOC HILL

Summary of Ferg's Study

Ferg (1979) documented "in excess" of 460 prehistoric petroglyphs on Tumamoc Hill, 408 of which could be assigned to design element categories and, thus, were included in his analyses; these were incorporated into 227 features. We use 460 elements as his total for comparative purposes. He noted that "it is believed that at least 90 percent of the glyphs on Tumamoc were found" (Ferg 1979:95). All of the glyphs were inferred to be Hohokam, and he concluded that all could be subsumed into two styles, a "Hohokam Pecked Style" and a style he first identified on Tumamoc as a "Hohokam Scratched Style." In addition, he recorded two examples of graffiti, one consisting of a pecked representation of the Pythagorean theorem (TH-F3295) (Ferg 1979:106, Fig. 4, upper left) and a panel of scratched elements that may represent a group of domed huts (TH-F2957). He did not record the hundreds of additional graffiti.

In terms of location on the hill, he concluded that there were at least as many prehistoric petroglyphs on the slopes of the hill as on the summit, and that the north slope, with its relatively gentle incline and prehistoric trail, was home to the vast majority of those glyphs that were not on the summit. He also noted that glyphs did not occur randomly on the hill, but that 90 percent were found on outcrops with the remainder on isolated single boulders (Ferg 1979:111).

In his analysis of spatial distribution, Ferg wrote that pecked-style glyphs were found on all outcrops, with three exceptions – two outcrops on the north slope were without petroglyphs and one outcrop on the west slope had only Scratched-style glyphs. [In addition to the many Scratched-style glyphs on this west slope outcrop, we recorded several pecked glyphs]. He also stated that outcrops without glyphs were located away from activity areas, "such as trails, walls, artifact clusters, mortar holes, or rock circles" (Ferg 1979:111). From this observation he concluded that "the best explanation for the distribution of Pecked style glyphs on the hill would appear to be that the decision-making processes governing location of glyphs were (1) the suitability of the rock surfaces, and (2) proximity to other activity areas. Poor rock or outcrops away from major activity areas were not desirable." He went on to conclude that, "This pattern is faithfully repeated on Martinez Hill and Black Mountain" (Ferg 1979:111-112). [The present authors note that Martinez Hill and Black Mountain are within the San Xavier District of the Tohono O'odham Nation. Both exhibit trincheras features including some rock art. During the 1974-1975 survey they could be accessed for informal examination. That is no longer the case. At present, a formal permit application must be completed and access granted by the Nation before any archaeological work can be done. We did not go through that process and, thus, do not include any comparisons with these locations.] In his spatial analysis, Ferg went on to note that the Tumamoc Scratched-style glyphs did not conform to this distribution pattern. The majority (26 in his tabulation) were located on an outcrop on the west slope while the remainder (six in all), were distributed relatively evenly over the hill.

Ferg (1979) recorded all elements on a sketch map showing their relationship to other elements and to nearby permanent or semipermanent objects. He also plotted all elements on a topographic map of the hill with 4-foot contour intervals. In addition, he made freehand sketches of most of the elements recorded on his survey and took color slides of 41 features (18 percent of the features he recorded), plus one panoramic slide that includes many elements on several features. Stephen M. Larson took black and white photos of 110 features (48 percent of the total). Many of these photos were duplicates, so the total number of features photographed is considerably fewer than the total number of slides and prints.

Ferg (1979:114-116) concluded with a section on the purpose of the glyphs. He briefly discussed ceremonialism, mnemonic devices, totem or clan symbols, and decoration. He concluded that there is little evidence to support the first three. He did note that "a string of hand-holding stickmen...might be interpreted as ceremonial, but they cannot be proven to be dancers, nor for that matter dancers at a ceremonial occasion" (Ferg 1979:115). He concluded further that decoration was the most likely purpose, that is, "[they] were created for the enhancement of the petroglyph maker's immediate surroundings" (Ferg 1979:116). Thus, in Ferg's view, the Tumamoc rock art could be considered a form of personal expression.

Miscellaneous Surveys

In addition to Ferg's (1979) thorough survey of the rock art, a few other research projects have located or mentioned rock art on the hill. In Table II.1 we provide designations from the other surveys and compare them with Ferg's designations and our designation. The first of these was Larson's (1972:99-100) preliminary report on the hill. He noted that petroglyphs were present and commented that they were "presumed to be of the 'Hohokam school'." A survey conducted by Lindsay and Metcalf (1973) on the north slope of the hill in connection with power line modifications also mentioned rock art. This survey did not record any specific rock art locales but noted the occurrence of prehistoric petroglyphs and some historic glyphs that mostly dated "between 1885 and 1905" (Lindsay and Metcalf 1973:8). As part of the Arizona Archaeological and Historical Society fieldwork in 1974-1975,

Table II.1. Previous Research Projects That Have Located or Mentioned Rock Art on Tumamoc Hill			
Larson 1972:99-100	Presence of prehistoric petroglyphs noted		
Lindsay and Metcalf 1973:8	Presence of prehistoric and historic petroglyphs noted		
Masse 1979:155, Fig. 6	Limited Activity Area 17, unrecorded by Ferg	=	our TH-F4451
Whitney 2005:27, 32-33	F. 4 = Ferg's ISO-1	=	our TH-F2997
	F. 8 = Ferg's Map 11, O-8	=	our TH-F197
	F. 9 = Ferg's Map 11, O-6	=	our TH-F195
	F.10 =Ferg's Map 11, O-4	=	our TH-F3349
Estes and others 2005:127	P-1 = unrecorded by Ferg	=	our TH-F4450
Burton (in Madsen 2008:29)	Associated with Structure 5, unrecorded by Ferg	=	our TH-F4450

archaeologist Bruce Masse (1979:155, Fig. 6) recorded prehistoric dry farming features on the western bajadas. In connection with that work he recorded a single petroglyph (an anthropomorph) on an isolated boulder cluster.

Another survey on the north slope of the hill in connection with a proposed overhead fiber optic line was conducted in May 2005 (Whitney 2005). Four petroglyph features were recorded, all of which had been previously recorded by Ferg (1979). Also in 2005 a report was published of a survey conducted on the western bajada in connection with the Kinder Morgan pipeline replacement project (Estes et al. 2005). This survey recorded a single glyph on an isolated boulder that had not been previously recorded. Finally, a historical inscription was recorded in 2008 by archaeologist Jeff Burton (Madsen 2008:28) on the west side of the hill. Burton was conducting a preliminary reconnaissance in connection with the *Tumamoc Hill Cultural Resources Policy and Management Plan* (Madsen 2008). The inscription he discovered had not been recorded previously and may represent the earliest historical inscription on the hill. All these glyphs were re-recorded in our study.

The 2006-2009 Survey

The present survey was conducted in response to a request by Suzanne Fish and Paul Fish, Curators of Archaeology, and John Madsen, former Associate Curator of Archaeology (now emeritus), with the Arizona State Museum. As part of research for a National Register nomination and a management plan of the hill, they were overseeing a precise survey of the archaeological features on the summit of the hill, using modern mapping techniques. Several graduate students under the direction of Suzanne and Paul Fish were responsible for accomplishing most aspects of the summit survey. However, to resurvey the rock art required a considerable output of time, more than the graduate students and undergraduate students could commit. Thus, the principal authors (GHH and PCB) were approached about undertaking a new survey and agreed to do so, under the auspices of the Arizona State Museum and with the volunteer help of members of the Arizona Archaeological and Historical Society (Figure II.2).

The rock art survey was conducted largely during three field seasons: late fall through early spring of 2006-2007, 2007-2008, and 2008-2009. During the first field season the

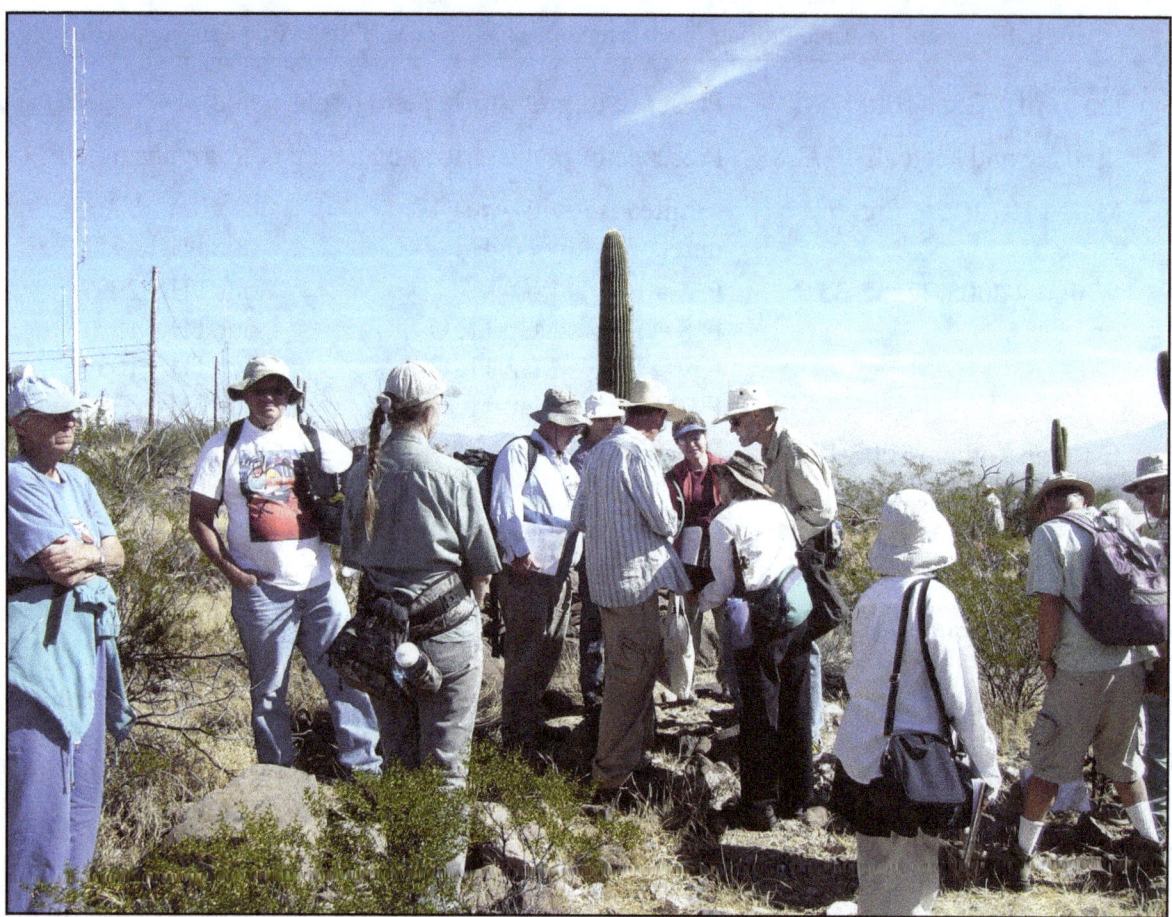

Figure II.2. Todd Pitezel orienting surveyors on the summit of Tumamoc Hill. (Photo by Katherine Cerino, 4 November 2006)

survey team varied in size from about eight to as many as 14; during the second and third season the team generally consisted of a core of eight members. The team contributed 2,041 person hours over the three field seasons. During the late spring and early summer of each year several members of the crew entered the data gathered during the previous field season into a Microsoft Access program as well as carrying out associated tasks, expending 1,112 hours. Thus, a total of 3,153 person hours were expended in the field and in the laboratory on the project. This summary of the time needed to gather and computerize the data emphasizes how time-consuming rock art recording can be.

The survey team, all volunteers with various levels of experience, worked diligently to record what they saw with care and precision. Because many different eyes and hands were involved in the initial recording, the principal authors not only participated in the survey but reviewed the recording forms for completeness and, when necessary, revisited features to make corrections. As time went on and everyone became more experienced, errors became fewer and, we believe, records became more comparable.

Tumamoc Hill is not an easy place to survey. On some days the wind blew so violently that work was called off for fear someone would fall off the edge of a summit cliff (Figure II.3).

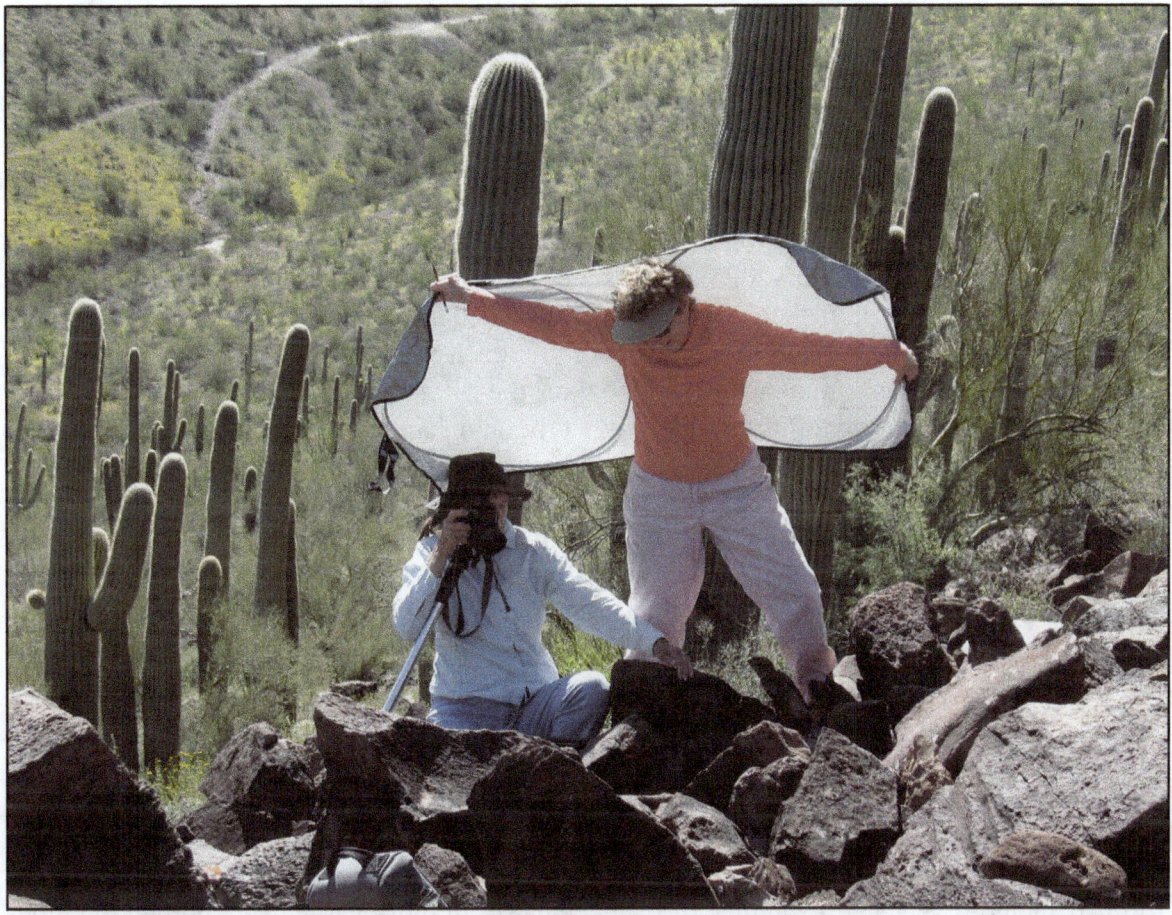

Figure II.3. Rock art recorders Janine Hernbrode and Valerie Davison with their photo shade on a windy day. (Photo by Gayle Hartmann, 11 March 2008)

Care had to be taken with unstable boulders, steep, uneven slopes, resting javelina, and, on one occasion, a sleeping rattlesnake.

METHODOLOGY

The goals of this project were (1) to re-record all previously noted rock images on the hill, (2) to record images that had been overlooked and (3) to document all historic graffiti and outright vandalism in order to provide a baseline for future comparisons. To use our time effectively, we made the decision to begin with what was already known, adding new features as we came upon them. Thus,

the fieldwork conducted for this paper did not consist of a new and complete survey of the summit and slopes of Tumamoc Hill. Instead, it was largely based on two bodies of information gathered previously: (1) rock art recorded as part of an undergraduate field school in 2005 and 2006 (largely on the summit of the hill) (University of Arizona Archaeological Field School at Tumamoc Hill 2005-2006) and (2) the published work of Alan Ferg (1979) along with his maps and photographs in the archives of the Arizona State Museum. In addition, we examined more recent surveys of the hill that were conducted for special purposes. (See details of the recent surveys in Table II.1) We include those in our tabulations. Finally, we discovered a considerable quantity of previously unrecorded rock art.

The recording form that we used was created initially for a 2005-2006 undergraduate field school that took place on Tumamoc and recorded some of the rock art on the hill (University of Arizona Archaeological Field School at Tumamoc Hill 2005-2006). It was created by Phil Leckman, then a graduate student in the Department of Anthropology at the University of Arizona, along with Suzanne and Paul Fish. The majority of its terminology and organization were taken from Ferg's (1979) recording system, while some was project specific. Before we began work on the hill, the list of design elements from that survey was expanded by graduate students Todd Pitezel and Dan Broockman. They added additional elements that were used by Henry Wallace and James Holmlund (1986) during their survey of the petroglyphs of the Picacho Mountains. The recording form may be found at the end of this article as Appendix I. Appendix II is the manual that assists recorders in filling out the form. It includes sketched examples of each design element and its designation.

We began our work by relocating glyphs that had been recorded by the undergraduate field school. We quickly discovered that the quality of the student work was variable. In many cases we heavily revised what they had done and checked our recording efforts against those previously done by Ferg. Because of the unreliability of the students' work, we did not include it as a baseline of comparison in the "General Survey Observations" section of this report. When we finished re-recording the students' work, we turned to the additional petroglyphs that had been recorded by Ferg. During our work, we had the advantage of modern technology in mapping and photography that was not available to Ferg. We recorded UTM coordinates for each feature, most of which were characterized by an uncertainty of 4 to 5 meters. This was not as precise as we would have liked but was the best we could achieve with the equipment available. More accurate UTM coordinates were recorded for some features by using a Trimble GPS, primarily those recorded previously by the field school. Also, each feature was photographed using a digital camera following guidelines developed by Janine Hernbrode, which are presented in Appendix III.

Each recording form included information on the number and type of glyphs; feature type and location; panel angle, aspect, and height; panel and element size; technique of production; line width; superimposition; patination; condition of the rock; amount and type of disturbance; and a drawing that recorded each glyph and the rock condition as faithfully as possible.

We discovered that graffiti were abundant, even more so than we had realized, especially in certain easy-to-reach locations. As we neared the end of the project we realized we did not have the time to devote an entire recording form to each set of modern initials, names, etc. So, in those cases, we recorded the modern graffiti in an abbreviated fashion. In all cases, each feature with graffiti was given a feature number and location as well as being drawn and photographed. Project records, photographs, and artifacts are curated at the Arizona State Museum (ASM Accession No. AP-2013-437: Tumamoc Hill Mapping and Excavation Project).

GENERAL SURVEY OBSERVATIONS

Here we focus on several general attributes of the prehistoric rock art—quantity recorded, spatial distribution, techniques employed, missing and disturbed glyphs, and design elements. Specific styles—Hohokam and Western Archaic Tradition—are described in the sections following this one. For perspective, this section also provides information about the quantity and location of graffiti recorded, but, otherwise, details regarding graffiti are discussed separately in a later section. A summary tabulation of the prehistoric rock art recorded by this survey is provided in Appendix IV.

Quantity Recorded

We used Ferg's maps to relocate glyphs and found both his sketch maps and topographic map to be accurate and helpful. As we proceeded with our recording efforts, we began to discover rock art that had been missed by previous recorders. In fact, by the time we finished the project we had added 135 features consisting of 274 elements to the body of recorded prehistoric rock art on the hill, bringing the total number of rock art features that include prehistoric rock art to 362 and the number of prehistoric elements to 734. Included in these 450 features are 56 features that contain both prehistoric rock art and graffiti elements. In addition, six features contain one element each of indeterminate age; that is, we could not determine whether they are prehistoric or historic. As a result, they are not included in the tabulations and discussion that follows. Those elements that could not be dated are listed in Appendix V.

The focus of Ferg's (1979) study was prehistoric rock art, but he also recorded two cases of graffiti he found of interest. We recorded 206 features with graffiti; these contained a total of 450 graffiti elements.

We want to reiterate that we did not conduct a thorough survey of the hill, so there are undoubtedly some rock art features that remain to be recorded. We did, however, visit virtually all parts of the hill with rock outcrops, talus slopes, and boulder fields with suitable rock surfaces. We believe we recorded a minimum of 95 percent of the rock art on the hill.

Spatial Distribution

As Ferg (1979) noted, the vast majority of rock art is on the summit and the more gentle north slope. Our tabulations indicate that 75 percent of the prehistoric rock art can be found within these two areas.

In our discussions of location we identify specific locales using Ferg's alphabetical list of clusters, to which we have added new data, both additional examples of prehistoric rock art and modern graffiti. (Ferg's clusters begin at the bottom of the hill with "A" and work their way up the north-slope to the summit; then they continue onto the other slopes.) Information about the spatial distribution of the rock art (both prehistoric and graffiti) is provided in Figures II.4-II.7 and in Table II.2.

In comparison with the overall rock art universe on the hill, scratched glyphs have a different spatial distribution (Figure II.8). Instead of being largely found on the north slope and the summit, the largest number of scratched elements are on a large outcrop on the lower west side of the hill. A much smaller number of Hohokam-style pecked glyphs also occur there. Other scratched glyphs are scattered on the north slope, the summit, and east slope. For reasons that we can only speculate about, scratched glyphs are frequently superimposed one on the other. We discuss scratched glyphs in more detail in a later section.

With the exception of the agricultural fields on the western bajadas, in general, the prehistoric rock art is close to the places on the hill where other human activities occurred— the summit and the north-slope trail. Ferg (1979:111) also noted that, although glyphs were in the areas most frequented by humans, they were not within or part of activity areas. We concur with this statement. Although we did not systematically record whether glyphs were on human-built structures such as walls, trails, or pithouses, we can report only a few such

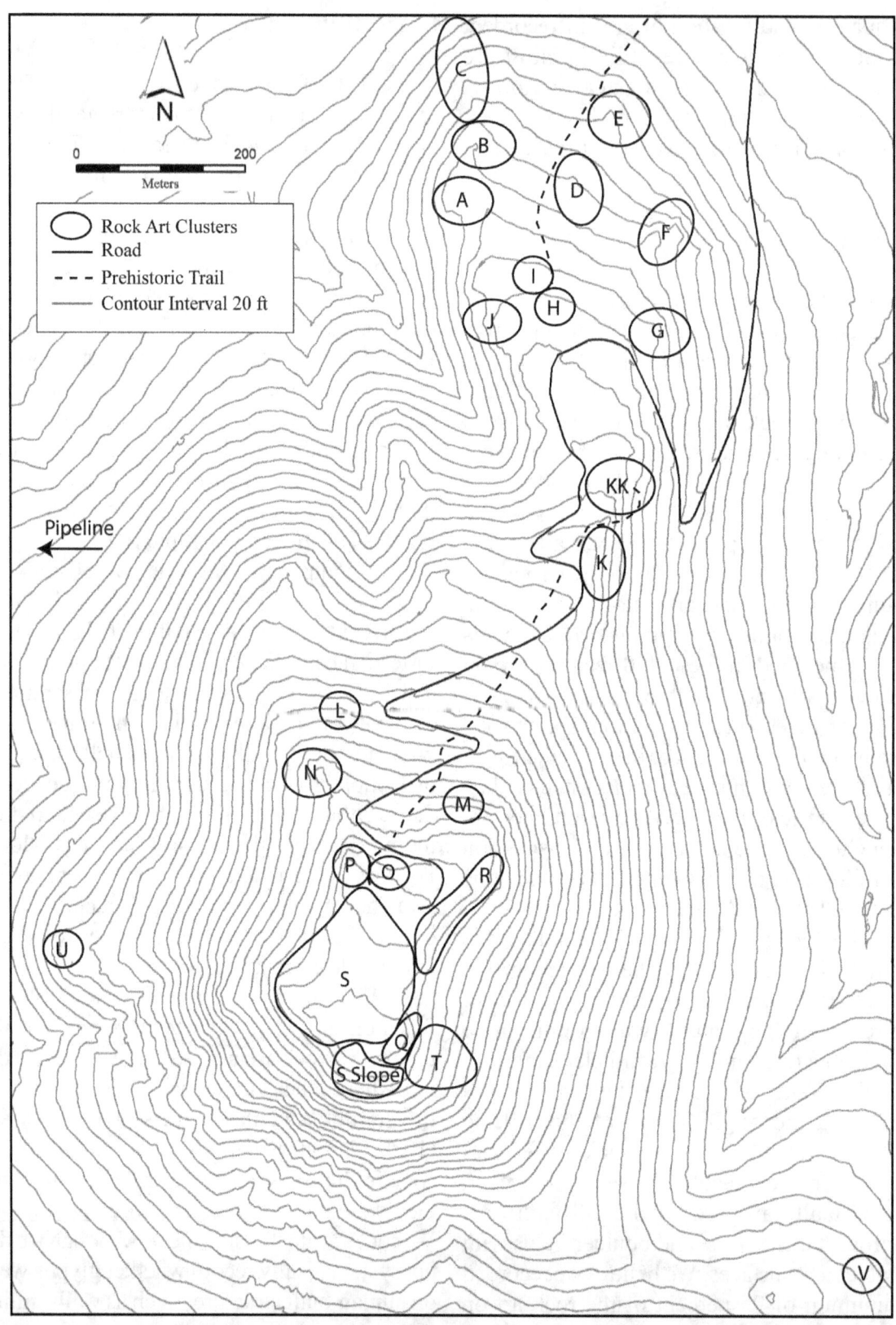

Figure II.4. Map illustrating locations of clusters. Cluster outlines are not precise; they provide only generalized locations. (Map by Todd Pitezel and Kelly Rehm)

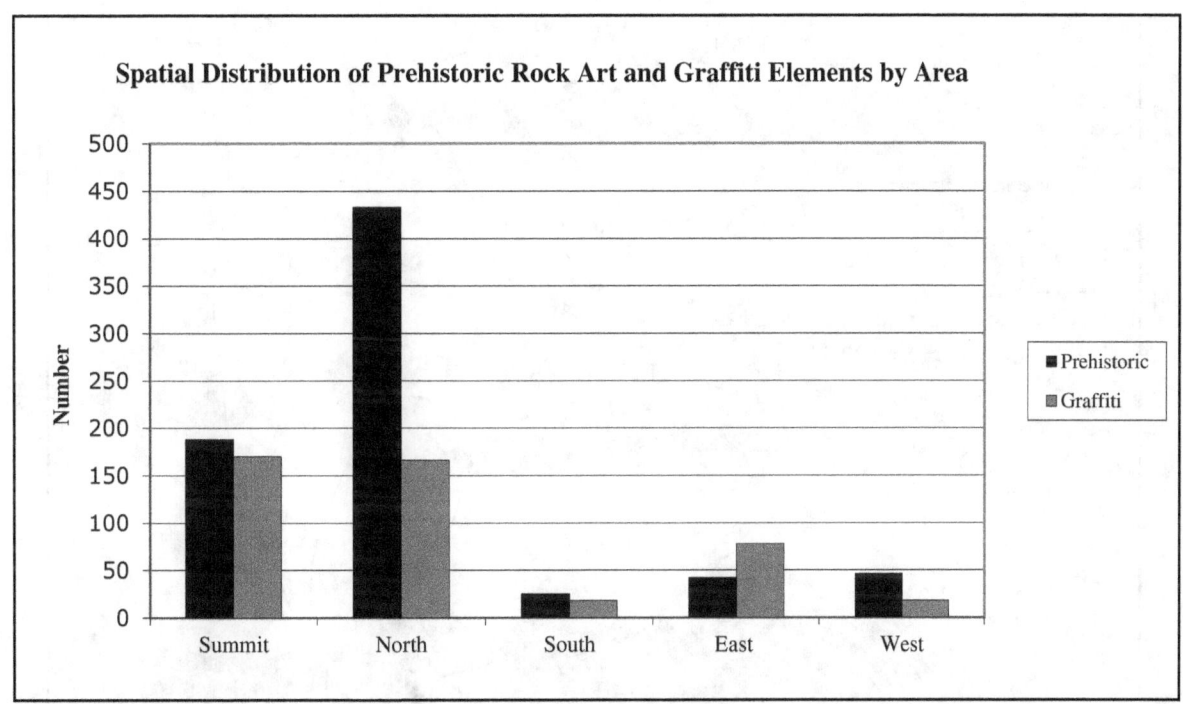

Figure II.5. Spatial distribution of prehistoric rock art and graffiti elements by area. Glyphs recorded as "South" are not far below the summit.

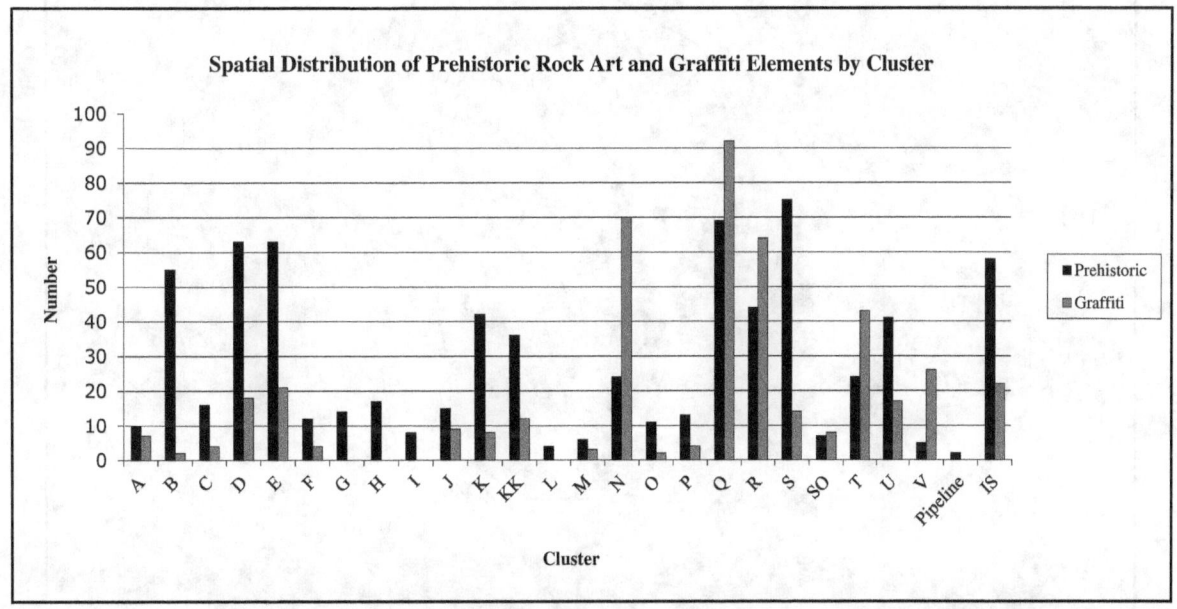

Figure II.6. Spatial distribution of prehistoric rock art and graffiti elements by Ferg's clusters.

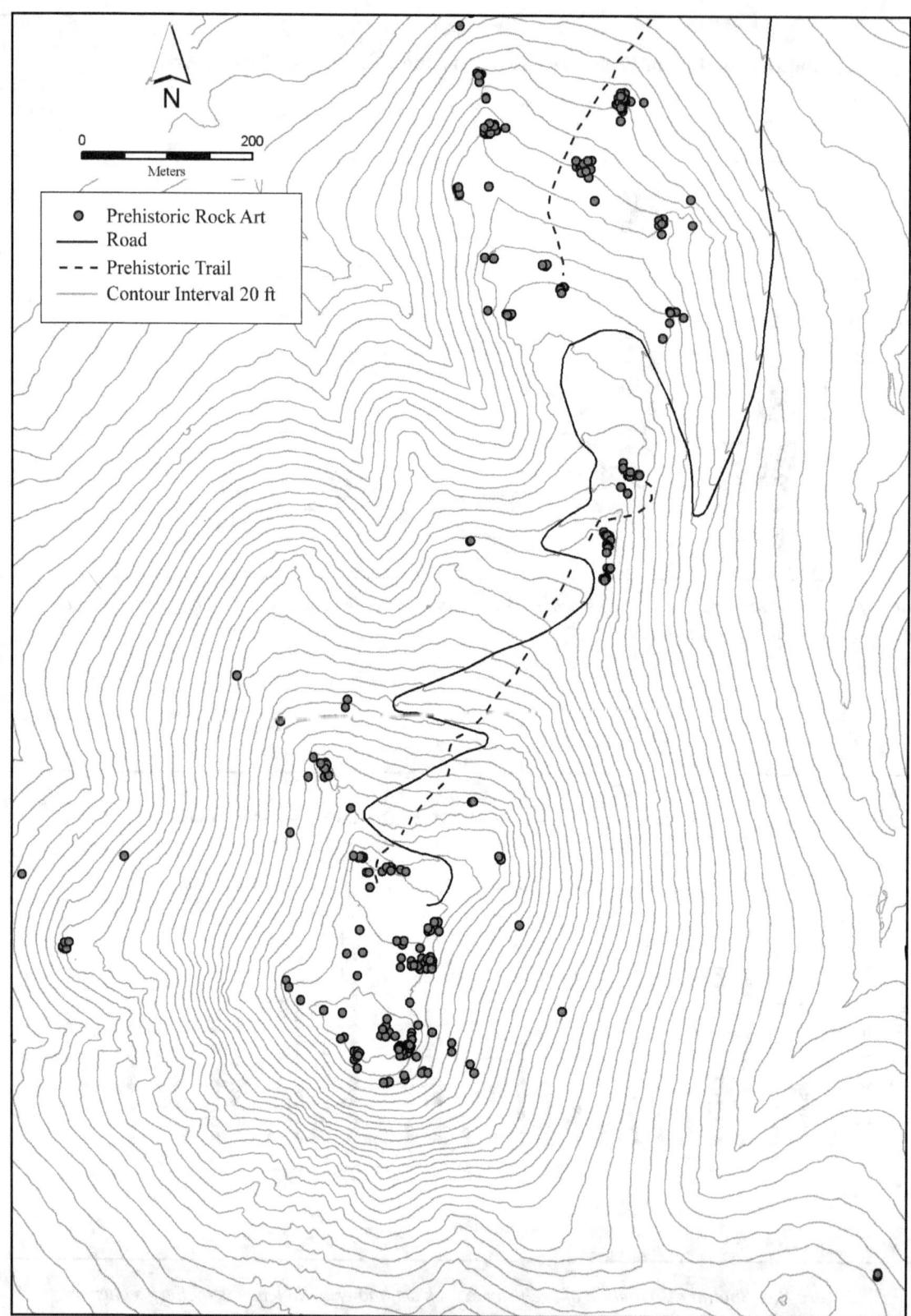

Figure II.7. Map illustrating distribution of prehistoric rock art. Note: Each circle represents a rock art feature. Some features contain more than one element. (Map by Todd Pitezel)

Table II.2. Spatial Distribution of Prehistoric Rock Art and Graffiti Elements by Ferg's Clusters

Ferg Cluster ID	Area	Prehistoric	Graffiti
A	North slope	10	7
B	North slope	55	2
C	North slope	16	4
D	North slope	63	18
E	North slope	63	21
F	North slope	12	4
G	North slope	14	0
H	North slope	17	0
I	North slope	8	0
J	North slope	15	9
K	North slope	42	8
KK	North slope	36	12
L	North slope	4	0
M	North slope	6	3
N	North slope	24	70
O	North slope	11	2
P	North slope	13	4
Q	Summit	69	92
R	Summit	44	64
S	Summit	75	14
T	East slope	24	43
U	West slope	41	17
V	East slope	5	26
So. Slope	South slope	7	8
Pipeline	West of hill	2	0
Isolates	Various	58	22
Total		734	450

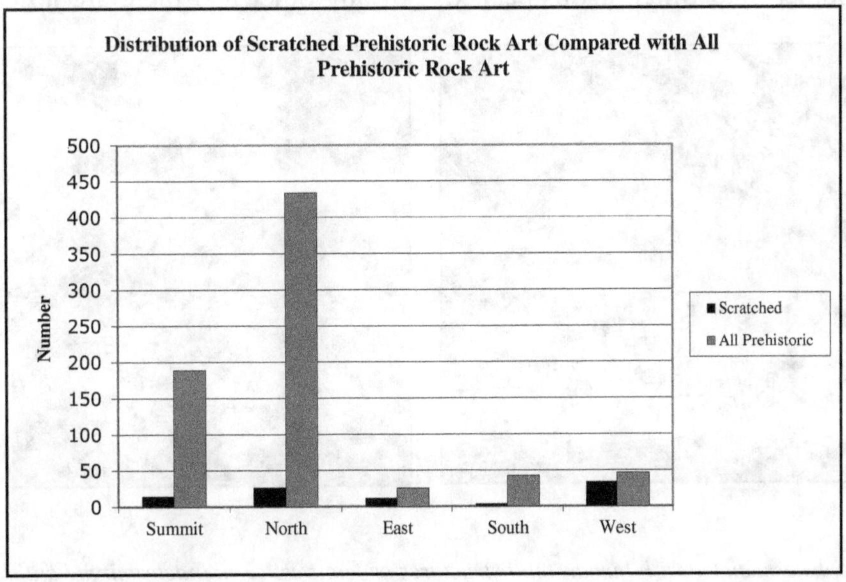

Figure II.8. *Spatial distribution of scratched prehistoric rock art compared with all prehistoric rock art. Glyphs recorded as "South" are not far below the summit.*

instances. We cannot rule out that there may be others, but if so we think there are only a few. In fact, we identified only three that fit in this category, two of which are illustrated in Figure II.9. One is associated with a trincheras feature, one with a probable trincheras feature, and the third is part of a circular rock structure.

The most prominent glyph of the three is an indeterminate anthropomorph pecked into a boulder that is part of the trincheras structure that extends along the east side of the summit (Figure II.9a). The second glyph consists of several parallel lines scratched into a probable trincheras feature that surrounds the southwest edge of the summit. The third is a small, very faint three-ring concentric circle (actually more of an oval) located on a boulder that is part of a circular structure (presumably a pithouse foundation) on the south portion of the summit (Figure II.9b).

These three glyphs bear no obvious relationship to each other and what, if anything, their presence on human-built structures may signify is unclear. It is important to recognize, however, that the first glyph definitely fits within the Hohokam Pecked style and thus would have been created centuries later than the trincheras boulder onto which it was pecked.

The second, the set of parallel lines, may belong to the Hohokam Scratched style, and, thus, also may have been created long after the probable trincheras feature was constructed. Because it is very faint, the third gives the impression of being of greater antiquity than the other two. It does not, however, meet our criteria for Archaic Tradition glyphs, as discussed below, so it could have been created during Hohokam times long after the construction and use of the pithouse.

The location of rock art in terms of its importance to the community versus the individual is discussed by numerous authors, for example Wallace (2008). This distinction is often referred to as "public" versus "private" rock art. In his discussion of the petroglyphs of Atlatl Ridge in the Tortolita Mountains, Wallace (2008:203) points out that glyphs in small sheltered areas "would likely have been important to the individual rather than to a community, ethnic group, or culture. This is especially true for isolated locations with no discernible landscape or cultural association." On Tumamoc there are no truly "isolated landscapes," since any spot on the hill is within relatively easy walking distance of any other and there are no caves or large

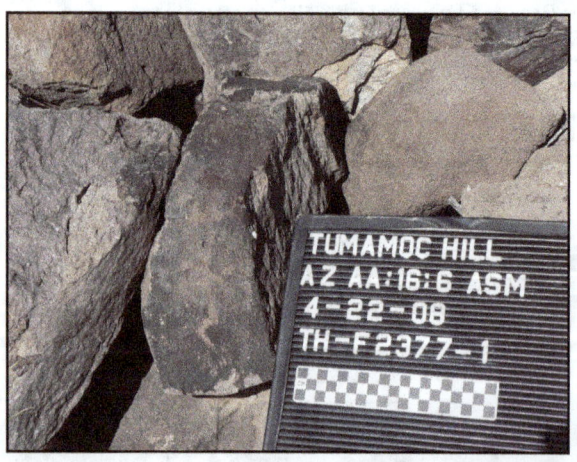

a

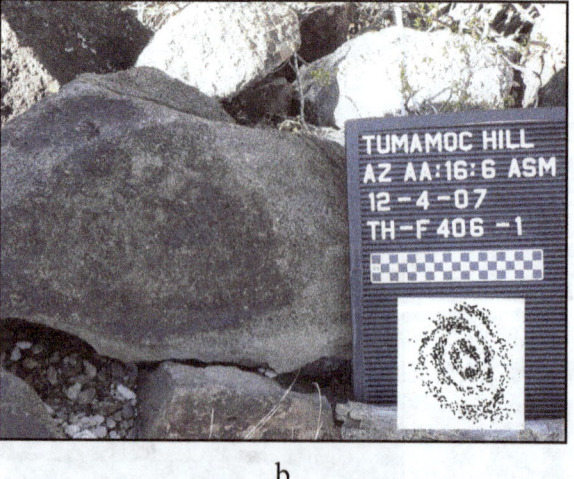

b

Figure II.9. Glyphs associated with human-built structures or features. a, an indeterminate anthropomorph pecked into a trincheras structure (TH-F2377-1); b, a faint three-ring concentric circle incorporated into a rock structure (TH-F406-1). (Photos by Janine Hernbrode; sketch by William K. Hartmann)

overhangs that provide secluded locations. In addition, there seem to be no glyphs in locales that are truly confined and sheltered. The vast majority is on outcrops or vertical rock faces visible from at least a few meters away. Of the pecked glyphs, a few recorded as isolates might have been created for individualistic reasons. Although they do not differ dramatically in motif from other Hohokam-style glyphs, and none is hidden, all are separated from the larger clusters of glyphs and, thus, might have been created in connection with some individual ideological rite. All are listed as "IS" (isolated) in Appendix IV.

If any area of the hill is a location of special significance for rock art activity, it is the southeast "corner" of the summit. The rock art on this portion of the summit is characterized by three factors: high density of glyphs, the presence of unusual motifs, and glyphs with possible astronomical significance. This area, Cluster Q as identified by Ferg (1979), covers about 1,634 square meters and includes 69 prehistoric glyphs. The remainder of the summit, in contrast, measures 56,506 square meters and contains 119 glyphs. Thus, Cluster Q contains a little over one-third of the glyphs on the entire summit.

The glyphs on this corner of the summit are not only abundant, but include motifs that are present nowhere else on the hill. There are, for example, one sun disk that incorporates a natural vesicle, two unusual zoomorphs (one that appears to be an arachnid and one a horned serpent), and three centipedes, the only ones found on Tumamoc. In addition, several of the more unusual elaborated anthropomorphs, which may represent deities or individuals of prominence in the community, were recorded here. (These are discussed in more detail in the section "*Elaboration among Anthropomorphs.*") Nowhere else on the hill is such a large number of unusual motifs present in such a small area. We provide a brief description of some of these motifs below.

One of the most prominent glyphs anywhere on the hill is the pecked sun disk just mentioned. The disk surrounds a natural circular vesicle with prominent pecked rays emanating out from the disk.

Finally, six of the most unusual anthropomorphs on the hill are located here, two of which are carrying objects and one of which is connected to a snake-like element. One of the anthropomorphs with material culture, a staff and another linear object, utilizes natural vesicles in the boulder as part of its body; it also faces east with a clear view to Sentinel Peak, the Santa Cruz River valley, and the eastern horizon. The other is the only example of an anthropomorph holding a bow; he may be shooting at a small sun disk about 26 cm away on the same large boulder. Another anthropomorph has a broad body and long incised digits (both fingers and toes); it is the only anthropomorph on the hill with incised digits. The final three anthropomorphs have broad bodies and prominent digits. Although none of these anthropomorphs is the largest on the hill, one (the individual holding a staff and another linear object) is among the largest.

This corner of the summit is also the location of several possible solar markers. During our survey, one of our members (Janine Hernbrode) began to question whether some petroglyph elements on the hill might have astronomical references. Also, several years earlier, Cherie Freeman (who worked on our survey during the first season) had made a similar suggestion. Thus, we invited astronomer John Fountain, who has had considerable experience in the field of archaeo-astronomy, to visit the hill. Over the 2006-2009 period he, Janine, and others visited several rock art features repeatedly on significant calendrical days and observed what they believe are glyphs that interact with sunlight in ways that appear to have astronomical significance.

John Fountain (personal communication, 2010) defines a solar marker as follows, "Light or shadow falling across a petroglyph in a distinctive way on a significant calendrical day." The preliminary result of Fountain and Hernbrode's research was the identification of eight probable markers on the southeast corner of the summit. Three of these were observed at winter solstice, two at the equinox, and three at summer solstice. The most credible markers are those that have interactions on more than one significant seasonal day. Two of the markers in this area exhibit these multiple interactions. The pecked sundisk and two of the elaborated anthropomorphs mentioned previously were included in this group of probable markers. In addition, on the slopes of the hill, Hernbrode identified several glyphs with interaction potential, but no direct solar markers have been confirmed. For a more detailed discussion of the results of this project see Fountain and Hernbrode (2008; this volume).

Techniques Employed

Pecked glyphs were made by direct percussion, the pecked motif being created from individual blows with a cobble that removed the exterior patina of the host rock and left small depressions or dints. We recorded 632 (86 percent) pecked glyphs, making pecking the most common technique, by far, for the 734 prehistoric elements. Considerably less common is scratching (n = 85, 12 percent), with a few examples of abrading (n = 5, less than 1 percent) and incising (n = 1, less than 1 percent). Eleven elements combine techniques: pecking and scratching (n = 8, less than 1 percent); pecking and incising (n = 1, less than 1 percent); pecking and abrading (n = 1, less than percent); and pecking, scratching, and possible abrading (n = 1, less than 1 percent).

Individual pecked lines range from 0.1 to 10 cm in width with a median and mode (typical width) of 1.0 cm. Our measurements of element size (width by length) indicate that the minimum dimension of individual pecked elements ranges from 1.0 to 84 cm, while the maximum dimension ranges from 3.0 cm to 126 cm. For the smaller dimension the median is 11 cm with a mode (or typical minimum) of 7 cm; for the larger dimension the median is 16 cm with a mode of 13 cm.

The scratched glyphs were created by dragging a tool stone across the rock face, often so gently that the line barely penetrated the exterior varnish of the rock surface. As Ferg (1979:97) notes, "The implement used [for scratching] was almost certainly a flake or complete tool made from silicious stone rather than from the local basalt. Using a sharp piece of basalt on the basalt produces at best a wide, shallow gash." Of the 85 we recorded, line width ranges from 0.1 to 2.5 cm with a median and mode of 0.1 cm. Element size ranges from a minimum dimension of 2 to 72 cm; while the maximum dimension ranges from 6 to 120 cm. For the smaller dimension the median is 13 cm with a mode of 14 cm; for the larger dimension the median is 20 cm with a mode of 15 cm.

In addition to the nature of their manufacture, scratched glyphs differ from pecked glyphs in other ways. The individual lines in each scratched element are narrower, generally about 0.1 cm in width, and the lines are close together, with the distance between lines generally ranging from about 0.5 cm to 2.0 cm. The lines in similar pecked motifs, that is, grids, diamonds, and bands, are generally about 5.0 cm apart. In addition, line width in scratched glyphs is very uniform with only five elements having a line width other than 0.1 cm. We should point out that we did not measure the distance between lines in the field, but rather estimated them from an inspection of a sample of the photos. In contrast to line width, element size is similar between the two techniques, exhibiting similar ranges, medians, and modes. Thus, although glyphs created by the two methods have similar overall dimensions, they have a very different gestalt and, were quite possibly made for different reasons.

Missing and Disturbed Glyphs

With two exceptions, we located all the glyphs recorded by Ferg (1979). Both of the missing glyphs, an anthropomorph located on a prominent outcrop just below the summit on the north slope, and a two-ring concentric circle on the west side of the hill, have clearly been removed since Ferg's survey. The outcrop on the north slope was popular with prehistoric artists and historic "artists" (only 24 of the glyphs on the outcrop are prehistoric while 70 are modern graffiti). By using the single photograph we had as a guide, we were able to locate the large, flat slab on which the anthropomorph rock had rested (Figure II.10).

The missing two-ring concentric circle was part of a large, complex feature located just above a vertical face on the west side of the hill (TH-F4341). In addition to being the home of one of the two missing glyphs, this feature, which is isolated from other rock art and not easily accessible from the north-slope road, also exhibited definite examples of vandalism that had occurred since Ferg's survey. Presumably, the individuals who visited this location entered the Tumamoc Hill property from Greasewood Road and walked across the bajada on the west side of the hill.

Feature TH-F4341 covers three boulders and consists of 12 elements (Figure II.11). Figure II.11a provides an overview of the entire feature showing the three large boulders that are included. In one instance of vandalism, an attempt was made to remove an element that appears to be a foot or a bear paw. Chisel marks and flake scars where rock chips were removed are evident around the element, but the attempt at removal was unsuccessful (Figure II.11b). This attempted vandalism post-dates Ferg's work as there was no evidence of chiseling in photos taken at the time. In the original photographs, a faint outline is visible around the glyph. Ferg (personal communication, 2009) has no memory of anything unusual at this location, but commented that he believes he would have made note of obvious vandalism. Thus, it seems probable that the outline is a natural crack. In a second case, a geometric indeterminate has been chiseled out, but left nearby (Figure II.11c). The rock fragment on which the element was pecked fits neatly into its original location (Figure II.11d). This glyph as it was put back into its original location can also be seen in the upper left part of Figure II.11a (above and to the left of the single circle glyph). In a third instance of vandalism, an attempt was made to remove a two-ring concentric circle and possibly some smaller indistinct elements (Figure II.11e), but the section of rock on which the glyph had been pecked broke into several pieces. At least some of the pieces were left nearby. Figure II.11f illustrates a few of the pieces being put together.

The final example of disturbed rock art consisted of a single boulder with two elements (a counterclockwise scroll and a geometric indeterminate) (TH-F2912) that was not in the position it had been when recorded by Ferg. After spending considerable time searching the small knoll on which the feature had been recorded, we discovered the boulder upside down (with the rock art on the bottom faces) about 1.5 m downslope to the east of its recorded location. Only two additional rock art elements are present on this knoll; both are prehistoric. The absence of graffiti and the distance from the north-slope road make this seem an unlikely location for modern visitors. Whether the boulder was moved by humans, animals, or environmental forces is uncertain, but its movement reminds us that even over a period as little as approximately 34 years, change occurs, especially on steep, unstable slopes.

Design Elements

Recording design elements (motifs) is a

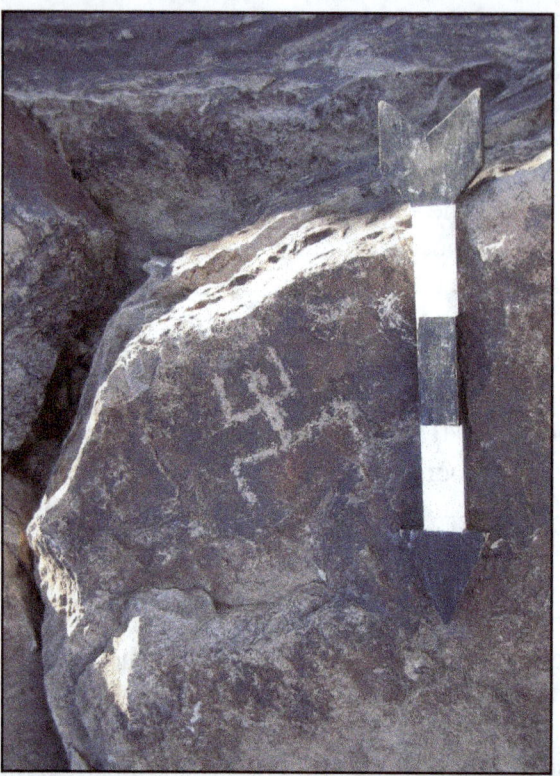

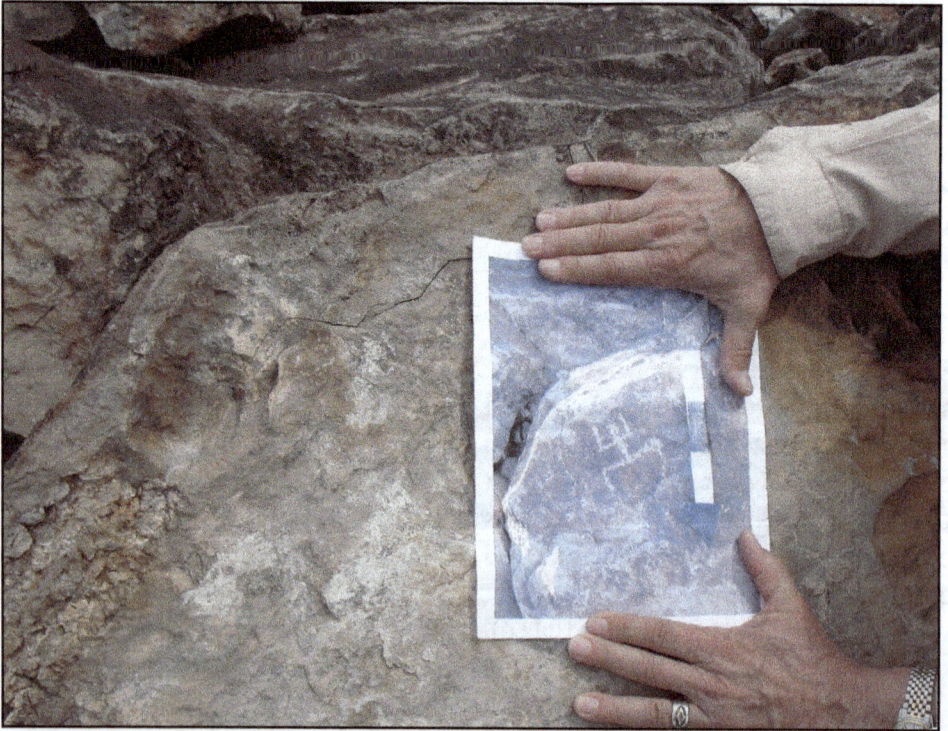

Figure II.10. One of the two prehistoric glyphs that has been removed from the hill. upper, the missing anthropomorph (TH-F13) (photo by University of Arizona Archaeological Field School at Tumamoc Hill, 2005-2006); lower, the photo of the missing anthropomorph showing the location where it rested on a large, flat slab (TH-F13-2). (Photo by Gayle Hartmann, 21 March 2011)

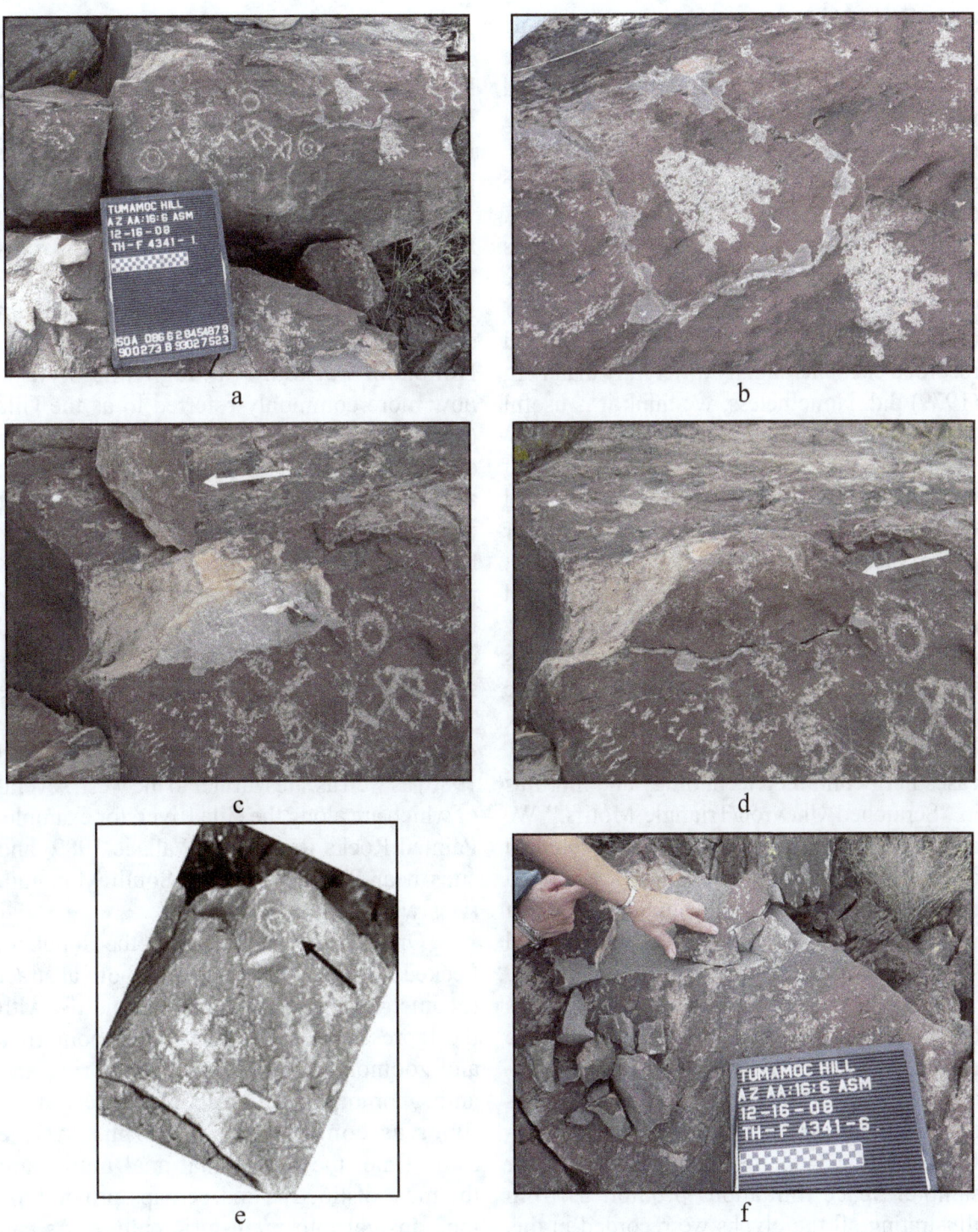

Figure II.11. The most serious case of rock art vandalism. a, overview of TH-F4341-1; b, foot/bear paw glyph (element 11) encircled by chisel marks (TH-F43314-10); c, a geometric indeterminate (element 2), as we found it, removed from its original location (TH-F4341-13); d, the same geometric indeterminate put back into its original location (TH-F4341-14); e, a two-ring concentric circle as photographed by Stephen M. Larson in 1974-1975, the prior location of this glyph (now missing) can be seen in the lower right corner of a; f, the location of the vandalized concentric circle shown in e with some of the pieces being put back into place (TH-F4341-6). (Photos c and d by Peter Boyle; a, b, and f by Janine Hernbrode)

subjective activity. Drawing and photographing any element depends on light conditions, the condition of the rock surface, the depth and width of the pecking within the element being recorded, and an assessment of superimposition, as well as other variables, such as the presence of lichens, which may obscure the rock art. Thus, we do not claim that the design elements that we saw and recorded are precisely the same as those that would be recorded by other individuals. In fact, in some cases we saw and recorded elements slightly differently than Ferg (1979) did. Nonetheless, we think it is useful to compare our two sets of data.

In Table II.3 we provide a comparison of the elements we recorded with those recorded by Ferg. In a few cases we recorded fewer design elements than Ferg did. That does not mean we did not locate the elements, instead it means we categorized them differently. For example, we used categories such as "Geometric indeterminate" and Geometric other," that were not used by Ferg (Appendix II). In addition we should note that in a few cases Ferg combined technology and motif as in "Scratched Chevron/Triangle Motifs." We added these scratched motifs to the relevant design element category. Finally, as noted earlier, we used a set of design elements that were primarily from Ferg (1979), but included some additional elements from other sources.

The primary difference between Ferg's design tabulation and ours is quantity. We recorded more examples in nearly every category. Thus, we confirm Ferg's basic findings regarding design elements with the main difference being we have a considerably larger sample. Space limitations prohibit us from illustrating all the glyphs we recorded in this report. However, photographs of all the glyphs (including graffiti) can be accessed on the Arizona State Museum website: www.state-museum.arizona.edu/research/pubs/archseries/companion_materials

HOHOKAM STYLES

Most of the prehistoric rock art on Tumamoc Hill can be divided into two basic styles: Hohokam Pecked and a Scratched style that is probably of Hohokam age and affinity.

Hohokam Pecked Style

As Ferg (1979) noted, the dominant rock art style on Tumamoc Hill is, in his terminology, Hohokam Pecked. Although this style is now more commonly referred to as the Gila (Hohokam) style as defined by Wellman (1979), Schaafsma (1980:83-99), and Wallace and Holmlund (1986:82-84), among others, we use Ferg's terminology, "Hohokam Pecked" because it is less cumbersome. Since Ferg's pioneering work, the Hohokam Pecked style has been recorded throughout southern and central Arizona including nearby locations such as Rillito Peak at the northern end of the Tucson Mountains (Wallace 1983) and the Picacho Mountains (Wallace and Holmlund 1986) as well as sites farther to the west, several of which are along the Gila River, for example, Painted Rocks Reservoir (Wallace 1989) and sites near Phoenix such as South Mountain (Bostwick 2002).

On Tumamoc as elsewhere, the Hohokam Pecked style is characterized by both abstract (geometric) and representational motifs, with the representational motifs (anthropomorphs and zoomorphs) being in the minority, and anthropomorphs being approximately three times as common as zoomorphs. At the same time, the representational motifs are the most distinctive and perhaps provide the most insight into prehistoric culture. As can be seen in Figure II.12, of the three design categories, geometric elements occur in the greatest frequency overall and are especially abundant on the north slope, with a little over one-third as many occurring on the summit.

Table II.3. Comparison of Design Elements Data from Ferg (1979) and from this Study

Design Elements	Ferg (1979) Number	This Study Number
Anthropomorphic		
Stick anthropomorph	94	93
Stick anthropomorph holding material culture	Included in category above	15
Anthropomorph other than a stick figure	1	19
Anthropomorph (not a stick person) with staff	1	1
Footprints	(Ferg listed 1 set of 2 footprints) 1	2
Anthropomorphic indeterminate	(Ferg did not use this term) NA	17
Anthropomorphic other	(Ferg did not use this term) NA	17
Total Anthropomorphs	97	164
Zoomorphic		
Centipede	3	3
Insect	1	0
Lizard with toes	1	1
Lizard without toes	7	11
Quadruped, horned	8	16
Quadruped, without horns	2	6
Tortoise	2	3
Zoomorphic indeterminate	(Ferg did not use this term) NA	8
Zoomorphic other	(Ferg did not use this term) NA	3
Total Zoomorphs	24	51
Geometric		
Arcs, concentric	2	2
Arcs, concentric, spoked	1	1
Asterisk	5	3
Bull's eye, 1 ring	4	11
Bull's eye, 2 rings (includes 2 of Ferg's "elaborated concentric circle motifs")	3	6
Bull's eye, 3 + rings (includes 1 of Ferg's "elaborated concentric circle motifs")	2	2
Chevron ladder	1	1
Chevron, nested (Includes Ferg's "scratched chevron motif")	4	9
Circle	35	49
Circle chain	6	15
Circle cluster	1	4
Circle pattern	2	4
Circle tailed	2	9
Circles, concentric, 2 rings	22	37

Table II.3. Comparison of Design Elements Data from Ferg (1979) and from this Study, cont'd

Design Elements	Ferg (1979) Number	This Study Number
Circles, concentric, 3 rings (includes 2 of Ferg's "elaborated concentric circle motifs")	6	10
Circles, concentric, 4 rings	1	2
Circles, concentric, 5+ rings	1	2
Circles, line connected (Equates with Ferg's "connected circles")	2	4
Circles, sectioned	5	3
Circles with arc	1	1
Cross	3	11
Cross hatch, band (includes Ferg's "scratched hachure band")	9	8
Cross hatch, diamond	5	20
Cross hatch, grid (includes Ferg's "scratched cross hatched grid)	28	22
Curvilinear abstract	40	38
Dot framing	0	1
Dot undefined pattern	0	1
Ladder	0	3
Line, curved	0	4
Line, straight	7	20
Lines, parallel	0	15
Line, zigzag or wavy (includes Ferg's 3 examples of "scratched straight, zigzag, & wavy lines")	17	22
Pipette	3	5
Rain cloud	1	1
Rake	1	2
Rake, double	0	3
Reticulate	3	0
Rectilinear abstract	23	24
Rectilinear meander	7	4
Scroll, curvilinear clockwise	5	8
Scroll, curvilinear connected [a,b]	3	5
Scroll, curvilinear counterclockwise [a]	8	15
Scroll, curvilinear interlocking	1	2
Scroll, rectilinear connected	0	1
Shell	0	1
Snake	2	3
Square (includes Ferg's "elaborated square motif")	3	4
Sun disk	6	11
Swastika	1	1

Table II.3. Comparison of Design Elements Data from Ferg (1979) and from this Study, cont'd

Design Elements	Ferg (1979) Number	This Study Number
Terraced element	1	1
Triangle (includes Ferg's "scratched")	3	4
Geometric indeterminate (includes 1 of Ferg's "elaborated concentric circle motifs")	1	77
Geometric other	NA	7
Total Geometric	287	519
Grand Total	408	734

[a] Ferg used the term "spiral" instead of "scroll."
[b] Ferg used "spirals joined to a common line," and "connected spirals." Ferg did not separate curvilinear from rectilinear spiral/scrolls.

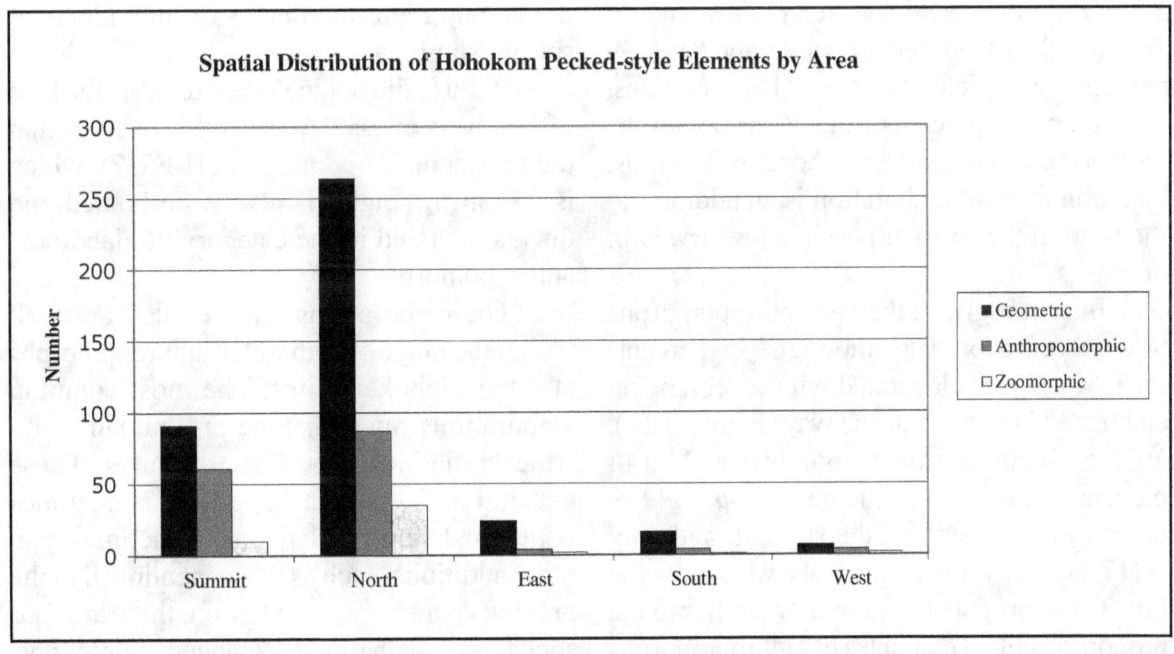

Figure II.12. Spatial distribution of Hohokam Pecked-style elements by area: geometric, anthropomorphic, and zoomorphic. Glyphs recorded as "South" are not far below the summit.

Anthropomorphs are significantly less common in all areas, but are also most common on the north slope with nearly two-thirds as many on the summit. They are uncommon on the other three slopes. Zoomorphs are even less abundant but with similar distribution. More detailed discussion of components of the Hohokam Pecked style is provided in Ferg (1979:104-

105). Wallace (1983) also discusses this style in some detail as it occurs on various sites in the Tucson Basin including Tumamoc Hill.

We continue our discussion of Hohokam style rock art by focusing on two discrete components of the style: elaboration among anthropomorphs and temporal affiliation of motifs.

Elaboration Among Anthropomorphs

At most sites a significant portion of the representational designs consists of anthropomorphs and Tumamoc is no exception. There are 164 anthropomorphs, about 22 percent of all the prehistoric glyphs on the hill. In his study of Rillito Peak, a portion of Los Morteros (AZ AA:12:57 [ASM]), Wallace (1983:220, 226) notes that there is considerable similarity between anthropomorphs there and at Tumamoc. He describes anthropomorphs from the two sites by saying most "are represented as stickmen without any elaboration of the body or head and without phallus, hands, feet or phalanges. The arm position and whether the figures are curvilinear, rectilinear, or both, is highly variable. Most figures are static and over 99 percent are depicted head-on." He also notes, "less than five percent of the anthropomorphs recorded are in some way elaborated. The most common form of elaboration is an addition to the head in the form of possible jewelry, hair, or masks."

Interestingly, of the 164 anthropomorphs now recorded on Tumamoc, 36 (22 percent) are in some way elaborated with several being elaborated in more than one way (Figure II.13). Of the elaborated anthropomorphs, 16 (44 percent) are located on the north slope, 14 (39 percent) are located on the summit, and only 6 (17 percent) are located elsewhere on the hill. These proportions are fairly similar to the proportions of all examples of anthropomorphs on the hill, with the distinction being that a somewhat smaller percentage of elaborated anthropomorphs is located on the summit relative to the north slope.

In defining "elaboration" we include wide bodies (as opposed to stick figures); expanded mid-bodies; the single hour-glass figure; presence of material culture including, for example, additions to the head, the presence of staffs and the single individual with a bow; use of cupules; use of cracks or natural holes;

and scenes with multiple figures. We do not consider "elaboration" to include variations in arm and leg positions, presence of hands, feet, digits, or phalluses. We note, however, that the instances of exaggerated digits on Tumamoc are generally associated with other elaboration. For example, Figure II.13a is wide bodied, is trailing something from one foot, has a circular object near one hand, and interacts with the sun on winter solstice (Fountain and Hernbrode, this volume, Figure III.2). In another example, Figure II.13b is wide bodied and has a serpent-like element attached to one leg. The upper portion of this figure has exfoliated away, but a few incised digits are still clearly visible. These anthropomorphs with large or unusual digits may represent deities or individuals of special significance.

We also did not include size as an attribute of "elaborateness." We note, however, that the largest anthropomorph (TH-F517), which is 65 cm in height, is also wide bodied and thus is included in the category of elaborated anthropomorphs.

The elaborations we recorded are well within the range of elaborated anthropomorphs at other Hohokam sites. The most common elaborations on Tumamoc are humans with wide bodies instead of stick figures. These generally also have a large head, sometimes with broad arms and legs, and sometimes with other additions, such as those mentioned in the previous paragraph. In addition, there are four stick figures with round, expanded midsections, one of which is illustrated in Figure II.13c. We note that, although an obvious interpretation of these figures would be that they represent pregnant females this may not be the case. Archaeologist Todd Bostwick (personal communication, 2010) has commented to us that the expanded midsections may be associated with high status males. At the same time, Figures II.13c, d and e include something between their legs that could illustrate a birth or afterbirth. In one instance an unusual hour-

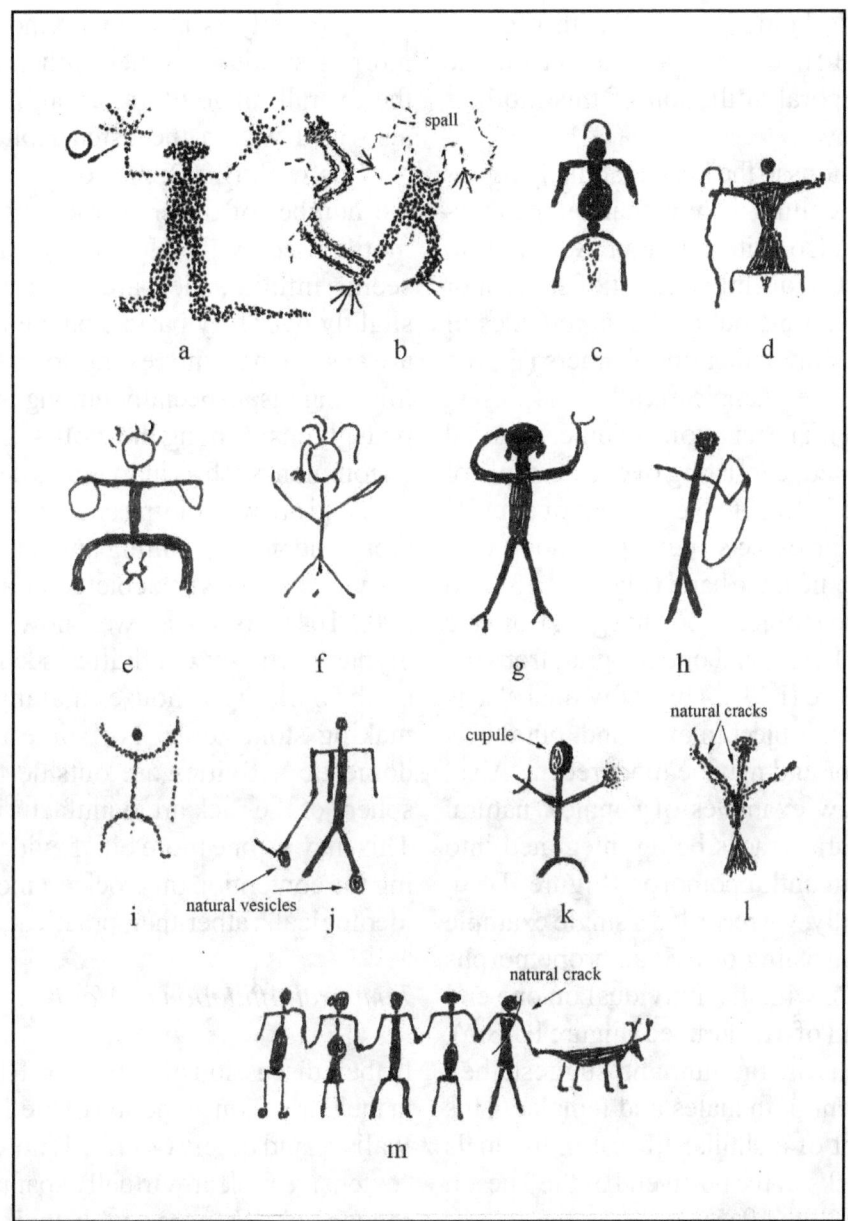

Figure II.13. Illustrations of some elaborated anthropomorphs: a, a wide-bodied figure with digits, a circular object near one hand, and a linear object attached to one foot (TH-F453); b, a wide-bodied figure with a serpent-like element attached to one leg and a few digits still visible extending from an exfoliated area (TH-F459); c, a figure with an expanded midsection, an arc over the head, and something between the legs – possibly a birth or afterbirth (TH-F4451); d, an hour-glass figure holding a staff with a crook, also with something between the legs (TH-F168); e and f, anthropomorphs with additions to the head, possibly feathers or wands (TH-F2934, TH-F2999), (e is also holding a circular object in one or both hands and like c and d has something between the legs); g, an anthropomorph with earbobs (TH-F519); h, an anthropomorph with a bow (TH-F695); i, an anthropomorph holding a linear object that extends down from one upraised hand (TH-F2918); j, an anthropomorph with a linear object hanging from the shoulder, perhaps a sash (the linear object held in the hand [the "hockey stick"] is lighter in color and, thus, probably more recent), this anthropomorph also uses a rounded, natural vesicle as a foot (TH-F413); k, an anthropomoph that uses a cupule as the head (TH-F707); l, an anthropomorph that integrates natural cracks into the body; (TH-F2959); m, five anthropomorphs holding hands with one holding the tail of a quadruped – the only example of a scene on Tumamoc Hill (TH-F2945). (Drawing by Valerie Davison)

glass figure is holding a staff with a crook (Figure II.13d). More information on the probable temporal affiliation of this motif is provided below.

Elaborations to the head that likely represent material culture—some that can be categorized—are also quite common. Additions to the head most frequently consist of straight or curved lines coming out of the top or sides of the head, possibly indicating feathers (Figure II.13e, f). A single example of earbobs is present (Figure II.13g). The repertoire of other material culture is limited, consisting of one example of a bow (Figure II.13h), two examples of circular or near circular objects (perhaps a hoop or a ball) held in or near the hand (Figure II.13a and e) and two linear objects, one hanging from the hand (Figure II.13i) and one hanging from the shoulder (Figure II.13j). This individual also is holding a linear object in one hand, but this is lighter in color and may be more recent. Also, there are a few examples of cupules, natural holes, or natural cracks being integrated into the body of an anthropomorph (Figure II.13j, k, and l). Finally, we recorded a single example of a scene consisting of five anthropomorphs holding hands, with the individual on one end holding the tail of a quadruped (Figure II.13m). The variations in the humans suggest they might represent both males and females. This is reminiscent of a similar line of individuals at Picture Rocks in the north end of the Tucson Mountains (White 1965).

Thus, the elaborated anthropomorphs constitute a sizeable fraction of the anthropomorphs on the hill, a considerably greater percentage than at other Tucson Basin sites. The range of elaborations is not great, but with a few exceptions, is similar to that at other Hohokam sites in the Phoenix and Tucson basins. Perhaps the most unusual examples are three anthropomorphs on the southeast corner of the summit (see Figure II.13a, b, and j) again suggesting the importance of this portion of the summit.

Not only is the range among anthropomorphs similar to other Hohokam sites, but the overall range of variation of all motifs is also well within the usual Hohokam range. As Bostwick (2002:20) points out, "although the number of different rock art elements or motifs used by the Hohokam in their rock art seems infinite, they are actually limited to slightly over fifty basic element types." It has always seemed interesting to us how limited this range is, especially among anthropomorphic glyphs. Among the motifs used, some are uncommon, such as individuals depicted with a bow and arrow, holding spears or canes, and in scenes depicting hunting and births, but many activities are never depicted at all (Bostwick 2002:104). As far as we know, there are no glyphs portraying activities such as weaving cloth, building a house, making pottery, or making stone tools. For some reason, most domestic activities are outside the accepted sphere of the rock art manufacturing tradition. This may be one more bit of evidence supporting the contention that rock art motifs focus on ideological, rather than practical, activities.

Temporal Affiliation of Motifs

In their discussion of Tumamoc Hill and its role in the Early Pioneer period of the Tucson Basin, Wallace and others (2007:94) note that there is "extensive rock art virtually spanning the local sequence." We agree with their observation and provide a brief discussion of certain rock art motifs that are temporally diagnostic and support this view.

Unlike Hohokam ceramics, which are now well defined from a temporal perspective (some types being tightly placed within a framework of decades), Hohokam petroglyphs are far less well understood temporally. Part of this difficulty stems from the fact that, compared to ceramic designs, petroglyphs are considerably less sophisticated in their production. Simply being pecked into the rock surface, they have minimal variation in technique, unlike ceramics, which are analyzed by the examination of temper, paste, and paint, among other attributes. In addition, Hohokam glyphs are generally scattered over a given rock face in what appears to be a haphazard manner; there are occasional scenes, but they are rare, especially on Tumamoc Hill. Thus, layout, which is an important criterion of analysis in ceramics, is generally not a useful consideration. So, we are left with patination and motif as the primary tools for temporal analysis. As we discuss in a later section, patination can provide assistance with relative dating, but is not very helpful in separating motifs created in closely associated time periods. Thus, motif is the most helpful attribute.

Numerous motifs from dated ceramic types appear as petroglyphs on Tumamoc Hill and elsewhere. Thus, an obvious approach in the assessment of temporal placement is to compare the two. There are, however, problems with this strategy. For example, just because some motifs are similar between ceramics and petroglyphs does not necessarily mean they are of the same age. For example, as Wallace (2004:78) notes in his analysis of the Middle Gila Buff Ware ceramic sequence, "The use of parallel-sided, hachure-filled bands – which commonly appear on Sweetwater and Snaketown time segment pottery – are also a standard part of the rock image repertoire." Bands of this sort are common, especially in the Hohokam Scratched style, but it is not at all certain that these motifs are limited to the Sweetwater and Snaketown phases (A.D. 500-750). Scratched motifs, which barely penetrate the outer rock surface, often show little evidence of repatination and, thus, do not suggest great antiquity. However, scratched motifs are, on occasion, both superimposed on Hohokam Pecked designs and superimposed by Hohokam Pecked designs suggesting that they may have been made over a considerable time span. In addition, many motifs and layouts used

on pottery, for example, complex banding filled with interlocking curvilinear or rectilinear scrolls or plaited layouts with complex filler designs, simply do not occur in the rock art of the Tucson Basin, including Tumamoc Hill. An additional difficulty is that much of the relevant motif and design analysis comes from the Phoenix Basin and deals with buffware as opposed to the brownware of the Tucson Basin. There is considerable overlap between the two wares, but they are by no means identical. Life forms and small geometric elements that are often found in rock art are less common on Tucson Basin pottery than on Phoenix Basin ware. Thus, we must be cautious if we use comparative data from the Phoenix Basin.

Nonetheless, even given these limitations, we present a few comparisons between dated ceramic motifs and petroglyph motifs. Our purpose is not to try to place specific petroglyph motifs within a tight temporal framework, but instead to suggest that the Hohokam Pecked Style petroglyphs on Tumamoc cover the entire local sequence from the Pioneer period through the Classic period and perhaps into Protohistoric and even Historic times.

Motifs that definitely begin in the Pioneer period are not plentiful, but they do occur. For example, reptiles (turtles and lizards in negative) are noted on Phoenix Basin ceramics as early as the Late Pioneer period (Haury 1976:234, Fig. 12.86). There are several examples of lizardlike designs on Tumamoc, for example, TH-F3272 (Figure II.14a), although none is as lifelike as those illustrated by Haury 1976 (235, Fig. 12.81). Another motif, the multiple-ring bull's eye, also first appears on Phoenix Basin ceramics in the Late Pioneer period (Haury 1976:246, Fig. 12.99). Several multiple-ring bull's eyes are present on Tumamoc; we illustrate one (TH-F590) in Figure II.14b. These examples do not prove, but at least suggest, that some Tumamoc rock art may date back to the Pioneer period.

Other motifs on Tumamoc are similar

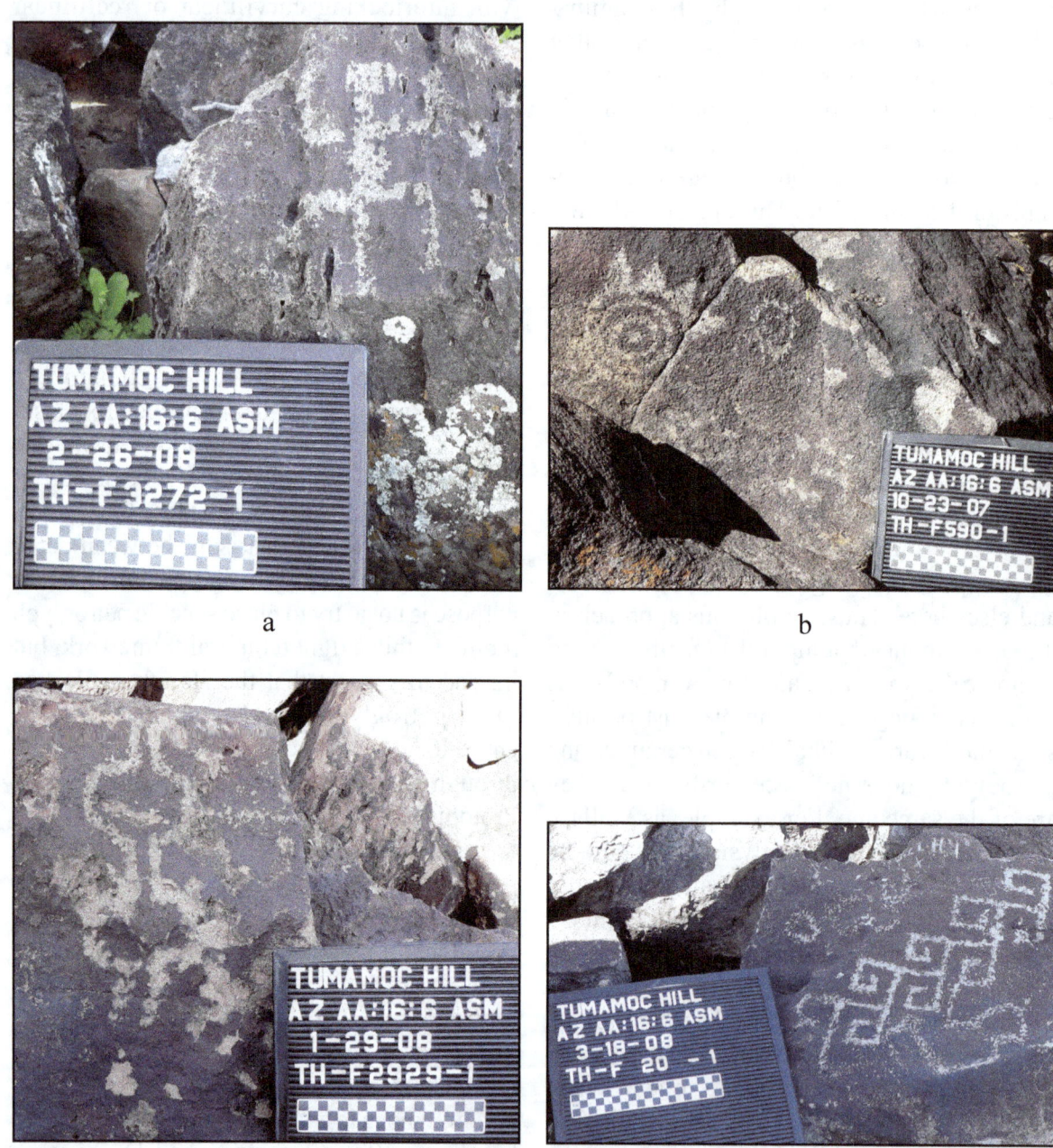

Figure II.14. Examples of motifs associated with specific periods in the Hohokam sequence. a, lizardlike motif (TH-F3272-1); b, multiple-ring bull's eye with elaboration (TH-F590-1). In the Phoenix Basin, these two motifs begin in the Late Pioneer period. c, pipette (TH-F2929-1). In the Phoenix Basin, this motif is associated with the Colonial through Sedentary periods; in the Tucson Basin it may be later. d, rectilinear scroll/rectilinear fret (TH-F20-1). This motif may date from the Sedentary period into the Classic period. (Photos by Janine Hernbrode)

to ones represented on pottery from the Colonial to Sedentary periods (A.D. 700-1150) in the Phoenix Basin. One of the most interesting examples is an hourglass-shaped anthropomorph holding a staff with a crook at the top (TH-F168; Figure II.13d). Anthropomorphs holding a staff with a crook at the top occur on pottery from the Gila Butte phase to the Sacaton phase at Snaketown (Haury 1976:238, Fig. 12.87). These motifs differ from the petroglyph on Tumamoc in that they are not hourglass-shaped and most are carrying a burden basket. The hourglass figures depicted on ceramics are not carrying a staff; still there is a strong similarity. The hourglass anthropomorph is superimposed by a simple stick figure that is clearly less patinated, and thus presumably younger. The hourglass motif is not at all common in the Tucson Basin, being represented only by the single example on Tumamoc Hill and an example in Saguaro National Park (Bostwick 1999:129); neither is it particularly common in the Phoenix Basin although at least a dozen have been recorded on South Mountain (Bostwick 1999). A second motif that apparently dates to this same time period is a human figure with a bow and arrow. Haury (1976:238, Fig. 12.87) illustrates examples from ceramics at Snaketown from the Gila Butte and Sacaton phases. The single example on Tumamoc Hill (TH-F695; Figure II.13h) is a clear depiction of a human with a bow, although an arrow is lacking. In regard to these and other human figures, Haury (1976:237) notes that they "faded sharply by the end of the Sedentary Period."

Several examples of a motif first recorded on Tumamoc Hill and described by Ferg (1979:109) as a "pipette" may also date to approximately this same time period; one example (TH-F2929) is depicted in Figure II.14c. On South Mountain, ceramics collected from in front of a pipette panel were identified as Santa Cruz or Sacaton Red-on-buff, and thus date to the late Colonial or Sedentary periods

(A.D. 850-1150) (Bostwick 2002:148). Golio and others (1995) in their excellent analysis of the pipette in Hohokam rock art, also conclude that, at least in the Phoenix Basin, the pipette is a Colonial through Sedentary period element. They do point out, however, that in the Tucson Basin this element is attributed to the later Classic period by Wallace and Holmlund (1986) and Ferg (1979). They (Golio et al. 1995:106) suggest that, "based on the large numbers of pipettes found in the Phoenix Basin," the "design [may have] originated in the Phoenix Basin and spread south at a later date." Thus, on Tumamoc Hill this design could be placed anywhere in time from the Colonial period to the Classic period.

In addition, there are motifs on Tumamoc that probably date from the Sedentary into the Classic period. A rectilinear scroll/rectilinear fret is depicted on Tumamoc (TH-F20; Figure II.14d), and Wallace (2004:110, Table 3.7), in his discussion of the Middle Gila Buff Ware ceramic sequence, notes that this motif appears from the Middle Sacaton phase to the Soho phase, that is, from the Middle Sedentary to the Early Classic periods. In support of this contention he references Haury's (1937: Plate XLIVb, d) work at Snaketown, Wasley and Johnson's (1965:101, Fig. 64) work at the Painted Rocks Reservoir, and his own work (Wallace 2001:Fig. I.37f) with Middle Gila Buffware at the Grewe Site. At the same time, it is notable that simple rectilinear fret motifs appear as early as the Pioneer period at Snaketown (Haury 1976:250, Fig. 12.106).

Finally, two motifs on Tumamoc may date to the Sedentary/Classic periods or later, and, as far as we know, neither is known from southern Arizona, either in ceramics or rock art (Figure II.15). First, there is a single example of a complex terrace motif (TH-F468), a motif may date to the Classic period or later (Figure II.15a), but extends into historic times, although some simple terrace designs from other parts of the Southwest and Mexico do date earlier.

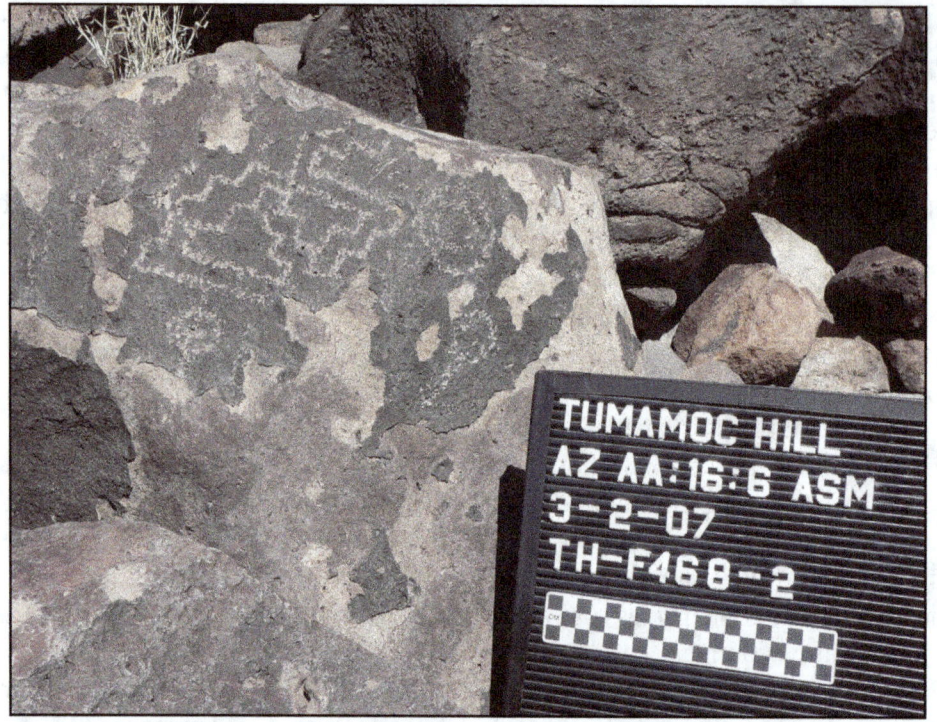

a

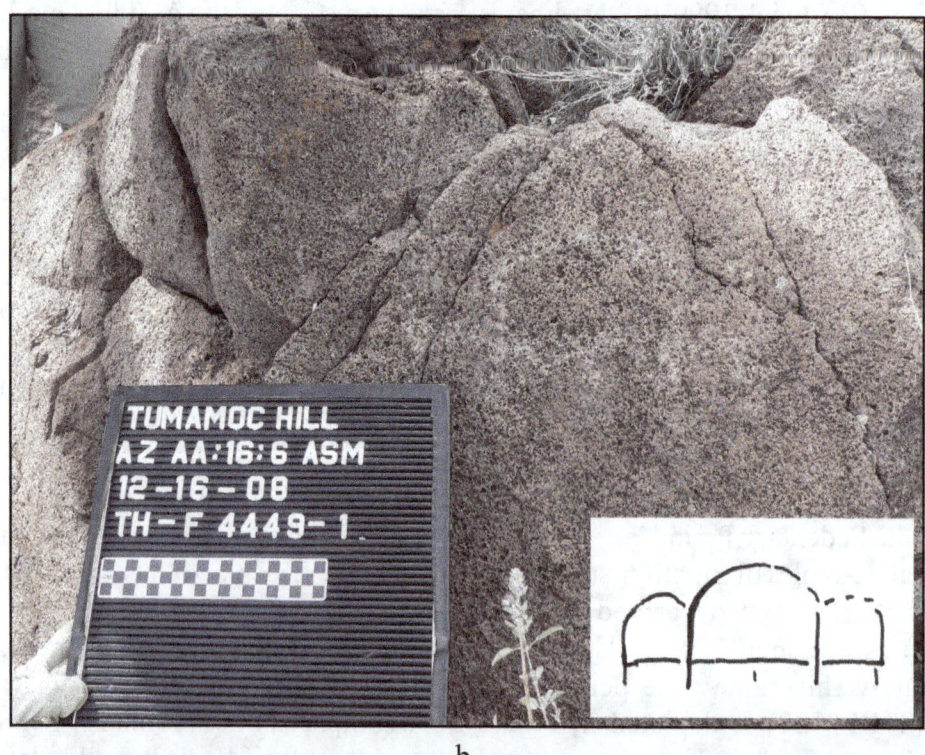

b

Figure II.15. Two glyphs probably from the Classic period or later. a, complex terrace motif (TH-F468-2); b, probable cloud motif (TH-F4449-1). (Photos by Janine Hernbrode; sketch by William K. Hartmann)

The simple version of this design, a stepped pyramid, is often referred to as a rain terrace or a cloud terrace, and by late prehistoric times, it is a very popular rock art design, especially in northern Arizona and northern New Mexico (McCreery and Malotki 1994:35). In the Pueblo IV period (A.D. 1300-1450), and later in historic times, the motif appears in a variety of venues including rock art (McCreery and Malotki 1994:56), as components of kiva murals from Kuaua (Dutton 1963), and on Hopi ceramics (Wade and McChesney 1981). We do need to point out, however, that this motif does appear in Jornada-style rock art sites, an interesting and complex style from southern New Mexico, Texas, and Chihuahua, that is generally dated from A.D. 1000 to 1450 (Schaafsma 1992:60, 72, Fig. 90; Schaafsma 1997:57, Fig. 36; Sutherland 1998:72, Fig. 10).

The second design, which we are interpreting as a probable rain cloud motif (TH-F4449), we believe to be known only from the Historic period, most commonly in Hopi designs (Figure II.15b). It appears as a Hopi rock art motif representing "water/cloud" as both a clan symbol and a totemic signature (Bernardini 2009:32, Fig. 3.8). It is also relatively common on Hopi ceramics; for example, it appears as a stand-alone element on Payupki Polychrome, which is dated from A.D. 1680-1800 (Wade and McChesney 1981:94, Plate III-a.) It also appears on Hopi kachinas, for example, on the face of the Talavai or Morning Singer kachina (Wright 1977:122, Plate 29A).

These two examples may significantly enhance the temporal extent and geographical breadth of the Tumamoc petroglyphs. It seems likely that one represents the late end of the prehistoric spectrum, while the second may have been created during historical times. At least as important, these are not local motifs, suggesting influence from cultures to the north, east, or southeast. In addition, the presence of these motifs suggests a shared perception

of the importance of the hill and the manner in which it was used (Wallace, personal communication, 2011). To summarize, while it is generally difficult to prove that specific rock art motifs date to a specific time period within the Hohokam sequence, we have made a probabilistic argument in favor of the inference that the Hohokam Pecked-style rock art on Tumamoc Hill spans the entire sequence from the Pioneer period into Historic times.

Hohokam Scratched Style

The other style described by Ferg (1979), the Hohokam Scratched style, was first identified by Heizer and Baumhoff (1962:208), in their seminal report on Great Basin rock art. They referred to it briefly as the "Great Basin Scratched Style" and noted that it was created with single strokes of a sharp rock to produce straight lines, sun figures, and crosshatching. They also commented that the glyphs were very crude, and they were of the opinion that the scratched glyphs were more recent than pecked glyphs. More recently this style has been described by Turpin (2001:372) who notes that "common motifs are cross-hatching, parallel lines, radiating lines, zigzags and chevrons, arcs, dashes, ladders and feather-like designs; curvilinear designs such as loops, scrolls, circles, ovals, and meanders; and rakes, squiggles, triangles, and anthropomorphs. More complex sites include cobwebs and zoomorphic creatures." In an excellent article that examines scratched glyphs in Arizona, Don Christensen (1992:104) notes that they are widely dispersed; in addition to being in the Great Basin they occur in California and the Southwest, including, of course, Arizona. Closer to home, archaeologists Aaron Wright and Todd Bostwick (2009:68) have recorded scratched glyphs on South Mountain in Phoenix and comment that "many…are stylistically consistent with those found on Tumamoc Hill."

The scratched glyphs on Tumamoc Hill

consist of many of the motifs listed by Turpin (2001:372) for the Great Basin Scratched Style, but by no means all. The 85 scratched elements that we recorded on Tumamoc are almost exclusively rectilinear geometrics and consist of the motifs listed in Table II.4. As would be expected, the motifs are similar to those in the smaller scratched-element universe recorded by Ferg (1979:97, 99) with the addition of a sectioned circle and a single anthropomorph that includes pecking and a small amount of abrading in addition to scratching. As can be seen by comparing Figures II.12 and II.16, the distribution differs markedly from that for Hohokam Pecked-style glyphs with the greatest number occurring on the west slope.

The single scratched anthropomorph is sufficiently unusual that it is worth a short discussion. It is located on a large outcrop on the west slope and is one of 40 prehistoric elements grouped into 13 features. Of the prehistoric elements 7 are pecked and 33 are scratched, making this the most abundant location for scratched glyphs on the hill. The anthropomorph consists of a poorly executed, wide-bodied human with raised arms, primarily defined by scratching (Figure II.17). In addition, some pecking and a small amount of abrading overlie the scratching, primarily on the torso. This scratched anthropomorph shares some similarities with scratched figurative elements on South Mountain, especially the "thunderbird" illustrated in Wright and Bostwick (2009:69, Fig. 11). At our request, Wright visited Tumamoc Hill and concurred that scratching was the principal technique in the Tumamoc example. He commented that, "If there were no scratches (on the Tumamoc example) it would not be an anthropomorph." At the same time, most of the scratched figurative elements from South Mountain do not include pecking or abrading and, thus, are somewhat different from our example.

In their discussion of scratched elements, Wright and Bostwick (2009:71) conclude that

"The scratched figurative petroglyphs in the South Mountains exhibit stylistic affinities to scratched designs in regions to the north and west, but such scratched figurative designs have yet to be identified in the Tucson Basin [emphasis added]; this spatial patterning may hint at different spheres of interaction between Hohokam communities in the Tucson and Phoenix basins." Now that at least one scratched figurative glyph is known from the Tucson Basin, this difference in "spheres of interaction" is less evident.

As to the age of the scratched style, the general consensus is that, in southern Arizona, it occurs during the time of the Hohokam culture or from around A.D. 700 to A.D. 1400. Wright and Bostwick (2009:71) note that scratched glyphs "co-occur with Gila style petroglyphs and are associated with Hohokam

Table II.4. Hohokam Scratched-Style Element Types

Element Code	Element Name	Number
17	Anthropomorphic other	1
36	Chevron, nested	5
47	Circles, sectioned	1
50	Cross hatch, band	7
51	Cross hatch, diamond	16
52	Cross hatch, grid	17
60	Ladder	2
62	Line, straight	6
63	Line, parallel	11
64	Line, zigzag or wavy	4
72	Rectilinear abstract	2
84	Square	1
89	Triangle	3
90	Geometric indeterminate	9
Total		85

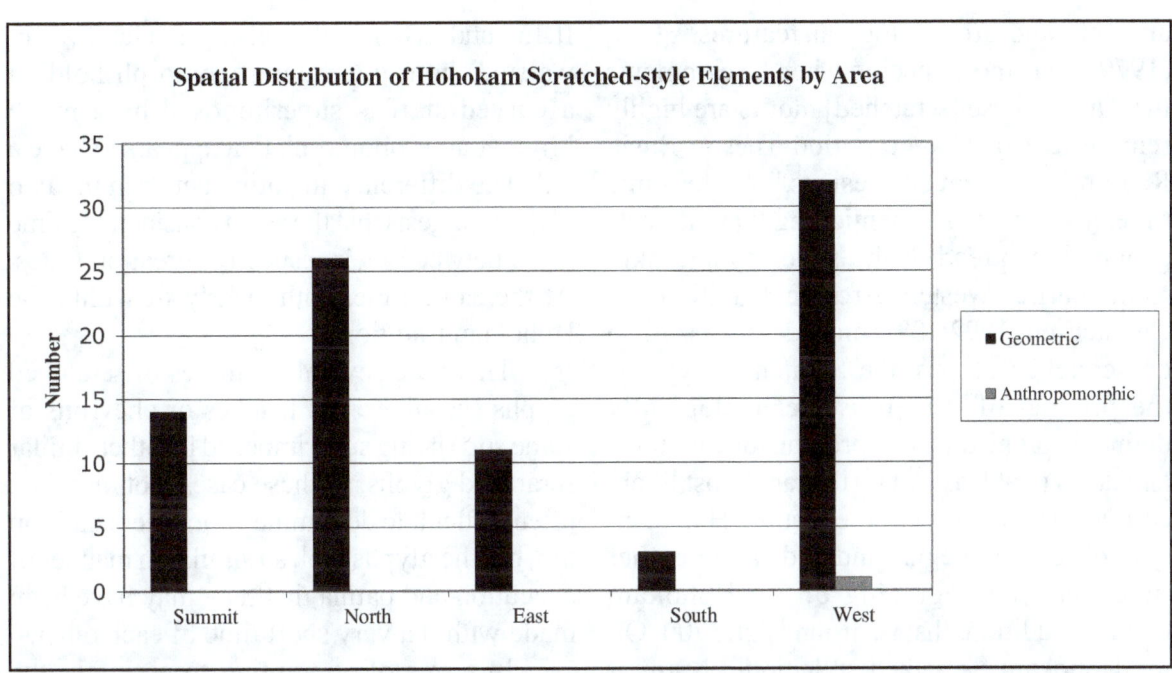

Figure II.16. Spatial distribution of Hohokam Scratched-style elements by area: geometric and anthropomorphic. Glyphs recorded as "South" are not far below the summit.

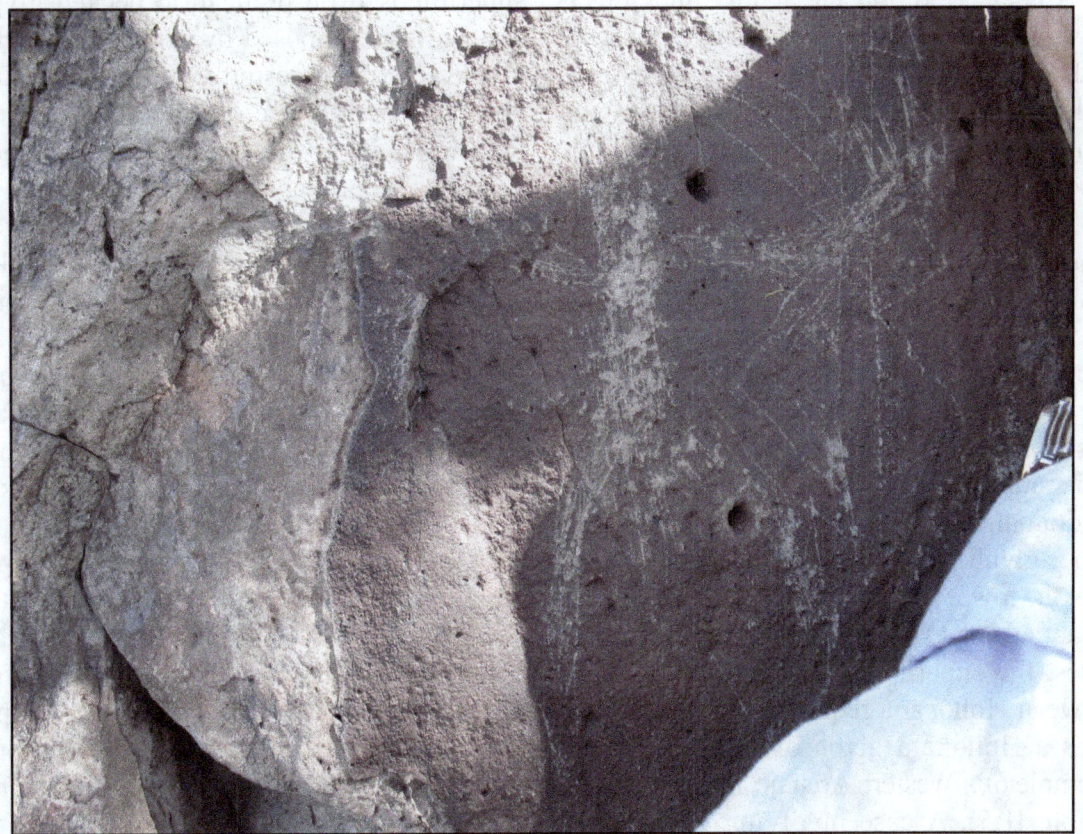

Figure II.17. An anthropomorph primarily created by scratching (TH-F3351-10). (Photo by Gayle Hartmann, 22 March 2010)

artifacts and archaeological features." Ferg (1979:99) is more specific when he comments that "all of these [scratched] motifs are highly reminiscent of Classic period Tucson Basin Red-on-brown pottery designs." At the same time, it seems worth mentioning that the wide geographic spread of the style is more akin to the earlier Western Archaic Tradition. As Christensen (1992:108) concludes in his article on scratched glyphs, the Scratched style "is the product of numerous archaeologically definable prehistoric and protohistoric cultures and dates to at least A.D. 1050 and most likely earlier." Thus, it is possible that the Hohokam Scratched style begins and ends at an earlier time than the beginning of the Hohokam cultural tradition, that is, around A.D. 700. Or, the Hohokam Scratched style could begin at an early time and continue through Hohokam times, as do a number of motifs associated with the Archaic Tradition. Or, and we think this is most likely, the Scratched style could be coeval with the Hohokam Pecked style. At best, the style is enigmatic and poorly understood and could benefit from additional careful recording, especially in the Hohokam cultural sphere.

Superimposition

The superimposition of one prehistoric glyph on another is not very common on Tumamoc Hill. We recorded only 24 cases, with the examples of superimposition scattered around the slopes and summit. Most of the examples are not at all dramatic. In fact, many have a sense of the upper glyph having been accidentally placed over the lower glyph, with only a small amount of actual superimposition occurring. In all cases, the superimposition appears to occur between Hohokam glyphs; that is, in no case does a Hohokam glyph overlie a probable example of a Western Archaic Tradition glyph (Table II.5). A case involving two pecked glyphs provides, perhaps, the most interesting example of superimposition on the hill (Figures

II.13d and II.18). In this example, a faint wasp-waisted, hour-glass anthropomorph holding a curved staff is superimposed by a much brighter anthropomorph that appears to have a tail. The difference in patina between the two glyphs suggests that there is a considerable time lapse between their respective creation times. At the same time, both clearly fit within the Hohokam tradition.

There are several examples of scratched glyphs (usually cross hatches or chevrons of some sort) being superimposed by other similar scratched glyphs. In these cases, not only is it often difficult to determine which element is on top, but the glyphs look so similar in manner of execution and patina that they may have been made within a very short time of each other.

In terms of attempting to ascertain the age of scratched glyphs, it would be helpful if all the examples on Tumamoc were either superimposed on prehistoric pecked glyphs or were superimposed by prehistoric pecked glyphs. Our analyses provide varying results, however, as do those of others from several locations, in both southern and northern Arizona. According to Christensen (1992:107) sites with scratched glyphs in northern Arizona are sometimes superimposed by pecked and abraded glyphs as well as the reverse. On South Mountain in Phoenix, Wright and Bostwick (2009:69) record examples where scratched lines superimpose Hohokam Pecked-style petroglyphs and other examples where scratched lines are superimposed by Hohokam Pecked-style petroglyphs.

In Ferg's (1979:99) analysis of super-imposition on Tumamoc he concluded that in all three cases (TH-F104, TH-F2991, and TH-F4324) where scratched and pecked glyphs interacted, the scratched glyphs were super-imposed by the pecked glyphs. We examined those three glyphs as well and concluded that in one case (TH-F4324) pecking was on top of scratching, while in a second case (TH-F2991) the reverse was true; in the third case

Table II.5. Prehistoric Elements Superimposed Over Other Prehistoric Elements

Feature ID	Ferg Cluster ID	Element Code	Element Name (Underneath)	Element Name (On Top)
104	R-3, Map 13	52	See Note 1	See Note 1
104	R-3, Map 13	52	See Note 2	See Note 2
168	M-2, Master Topo Map	14	Person (not a stickperson) with a staff	Anthro. arms down (None 2)
520	P-1, Map 11	52	Cross hatch, grid	Geometric indeterminate
2926	B-13, Map 2	26	Zoomorphic indeterminate	Geometric indeterminate
2959	E-2, Map 5	13	Anthropomorphic other than a stick figure	Geometric indeterminate
2962	E-5, Map 5	90	Geometric indeterminate	Bull's eye, 2-ring; Circle
2991	G-2, Map 7	37	Circle	Rectilinear abstract
2995	G-6, Map 7	90	Geometric indeterminate	Geometric indeterminate
3294	K-25, Map 9	42	Circles, concentric, 2 rings	Geometric indeterminate
3318	KK-New	53	Curvilinear abstract	Line, parallel
3351	U-2, Map 16	36	Chevron nested	Anthropomorphic other
3351	U-2, Map 16	52	Cross hatch, grid	Dot undefined pattern
3352	U-3, Map 16	50	Cross hatch, band	Cross hatch, grid
3352	U-3, Map 16	50	Cross hatch, band	Cross hatch, grid
3356	U-7, Map 16	36	Chevron nested	Cross hatch, grid
4324	V-3, Map 17	52	Cross hatch, grid	Anthro. arms down (None 2)
4341	L-Near, IS-3, Master Topo Map	1	Anthro. arms up (None 1)	Rectilinear abstract
4399	R-New	51	Cross hatch, diamond	Cross hatch, diamond

Note:
Four pecked elements (Concentric Circle, 3 rings; Circle; Circle; Concentric Circle 2 rings) interact with a single cross-hatched grid. We cannot determine which is on top and which is underneath.
Two pecked elements (Circle; Line) interact with a second cross-hatched grid. We cannot determine which is on top and which is underneath.

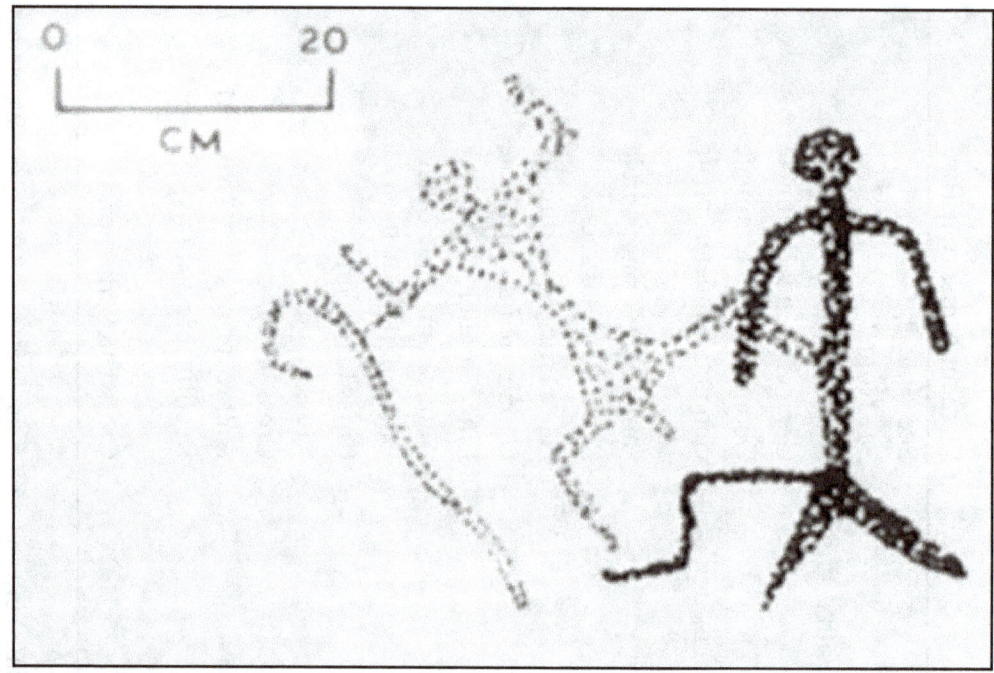

a

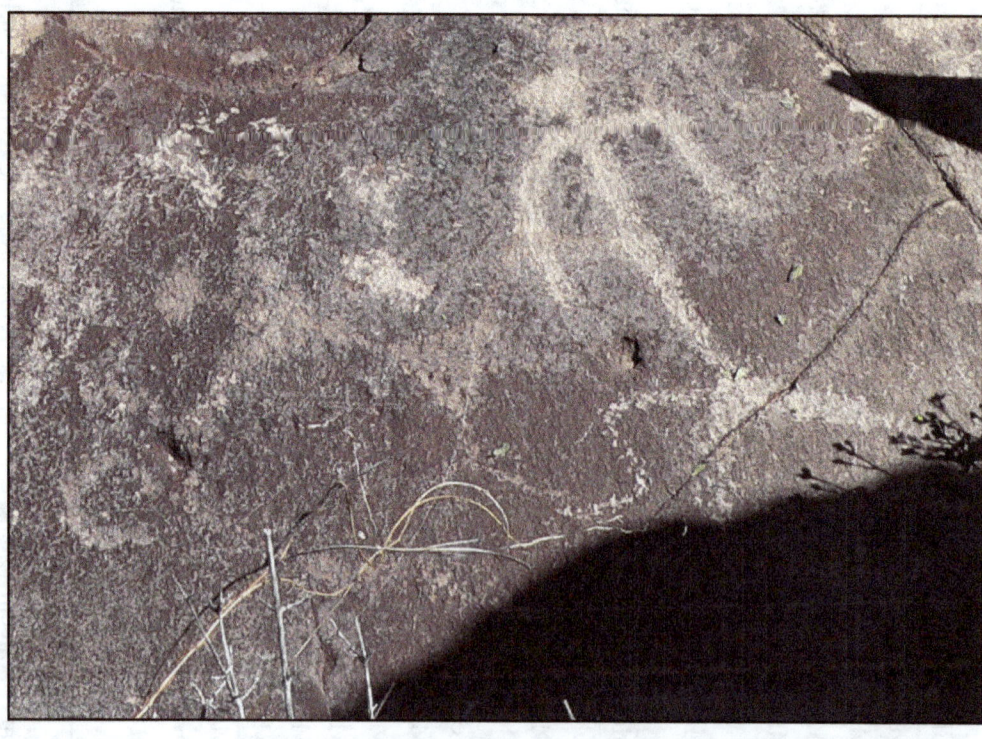

b

Figure II.18. The best example of superimposition on Tumamoc Hill. a, drawing of the two anthropomorphs, the arm of one superimposed over the leg of the other (adapted from Ferg 1979, Fig. 5). (Courtesy AltaMira Press and Arizona Archaeological and Historical Society); b, photograph of the two anthropomorphs (TH-F168-1). (Photo by Janine Hernbrode)

(TH-F104), discussed in more detail below, we could not determine which glyphs were on top. Including the two cases just mentioned we recorded seven cases of interaction between pecked and scratched glyphs where we could determine which glyph was on top. In five cases scratched glyphs superimpose pecked glyphs; in two cases the reverse is true. Therefore, like Christensen (1992) and Wright and Bostwick (2009) we conclude that in some cases scratched glyphs superimpose pecked glyphs and sometimes the pecked glyphs are on top. In addition, we recorded six cases of pecked glyphs superimposed over other pecked glyphs and five cases of scratched glyphs superimposed over other scratched glyphs.

Unfortunately, in one of the more dramatic examples of superimposition, we were uncertain how scratched lines interacted with pecked circular motifs. In this case (TH-F104), there is one example where four pecked glyphs interact with a single scratched cross hatched grid and a second example where two pecked glyphs interact with another scratched cross hatched grid (Figure II.19). When looking at these glyphs in the field it was difficult to tell whether the scratched lines or the pecked elements were on top. After enlargement and contrast enhancement of the photos we still could not be certain which elements were on top and which were underneath. The only obvious difference between the pecked and scratched elements is that the scratched lines are slightly darker than the pecked circles. We believe this difference results from the scratched lines not penetrating the rock's outer dark crust rather than being an indication of greater age.

WESTERN ARCHAIC TRADITION

One goal of this study was to attempt to understand whether any of the rock art could be classified as belonging to the Western Archaic Tradition. As was noted previously,

the original study by Ferg (1979) was one of the first systematic examinations of rock art in the region. At that time, temporal studies were in their infancy. Ferg (1979:107-111) relied on a stylistic comparison between some glyphs and the limited ceramic evidence available on Tumamoc to conclude that in the Tucson Basin, and on Tumamoc Hill, the petroglyphs belonged to the Hohokam culture and "were produced in the greatest numbers in the Classic period" (Ferg 1979:111). This concurred with conclusions reached by Wilcox et al. (1979) that Tumamoc Hill was primarily a Classic period site. Since that time new research has shown that Tumamoc was first used and occupied during the Cienega phase of the Early Agricultural period (ca. 800 B.C. to A.D. 150) and again somewhat later in the Tortolita phase of the Hohokam Pioneer period (ca. A.D. 475 to 700) (Fish et al. 1986; Wallace et al. 2007).

Also, research into rock art styles has come a long way since the 1970s. A geographically broad Archaic style, originally called the "Great Basin Abstract Style" by Steward (1929) and Heizer and Baumhoff (1962) has been refined by Schaafsma (1980) and Hedges (1973, 1982) and more recently by Wallace and Holmlund (1986) in the Picacho Mountains and Wallace (1989) at the Painted Rock Reservoir. This style is now generally referred to as the Western Archaic Tradition, a term first utilized by Hedges (1982), not only because of its wide geographic spread but because, he believed, it encompasses more than one local style (see Wallace and Holmlund (1986:84-86) for a cogent discussion of the Western Archaic Tradition). These studies mentioned provided us with considerably more information regarding issues of time and cultural affiliation than was available to Ferg. Thus, we are in a position to ask more detailed questions concerning rock art chronology.

As we noted previously, Wallace et al. (2007:94) commented that the rock art on Tumamoc Hill virtually spans the local

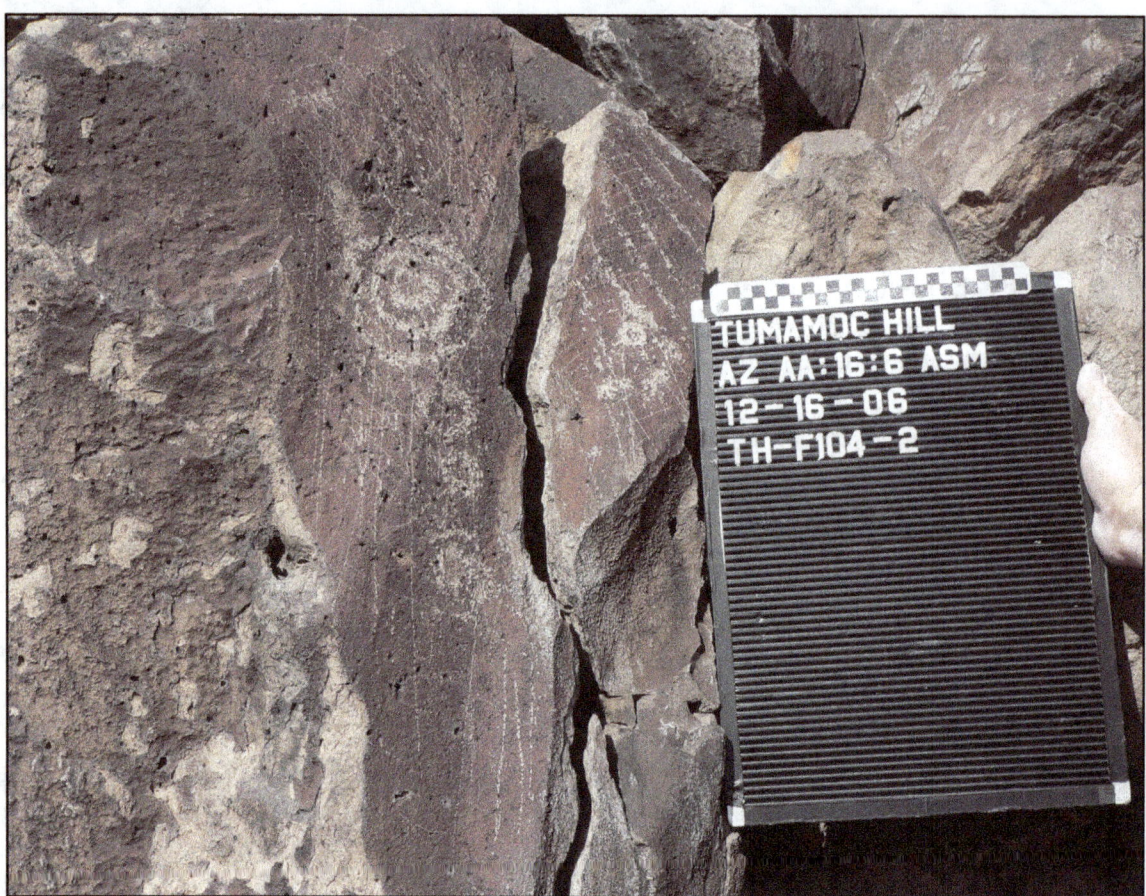

Figure II.19. An example of Hohokam Scratched-style glyphs interacting with Hohokam Pecked-style glyphs (TH-F104-2). (Photo by Janine Hernbrode)

sequence. With that thought in mind, and our own observations suggesting that some of the rock art might have considerable time depth, we attempt to identify rock art elements that may belong to the Western Archaic Tradition. We discuss motifs that fit the Western Archaic Tradition and, thus, may have been produced as early as the Cienega and Tortolita phases. We do not attempt to differentiate between motifs that may have been made in the Early Agricultural period versus the Hohokam Pioneer period. That is because, as Thiel (1995:63) notes, the Western Archaic rock art tradition may have continued until about A.D. 800, that is, into the Hohokam Colonial period. As was mentioned earlier, most of the rock art on the hill fits into the Hohokam Pecked style with the earliest examples belonging to

this style possibly created as early as the Late Pioneer or Early Colonial periods (that is, ca. A.D. 700-850). Thus, there may be some temporal overlap between the Western Archaic and Hohokam rock art traditions.

Criteria Approach

To extract Archaic glyphs from the large prehistoric rock art universe on Tumamoc Hill, we use two different approaches. The first approach relies on five field criteria used by numerous authors including Schaafsma (1980), Thiel (1995), and Wallace (2008) as hallmarks of the Western Archaic Tradition. These are the following: (1) belonging to an agreed upon Western Archaic set of motifs, (2) displaying heavy repatination, (3) consisting of broad lines, (4) following the shape of the boulder or wrapping from one surface to another, and (5) being superimposed by another prehistoric image. A brief discussion of these five criteria follows.

Motifs

The motifs used in criterion one are listed in Table II.6. This is a conservative list that includes motifs agreed upon by several researchers (noted previously); other researchers may include additional motifs. In addition, it is important to note that, although these motifs were definitely produced during Archaic times, virtually all researchers agree that most were not produced exclusively during the Archaic period. No motifs found on Tumamoc are specifically diagnostic of the Western Archaic Tradition. As Thiel (1995:64) points out, "Most Archaic period elements resemble those created by the later Hohokam. These include circles, bull's-eyes, concentric circles, sun disks, and parallel lines." Thus, what appears to be most important in identifying Archaic glyphs on Tumamoc Hill is not just the presence of a specific motif but the combination of some or all of the five criteria. We note, however, that to be admitted into our universe of potential Archaic glyphs, any glyph must be a motif listed in Table II.6. For example, a stick-figure anthropomorph, even if meeting the other criteria, would not be admitted into our list of candidates. On Tumamoc, 355 elements are included in this criterion.

Repatination

The second most important criterion is heavy patination—defined as "medium-heavy" or "heavy" on our recording forms. Fifty-one elements meet this criterion. It is important to note, however, that equating heavy patination with considerable time depth can be problematic. The nature of the repatination depends on rock type, local micro-climate and other factors, as well as age. As Wallace and Holmlund (1986:76) point out, "certain lithologic types seem to be preferred by the makers of prehistoric petroglyphs." In our case, basaltic andesite is the common rock type and most of the petroglyphs penetrate through the dark varnished surface exposing the rock's lighter interior. The exterior surfaces range in color from brown to black with some areas of dark red. Most rocks have large vesicles and cracks, but smooth surfaces are common and were favored for rock art creation. Once the glyph was created, repatination begins. As Wallace and Holmlund (1986:76) note, "the darker the patina (not the rock itself), the older the rock surface." We did not attempt a quantitative measurement of the patination, but instead estimate the amount of patination qualitatively.

Broad Lines

The third criterion is broad lines with 115 elements meeting this criterion. Line widths recorded during our survey ranged from 0.1 cm to 10 cm and we define broad lines as those being 1.5 cm or wider. Other researchers have concluded that well-defined lines (both broad and heavy) are a hallmark of the Western Archaic Tradition. For example, Schaafsma (1980:36) in her discussion of "Archaic Petroglyphs of the Western Arizona Desert" notes that when the abstract style occurs it is pecked in "heavy, clear lines through the black patina." As in the case of repatination, the interpretation of line width can be problematic. For example, the Western-Archaic-Tradition-style glyphs from the Growler Valley in southwestern Arizona discussed by Schaafsma (1980:36-41) exhibit broad and very well-defined lines, whereas the Tumamoc Hill Archaic candidates are broad, but a little less well defined. Nonetheless, in applying this criterion we argue that the glyphs consisting of broad lines are more likely Archaic in age.

Table II.6. Western Archaic Tradition Motifs	
Anthropomorph, large, unusual	Dint pattern
Atlatl	Double-tailed circle
Bull's eye, 1 ring	Double rake
Candelabra	Footprint
Centipede	Grid/Crosshatched design
Chevron/Triangle motifs	Ladder
Circle	Line, curved
Circle chain	Line, straight
Circle cluster	Paired circles/Figure eight
Circle, sectioned	(coded "circle chain" in our analysis)
Circles, line connected	Parallel lines
Concentric circle, 2 rings	Rake
Circle, double tailed	Rectilinear abstract
Circle, tailed	Scroll, curvilinear clockwise
Cross	Shell
Curvilinear abstract	Sundisk
(coded curvilinear meander in our analysis)	Triangles
Diamond	Wavy line or lines
Dint line or meander	Zigzag line or lines

Note: Any glyph identified as one of these motifs was considered as satisfying criterion one. We note that at least three Western Archaic Tradition motifs (atlatl, candelabra, and "large, unusual anthropomorph" [as defined by Schaafsma 1980:41]) are not included in our recording form, but we are certain that none exist on the hill. In addition, "barbell" as a separate design element was not on our recording form; it was coded as "Geometric other" and we are aware of one clear example (TH-F496). Motifs are listed in alphabetical order. (Sources of motifs are Schaafsma 1980:41; Thiel 1995:64, Table 3.1; Wallace 2008:191.)

Following the Shape of a Boulder or Wrapping from One Surface to Another

To meet the fourth criterion an element must follow the shape of a boulder or wrap from one surface to another; on Tumamoc 32 elements meet this criterion. Again, we are adapting this criterion from Schaafsma's (1980:45) discussion of the Western Archaic Tradition in the deserts of western Arizona. She notes that there is the occasional tendency for "deliberate adaptation of the design to the shape of the surface being decorated." An element meets the criterion of following the shape of the boulder if a portion runs along the boulder's edge. Wrapping from one surface to another is self-explanatory. This criterion is also problematic. For example, in the Growler Valley case, glyphs wrap farther around the boulders and follow the edges more deliberately than do our candidates.

Superimposition

Nine elements meet the fifth criterion, that is, they are superimposed by another prehistoric image. This, of course, does not by itself prove that the underlying image is significantly older. In principal, the lower element could have been created only minutes or days before the upper one. However, taken in combination with the other criteria, especially heavy repatination, superimposition can provide compelling evidence that the underlying element may be of considerably greater time depth. There is one example (TH-F2962) in which motifs that could be either Archaic or Hohokam (a circle and a two-ring bull's eye) overlay very faint, heavily repatinated elements. The underlying elements were coded as geometric indeterminate because we could not clearly identify them. They are so heavily repatinated that it seems likely that they were made during Archaic times, but they are so indistinct that we do not classify them as Archaic.

Independent Evaluation Approach

The second approach in our effort to ferret out Western Archaic Tradition rock art involved calling on expertise in the regional rock art community and was, thus, a more subjective approach. We asked the two acknowledged experts in the field, Henry Wallace from Tucson and Todd Bostwick from Phoenix to assist us (related correspondence is in the ASM Archives [ASM Accession No. AP-2013-437]). We gave each of them drawings and photographs of 48 glyphs from Tumamoc Hill and asked them to provide their opinions regarding the approximate age of each glyph using whatever criteria they liked. Although both Wallace and Bostwick kindly accepted the challenge, each had caveats. Bostwick (personal communication, 2009) stated that he made his decisions based only on motif and repatination while Wallace (personal communication, 2009) made it clear that drawing conclusions from the drawings and moderate-resolution photos would be difficult. Wallace pointed out that it was not possible to examine motifs for

repecking and also noted that it was difficult to discern underlying elements. We agree with the limitations of analysis based on photos and drawings, but believe that the opinions of these two experts are valuable to us and to our readers.

Results of the Two Approaches

The results of the two approaches are discussed here. In brief, results are similar, though not identical. First, no glyph meets all five criteria. We can say with some confidence, however, that at least four glyphs, all located on the summit, were produced during Archaic times, while there is fair probability that an additional 27 also belong to the Western Archaic Tradition (Figure II.20, Table II.7. The four glyphs that are the best Archaic candidates meet four of the five criteria while the additional 27 glyphs meet three of the five criteria. Finally, seven glyphs meet fewer than three of our criteria, but are rated Archaic or possible Archaic by Wallace and/or Bostwick (Table II.8). The glyphs listed in Tables II.7 and II.8 are illustrated on the Arizona State Museum website: www. statemuseum.arizona.edu/research/pubs/ archseries/companion_materials

Candidates Meeting Four Criteria

A Curvilinear Abstract (TH-F136). This complex, curvilinear abstract design is pecked with broad lines (2 cm in width) into a flat-lying bedrock slab. Its repatination is coded as medium-heavy and a portion of the glyph is parallel to the edge of the boulder. Bostwick estimated the glyph to be of Archaic age based on design and patination while Wallace defined it as "unknown," but wrote, "Patination suggests it might be Archaic but the motif is more elaborate than what would be typical" (Figure II.20a). (Note: When we quote Bostwick and Wallace we are referring to the correspondence we received from them in 2009 that included

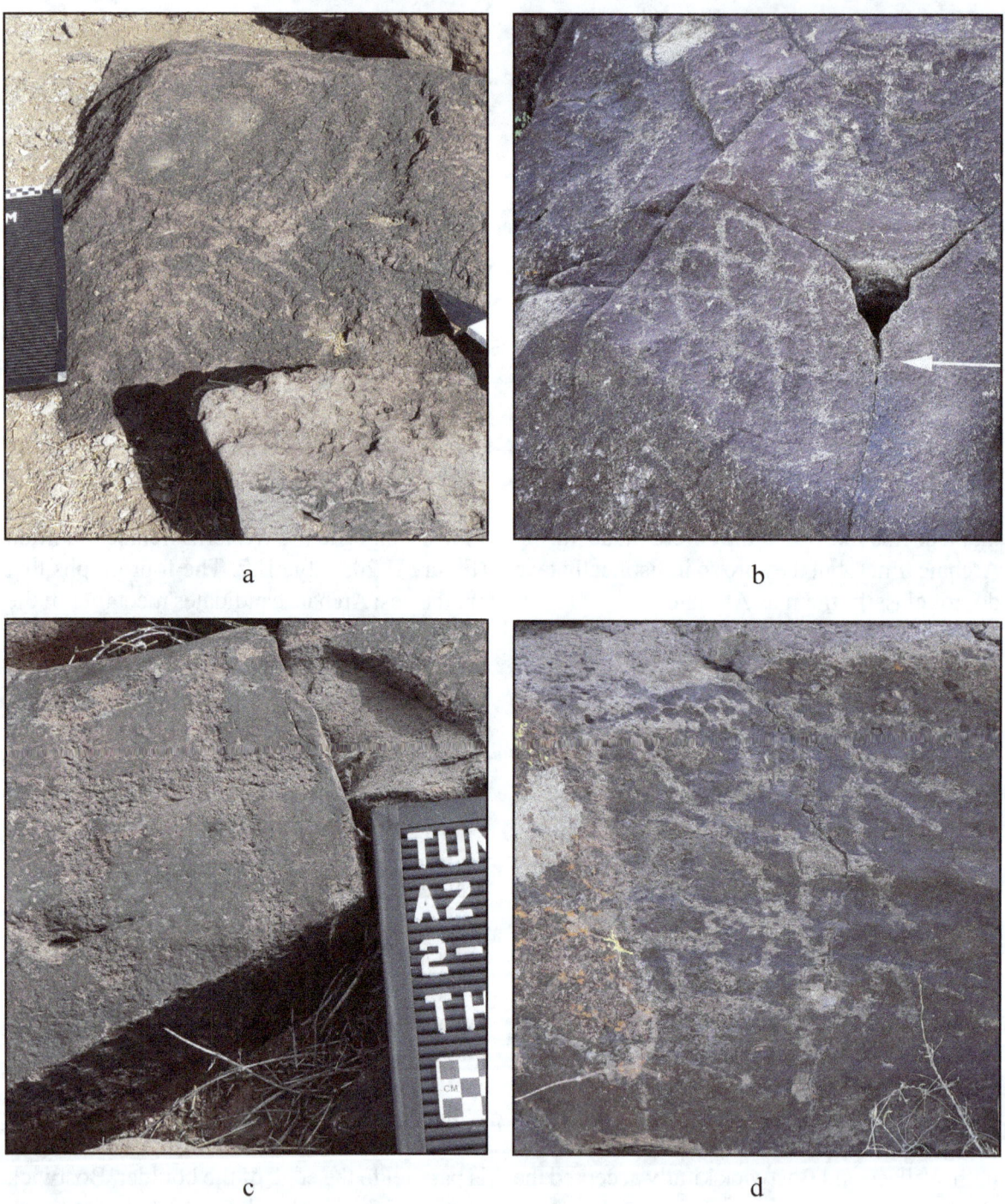

Figure II.20. Best candidates for Western Archaic Tradition glyphs. a, a curvilinear abstract (TH-F136) December 16, 2006; b, a crosshatched diamond (TH-F403, element 15) February 9, 2007; c, a rectilinear abstract (TH-F515) Feb. 9, 2007; d, a rectilinear abstract (TH-F4343) October 7, 2008. (Photos by Janine Hernbrode)

Feature ID*	Patination	Element Name	Technique	Line Width	Under Prehistoric	To / Around Edge	Criteria Met
		Table II.7. Probable and Possible Western Archaic Tradition Glyphs Based on Five Criteria					
403	h	Cross hatch, diamond	Pecked	1.5		X	4
136	h-m	Curvilinear abstract	Pecked	2		X	4
515	h	Rectilinear abstract	Pecked	2		X	4
4343	h	Rectilinear abstract	Pecked	1.5		X	4
Total							4
459	m	Centipede	Pecked	1.75		X	3
2962	h-m	Circle	Pecked	2			3
2926	h-m	Circle	Pecked	1.5			3
2962	h-m	Circle	Pecked	1.5			3
2942	m	Circle cluster	Pecked	5		X	3
2926	h-m	Circles, concentric, 2 rings	Pecked	1.5			3
2926	h-m	Cross	Pecked	1.5			3
3023	h	Cross	Pecked	2			3
4399	m	Cross hatch, diamond	Scratched	0.1	X	X	3
4324	h	Cross hatch, grid	Scratched	0.1	X		3
459	m	Cross hatch, grid	Pecked	2		X	3
520	m	Cross hatch, grid	Pecked	1.2	X	X	3
403	h	Curvilinear abstract	Pecked	2			3
3277	h	Curvilinear abstract	Pecked	2			3
3317	h	Curvilinear abstract	Pecked	2			3
403	h	Curvilinear abstract	Pecked	1.5			3
4349	h	Curvilinear abstract	Pecked	1.2		X	3
403	h-m	Curvilinear abstract	Pecked	2			3
444	h	Line, straight	Pecked	4			3
3277	h	Line, straight	Pecked	2			3
4386	h	Line, zigzag or wavy	Pecked	1.5			3
136	h-m	Line, zigzag or wavy	Pecked	2			3
3277	h	Rectilinear abstract	Pecked	2			3
3317	h	Rectilinear abstract	Pecked	2			3
2927	m	Rectilinear abstract	Pecked	2		X	3
3273	m	Rectilinear abstract	Pecked	1.5		X	3
2926	h-m	Sun disk	Pecked	1.5			3
Total							27

*These rock art features may be viewed on the ASM website, and are labeled as "TH-F" followed by Feature ID number (ASM website: www.statemuseum.arizona.edu/research/pubs/archseries/companion_materials).

Table II.8. Probable and Possible Western Archaic Tradition Glyphs Based on Independent Evaluation

Feature ID*	Element Code	Element Name	Technique	Criteria Met	Henry Wallace	Todd Bostwick
403	51	Cross hatch, diamond	Pecked	4	A or H	A
136	53	Curvilinear abstract	Pecked	4	U	A
515	72	Rectilinear abstract	Pecked	4	A	?
4343	72	Rectilinear abstract	Pecked	4	H	A
520	52	Cross hatch, grid	Pecked	3	H	A
403	53	Curvilinear abstract	Pecked	3	A or H	A
4349	53	Curvilinear abstract	Pecked	3	A	A
2927	72	Rectilinear abstract	Pecked	3	H	?
4	36	Chevron nested	Pecked	2	A	A
35	82	Shell	Pecked	2	A?	?
403	36	Chevron nested	Pecked	2	A or H	H
408	72	Rectilinear abstract	Pecked	2	A	A
483	53	Curvilinear abstract	Pecked	2	A?	A
2994	69	Rake	Pecked	2	A?	A
4461	53	Curvilinear abstract	Pecked	2	H	A

Key: A = Archaic; H = Hohokam; U = Uncertain
*These rock art features may be viewed on the ASM website, and are labeled as "TH-F" followed by Feature ID number (ASM website. www.statemuseum.arizona.edu/research/pubs/archseries/companion_materials).

their evaluation of the Tumamoc glyphs. Bostwick included an age/culture estimate [sometimes a question mark] for each element and an occasional comment, while Wallace included an age/culture estimate [sometimes "unknown"] for each element as well as comments for each element. This correspondence is curated at the Arizona State Museum, Accession No. AP-2013-437.

A Crosshatched Diamond (TH-F403, Element 15). This crosshatched, diamond design is pecked with lines 1.5 cm in width into a very large boulder near the southeast corner of the summit. The design is heavily repatinated and extends to the edge of the surface into which it is pecked in several places. This boulder contains the largest number of elements of any prehistoric feature recorded (20) and appears to exhibit a combination of Western Archaic and Hohokam elements. Bostwick estimated this element to be of Archaic age while Wallace identified it as either Archaic or Hohokam and noted, "This could go either way based on style. Patina looks pretty heavy but not knowing the local sequence, I am not prepared to assume Archaic on that alone" (Figure II.20b).

A Rectilinear Abstract (TH-F515). This rectilinear abstract design is pecked with lines 2 cm in width into a flat-lying bedrock slab. Portions of the design extend to the edge of the slab and the pecking is heavily repatinated. Bostwick provided a question mark as an age estimate while Wallace estimated the glyph to be Archaic, "based on patination and very wide, well-pecked design" (Figure II.20c).

A Rectilinear Abstract (TH-F4343). This rectilinear abstract design is pecked with lines 1.5 cm in width. The repatination is heavy and portions of the design extend along the edge of the boulder. Bostwick estimated this element to be Archaic while Wallace identified it as Hohokam and noted that if it were Archaic, "it would wrap onto the adjacent panel and it would be more curvilinear" (Figure II.20d).

Candidates Meeting Three Criteria

Twenty-seven elements meet three of our five criteria. Each, of course, is a motif identified as being made during the Archaic period (see Table II.6). In addition, most show medium to heavy or heavy repatination. Line width varies, although the majority is 1.5 cm in width or wider, a few of the designs extend to the edge of the boulder and one wraps around the edge of the boulder (Table II.7).

Four of these were included in the sample we sent to Bostwick and Wallace, and their comments generally corroborate an Archaic classification for these elements. TH-F520 (a cross-hatched grid that is netlike) was classified by Bostwick as Archaic while Wallace commented, "grids could be either Hohokam or Archaic, but this is not well pecked, it does not conform to the rock edges or spill over the edges, and it is relatively lightly patinated." Bostwick was not sure how to categorize TH-2927 (a rectilinear abstract), while Wallace favored Hohokam, but noted "I am assuming the Archaic here [the local sequence] does not have patination this light. If wrong, then this could be either Archaic or Hohokam." Finally, TH-4349 (a curvilinear abstract) was classified as Archaic both by Bostwick and Wallace, with Wallace commenting that he based his conclusion on its "deep pecking and patination."

Candidates Meeting Fewer than Three Criteria but Independently Evaluated as Archaic or Possibly Archaic

A final group consists of seven glyphs that met the motif criterion but satisfied fewer than three of our criteria, and were rated as Archaic or possible Archaic by either Bostwick or Wallace. We do not have space to discuss these in detail, but the information on all seven is provided in Table II.8 and illustrations can be accessed on the Arizona State Museum website. We do include Wallace's comments on the two elements that both he and Bostwick agreed definitely belong to the Western Archaic Tradition. These two elements (TH-F4 and TH-F408) as well as TH-F4349 are illustrated in Figure II.21. For TH-F4 (nested chevrons) Wallace notes, "Despite the relatively light patina, the design is most likely Western Archaic for three reasons: it wraps around the corner of a panel, it is a typical Archaic repetitive motif and chevrons are uncommon in Hohokam, and the patina is similar to the light patina on the panel's surfaces so there is not the expectation of dark patination on the glyph." For TH-F408 (a rectilinear abstract) he notes, "This reminds me of the sectioned rectangles present at Shelter Gap [in the Picacho Mountains], an almost purely Archaic site. Not at all typical of Hohokam, so I think this is a safe call."

In conclusion, although glyphs belonging to the Hohokam Pecked style and the Hohokam Scratched style are far more common on Tumamoc Hill than those that can be identified as Western Archaic, some rock art on the hill may have been created during Archaic times. It is interesting to note that, just as with the Hohokam glyphs, the summit and north slope were the preferred location for Archaic or possible Archaic glyphs (Figure II.22). Of 31 glyphs possibly belonging to the Western Archaic Tradition based on our five criteria analysis, 13 (42 percent) are on the summit while 16 (52 percent) are on the north slope. One each is located on the east and south slopes. The concentrations on the summit and north slope are not surprising since these locations were the locus of the trincheras, pithouse, and trail building activities during the Cienega and Tortolita phases. It is also noteworthy that the probable/possible Western Archaic glyphs comprise only a small number of motifs. Of the 36 motifs listed in Table II.7 that belong to the Western Archaic Tradition, only 12 were used on Tumamoc Hill, in the sense that they met either three or four of our Archaic criteria. This repertoire of Archaic motifs is small compared

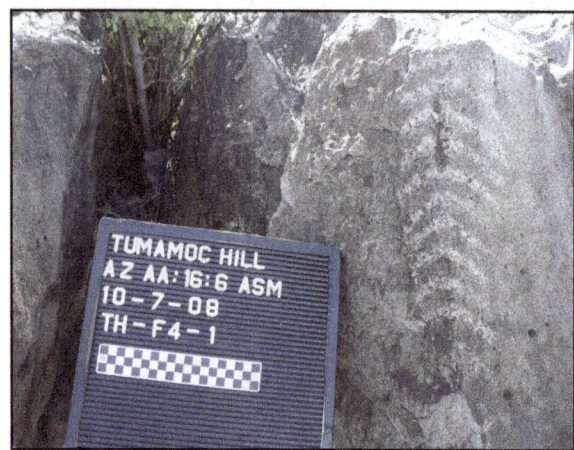

a

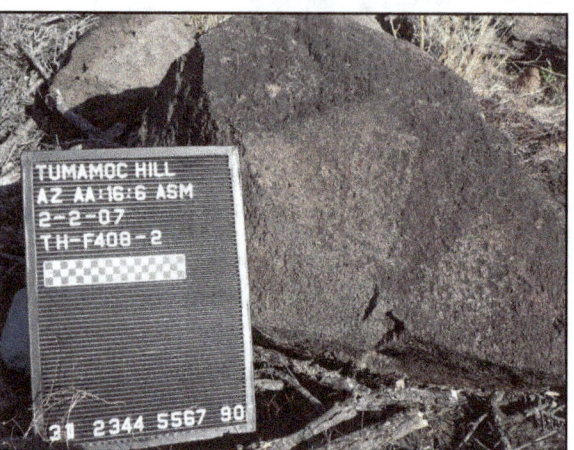

b

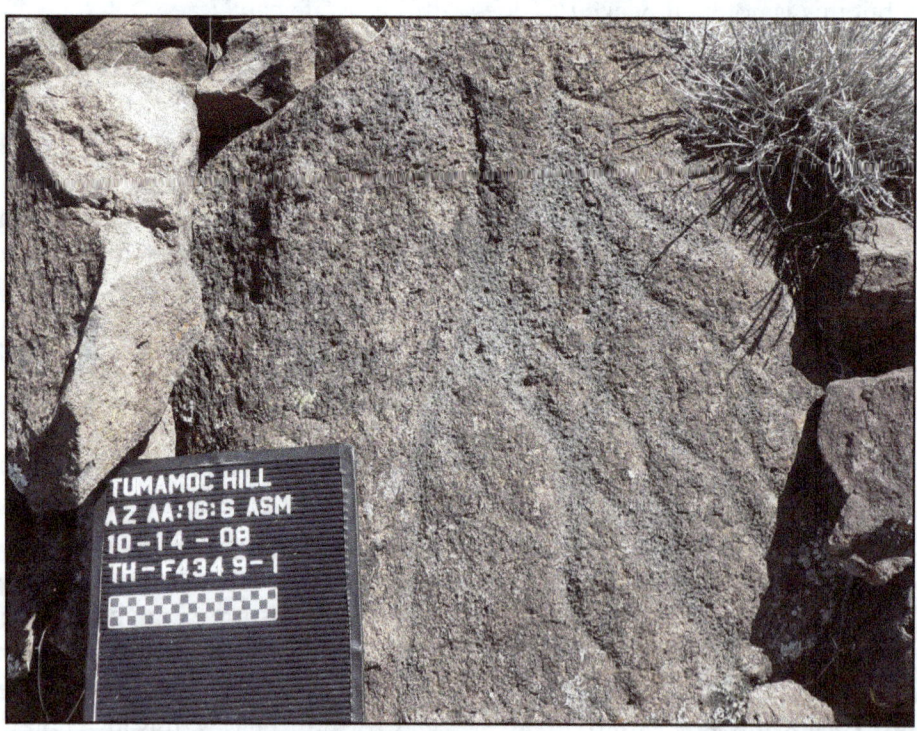

c

Figure II.21. Glyphs classified as Western Archaic by independent evaluation. a, nested chevrons (TH-F4) October 7, 2008; b, rectilinear abstract (TH-F408) February 2, 2007; c, curvilinear abstract (TH-F4349) October 14, 2008. (Photos by Janine Hernbrode)

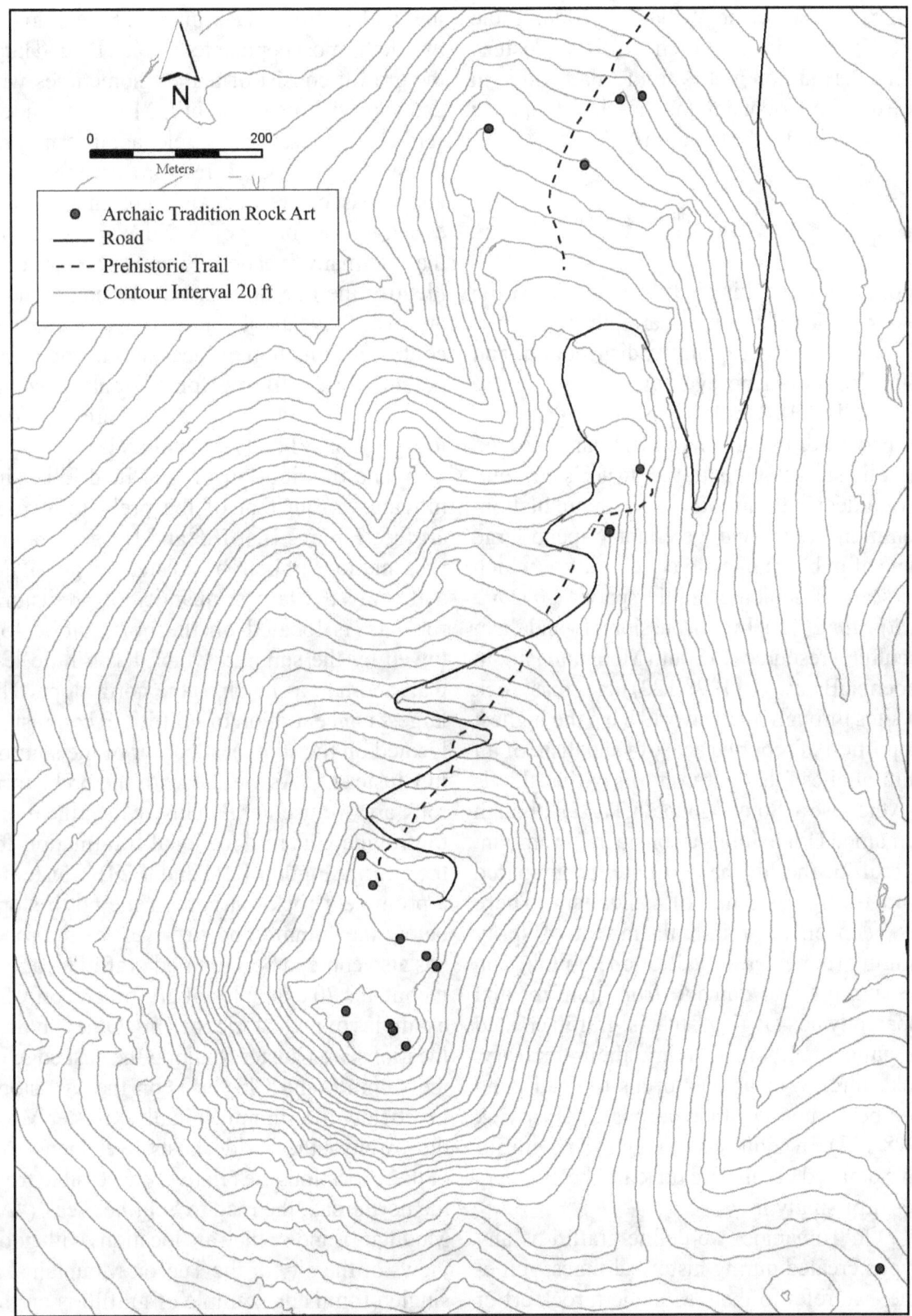

Figure II.22. Map illustrating distribution of probable/possible Western Archaic Tradition glyphs. Note: Each circle represents a rock art feature. Some features contain more than one element. (Map by Todd Pitezel)

to those discussed in Wallace's (2008: Table 4.8, 192) report in which he lists Western Archaic Tradition motifs from Atlatl Ridge in the Tortolita Mountains, the Picacho Mountains and the Gila Bend Mountains.

GRAFFITI

Another goal of this study was to record the 450 examples of graffiti as carefully as possible so changes in their quantity, distribution, and condition could be evaluated in the future (Appendix VI). Graffiti, which are generally defined as drawings or inscriptions made on a public surface without the owner's consent, have a decidedly negative social connotation. Communities around the country spend large sums of public money to cover graffiti, which are seen as defacing public spaces (*Arizona Daily Star* 2008). In a discussion of vandalism to cultural resources in South Mountain Park in Phoenix, Bostwick (1998:122) notes that "rock art sites throughout the world have the highest proportion of reported acts of vandalism of all cultural sites." He goes on to say that this is also the case at South Mountain Park. Although Tumamoc Hill exhibits a considerable amount of graffiti, the hill has, to date, been spared from the worst kinds of vandalism. There has been only a minimal amount of spray painting (the exterior wall of one building on the summit), no damage from gunfire, and apparently no "tagging," that is, graffiti created by gang members to mark their territory, make threats, or as memorials to dead gang members, among other purposes (Bostwick 1998:123). In addition, although some graffiti have defaced prehistoric rock art, the numbers are surprisingly low.

On Tumamoc, we define graffiti as any glyphs created during historical times; sometimes we refer to them as modern rock art or inscriptions. Six techniques are employed—scratching, pecking, abrading, incising, paint-ing, and use of a black marker. Scratching is, by far, the most popular technique. By and large the graffiti consist of names, sometimes with dates, of visitors to the hill. Most are crudely scratched, but several are elegant inscriptions, a few are pictorial, a few are pornographic, and at least one records an important historical event, the beginning of World War II (the date that Germany invaded Poland). We can only identify the age of 122, but we note that 75 are over 50 years old and a few of these may contain information of local significance, thus potentially qualifying for National Register evaluation. Data on the graffiti are provided in Appendix VI and Appendix VII.

The distribution of graffiti differs significantly from that of the prehistoric rock art (see Figures II.4, II.5 and II.6 for graphic presentations of both by cluster and area). Far and away the largest quantity of prehistoric rock art is located on the north slope followed by the summit, which has a little less than one-half as much as the north slope. The largest concentration of graffiti, in contrast, is located on the southeast corner of the summit in Cluster Q. (As we did with the prehistoric rock art, we use Ferg's cluster identifications to provide general locational information for the graffiti; Figures II.23 and II.24). Cluster N, a prominent rock outcrop on the north slope below the summit and just west of the road, has also come to be a favored graffiti location; it contains 70 examples of graffiti and only 24 examples of prehistoric rock art. Other favored locations are Cluster R, along the east edge of the summit, and Cluster T, on the east slope just below the summit. Finally, Cluster V, on the lower southeast side, hosts 26 elements. All of these locations are relatively accessible from the north road, the road to Sentinel Peak ("A" Mountain), and/or they are locations with good views of the city or the Tucson Mountains. A single prominent example of graffiti is on the upper south slope and consists of rocks painted white by Cholla High School students. At one

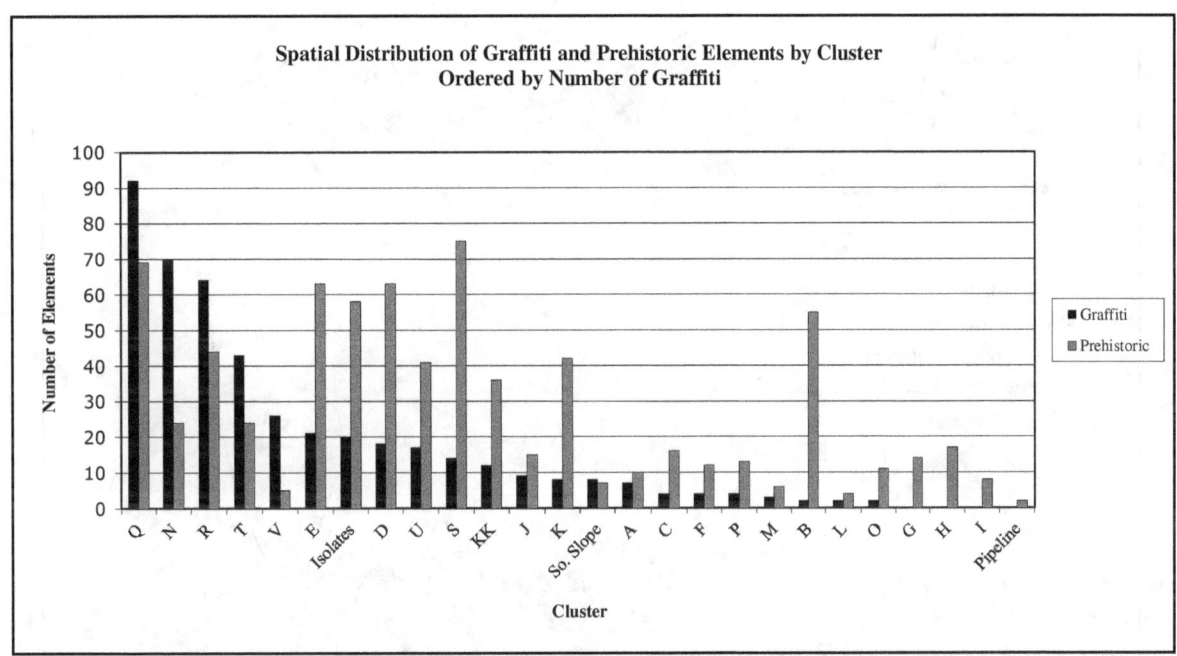

Figure II.23. Spatial distribution of graffiti and prehistoric elements by cluster, ordered by number of graffiti.

time we were told it said "CH," but now the letters cannot be distinguished. The popularity of these locations clearly illustrates that the decision making process for graffiti differs from that used in the creation of prehistoric glyphs.

We were especially interested in the impact of graffiti on prehistoric rock art. Of the 734 prehistoric elements on Tumamoc, 36 (5 percent) have been defaced by graffiti; that is, graffiti are superimposed over prehistoric glyphs. Clusters D and E, on the lower north slope, have the most examples (13), while Clusters T and Q, on or near the southeast portion of the summit, exhibit five examples each.

Although the number of cases where graffiti overlie prehistoric glyphs is disturbing, it constitutes a small percentage compared to South Mountain, the other extensive rock art site in south-central Arizona that is visited by the public in large numbers. There, according to research conducted by J. J. Golio and friends (1993), "approximately 22 percent

of the panels had been stolen or damaged, including petroglyphs destroyed by graffiti and gunfire. Boulders containing petroglyphs had been stolen and individual petroglyphs elements had been removed from panels" (reported in Bostwick 2002:14-15). If we add the five elements on Tumamoc that are missing, vandalized, or moved to the 36 overlain by graffiti this totals only 5.4 percent of the prehistoric total (n = 734).

Table II.9 is a summary of the graffiti that overlie prehistoric glyphs including their location and the motifs that they superimpose. A detailed discussion of each of these is not warranted, but to give an example we illustrate in Figure II.25 a three-ring bull's eye superimposed by an initial with many other initials nearby. It is interesting to note that the graffiti on this feature were all visible in a 1974-1975 photo by Larson (No. 53815). The only other photo taken by Larson that shows graffiti (TH-F20) illustrates that graffiti production is ongoing. In addition to five prehistoric motifs, two examples of graffiti are visible

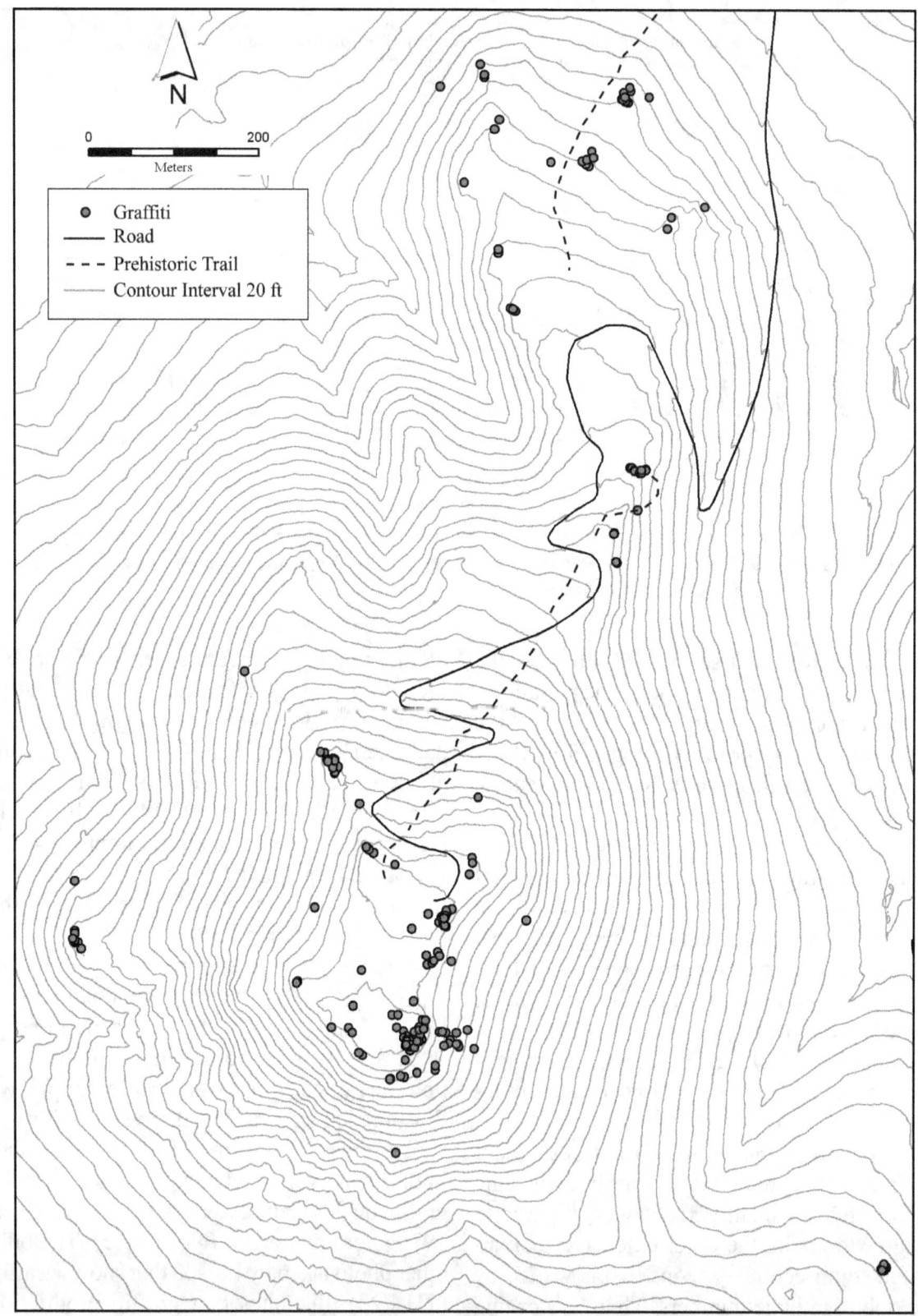

Figure II.24. Map illustrating distribution of graffiti. Note: Each circle represents a rock art [graffiti] feature. Some features contain more than one element. (Map by Todd Pitezel)

Feature ID*	Ferg Cluster ID	Element Code	Element Name
3256	A	22	Lizard without toes
2925	B	32	Bull's eye, 1 ring
2930	B	4	Anthro. arms up with phallus (None 4)
2945	D	74	Scroll, curvilinear clockwise
2945	D	76	Scroll, curvilinear counterclockwise
2941	D	46	Circles, line connected
2944	D	53	Curvilinear abstract
2944	D	62	Line, straight
2975	E	53	Curvilinear abstract
2961	E	53	Curvilinear abstract
2961	E	76	Scroll, curvilinear counterclockwise
2962	E	33	Bull's eye, 2 rings
2962	E	90	Geometric indeterminate
3023	E	49	Cross
3020	E	53	Curvilinear abstract
3020	E	64	Line, zigzag or wavy
4341	L	1	Anthro. arms up (None 1)
4341	L	72	Rectilinear abstract
168	M	14	Person (not a stickperson) with a staff
20	N	42	Circles, concentric, 2 rings
20	N	64	Line, zigzag or wavy
16	N	16	Anthropomorphic indeterminate
2387	N	90	Geometric indeterminate
694	Q	90	Geometric indeterminate
413	Q	12	Any stickperson holding material culture (Not person with staff; i.e., Not 14)
4488	Q	13	Anthropomorphic other than a stick figure
422	Q	60	Ladder
429	Q	91	Geometric other
403	S	53	Curvilinear abstract
3335	T	51	Cross hatch, diamond
3335	T	51	Cross hatch, diamond
3335	T	51	Cross hatch, diamond
3335	T	52	Cross hatch, grid
3335	T	63	Line, parallel
3357	U	62	Line, straight
4322	V	34	Bull's eye, 3+ rings

Table II.9. Graffiti Superimposed Over Prehistoric Elements

*These rock art features may be viewed on the ASM website, and are labeled as "TH-F" followed by Feature ID number (ASM website: www.statemuseum.arizona.edu/research/pubs/archseries/companion_materials).

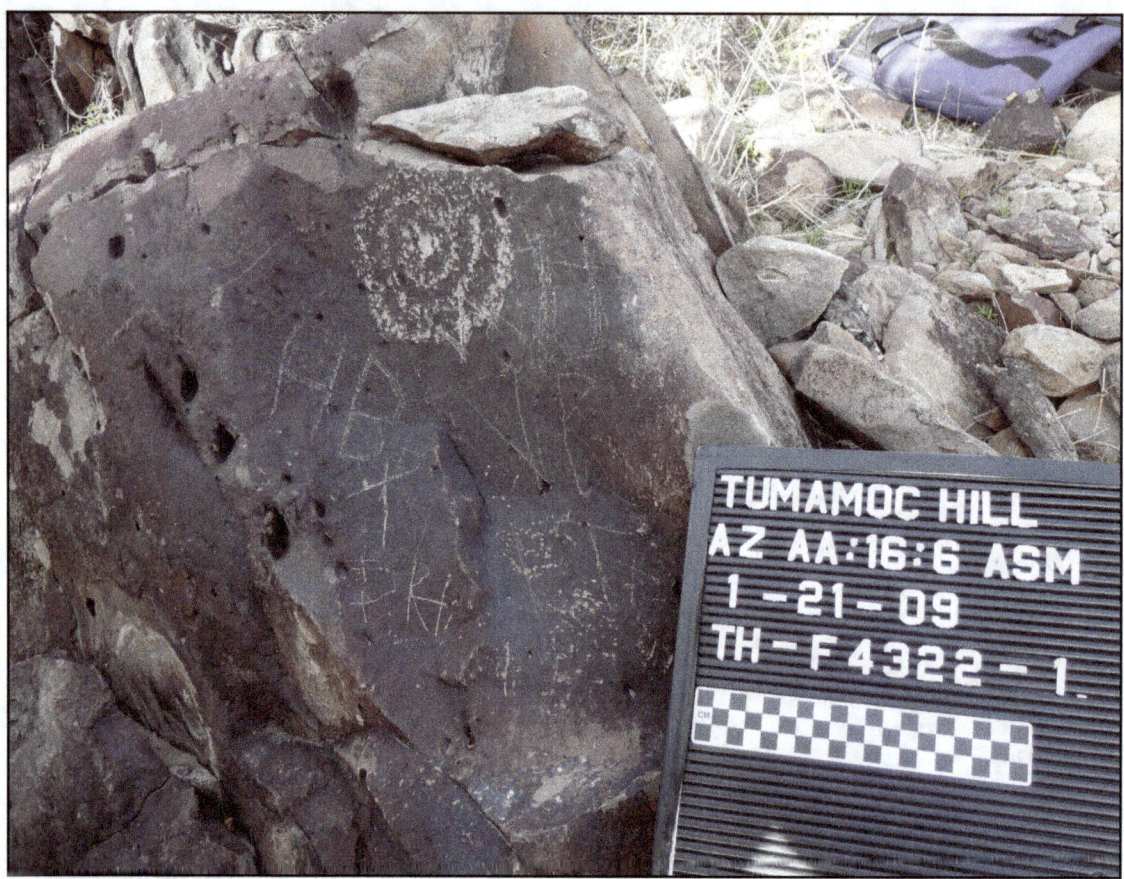

Figure II.25. Graffiti superimposed over a prehistoric glyph (TH-F4322). (Photo by Janine Hernbrode)

in the Larson photos (Nos. 53748, 49, 50). In our recording of this feature, two additional examples are now visible.

Figure II.26 illustrates the distribution of vandalized elements. As can been seen, for the most part they are concentrated on outcrops on the north slope and are on or near the summit.

Temporal Range and Changes over Time of Graffiti Production

In terms of temporal range of graffiti, we recorded 122 examples of names with dates or dates alone. This sample of the age distribution of the graffiti on the hill is depicted in a histogram in Figure II.27. We have no way of knowing the temporal distribution of the total number of graffiti. Assuming a similar distribution over

time, however, we can calculate a ballpark estimate of total graffiti production from the dated sample. Unfortunately, after three decades of relatively low graffiti creation, the most intense period of production occurred in the most recent decade, or more accurately until 2009. This consisted of 17 dated graffiti or 14 percent of the 122 dated examples in a nine-year period. Thus, we can estimate that 14 percent of the total sample of 450, or 63 graffiti, were created in this recent eight-year period. We emphasize that these figures are only estimates. We note that, in addition to the 122 examples cited, four historical inscriptions include what we believe to be bogus dates, that is, dates that seem unreasonably early either because of the haphazard style or accompanying words. We did not include these in our sample (Appendix VII). As a final note regarding graffiti production, on a visit to the

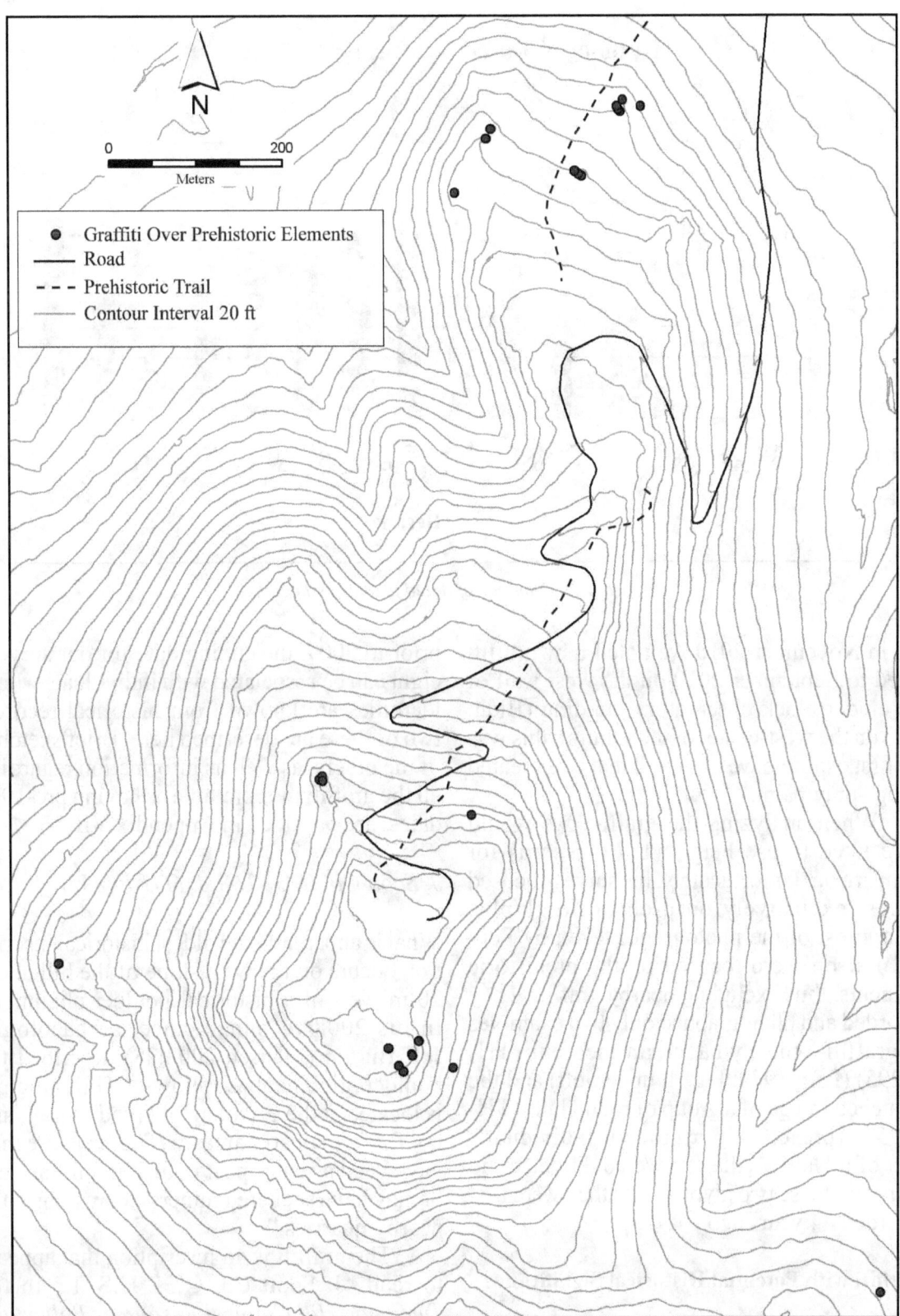

Figure II.26. Map of graffiti superimposed over prehistoric glyphs. Note: Each circle represents a rock art feature. Some features contain more than one element. (Map by Todd Pitezel)

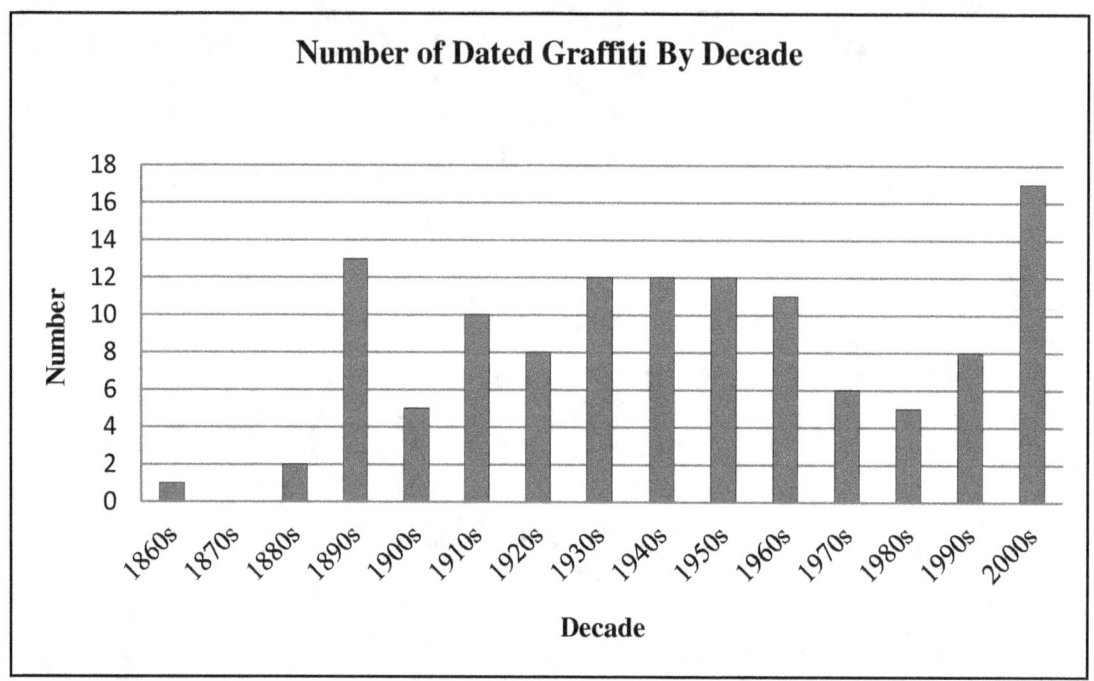

Figure II.27. Number of dated graffiti by decade.

hill in November 2010 we noted new graffiti dated to September 2010 on the west wall of the cinder-block observatory building (Bldg. 851) on the west-center of the summit; this was the first example we observed that was created using spray paint.

When analyzing the graffiti, we would have liked to use Ferg's (1979) records for comparison. Unfortunately, his survey focused almost exclusively on prehistoric glyphs. Also, most of the photographs taken by Ferg and Larson were focused on the prehistoric elements, thus excluding nearby graffiti. They recorded and photographed only two examples of graffiti—the Pythagorean theorem (TH-F3295) (Ferg 1979, Fig. 4, upper left) and the scratched image of a group of round huts (TH-F2957) (presumably a modern individual's idea of a Native village). We could detect no change in these two glyphs since they were first recorded 34 years ago.

Graffiti with Potential Historical Significance

Of the 75 graffiti that can be definitely dated as older than 50 years (that is, more than 50 years

prior to 2009, the ending date for our survey) eight can be associated with individuals whose identities are known from historical records; two of these are described here. Brief sketches of the others, as well as information regarding all the graffiti interpretable as having pre-1959 dates, are provided in Appendix VII.

J. Scott Co. C. 32 U.S. I. (TH-F4452)

What is apparently the oldest historical inscription occurs on the west slope of the hill about 20 m west of a historical boulder alignment. In his 2008 reconnaissance, archaeologist Jeff Burton (Madsen 2008:28) described the boulder alignment as follows, "This structure is located at the end of an old road or trail, and not far from quarry areas....The structure may have been a sentry post related to military use or may have sheltered miners excavating at the nearby quarries."

The graffiti is an inscription that appears to read "J. Scott Co. C 32 U.S. I." In the *Tumamoc Hill Cultural Resources Policy and Management Plan* (Madsen 2008:28) Burton references Larry Ludwig, the site manager at Fort Bowie National Historic Site, who concludes that this inscription must have been created by a member of Company C, 32nd U. S. Infantry. This company was stationed at Camp Lowell, which was in downtown Tucson from January 1867 until March 1868. The company's main duties were escorting government trains to and from posts dependent on supplies stored at the Tucson depot (Randall 1991). No one with the surname "Scott" appears in the post records, an indication that he was not an officer, as only the officers are listed (Figure II.28a).

Georgia Hazel Scott
(TH-F4410, TH-F4413)

One of the most prominent historical inscriptions on the hill, just below the east side of the summit, appears three times as a full name, once as "Hazel," and once as "GHS" (Figure II.28b). Twice "Georgia Hazel Scott" and the date "1891" appear to be associated with "Hugh McAnally," however, since Hugh was born about 1918, he presumably wrote his name at a later date (Appendix VII). With help from historical archaeologist Homer Thiel, Katherine Cerino learned that Georgia was the daughter of a pioneering Tucson family. Cerino (2009:4-6) published Georgia Hazel Scott's story in *Glyphs*, the monthly newsletter of the Arizona Archaeological and Historical Society. In the exuberance of Georgia's eighteenth year, she apparently had a good time inscribing her name in several locations near the summit of Tumamoc Hill. Because she was an individual of some importance in Tucson history, her story and that of her parents is summarized here (Cerino 2009:4-6).

Georgia Hazel Scott, who is referred to in all published literature as "Georgie," was born in 1873, in Tucson, and was christened by the territorial governor, A.P.K. Safford. Her father, William Fisher Scott, was a Scottish lawyer and judge; Scott Street bears his name. Her mother was Larcena Pennington; Pennington Street was named for her family. The Penningtons arrived in 1857, first settling near present-day

Benson. In 1859, while living at Fort Buchanan (near present day Sonoita), Larcena met and married John Page. A year later, while cutting wood in Madera Canyon, Larcena and two friends were captured by Apaches. Unable to keep up with her captors, she was stabbed multiple times and left for dead. After two days and nights [the number of days differs in different accounts; in some accounts it is as long as 17 days] she found water and got to a place where she could get help. A year later, her husband was killed by Apaches. Larcena was pregnant with Georgie's half-sister, Mary, at the time. After John Page's death, Larcena moved to Tubac with her father and brothers. By 1864, at the height of the Civil War, they were the only residents left in town. Then her father and two of her brothers were killed by Apaches. Eventually her only remaining brother moved to Texas. Larcena, however, remained in Arizona, marrying William Scott in 1870 (Banks 1999).

Larcena's daughter, Georgie, learned Spanish from a Mexican nurse as her first language, and she initially attended a Spanish-speaking private school. Later, she entered the earliest public schools in the Arizona Territory. Her obituary states that she entered the University of Arizona when it accepted its first class in 1891, but she is not listed in university records. Georgie became a rural school teacher and taught in the Huachuca Mountains and at Tanque Verde under very rugged conditions. Once, she shot a mountain lion who invaded the home where she was "boarded around" (*Arizona Daily Star* 1946).

Eventually she met Robert Humphrey Forbes, who was to play an important role in Arizona and especially at the University of Arizona. Dr. Forbes arrived in Tucson in 1894 from Illinois with a U of A teaching appointment. Robert and Georgie were married in 1902, when Georgie was 29. The story goes that she agreed to marry Robert if he succeeded in reaching the summit of Baboquivari Peak. It took him five attempts, but he and his

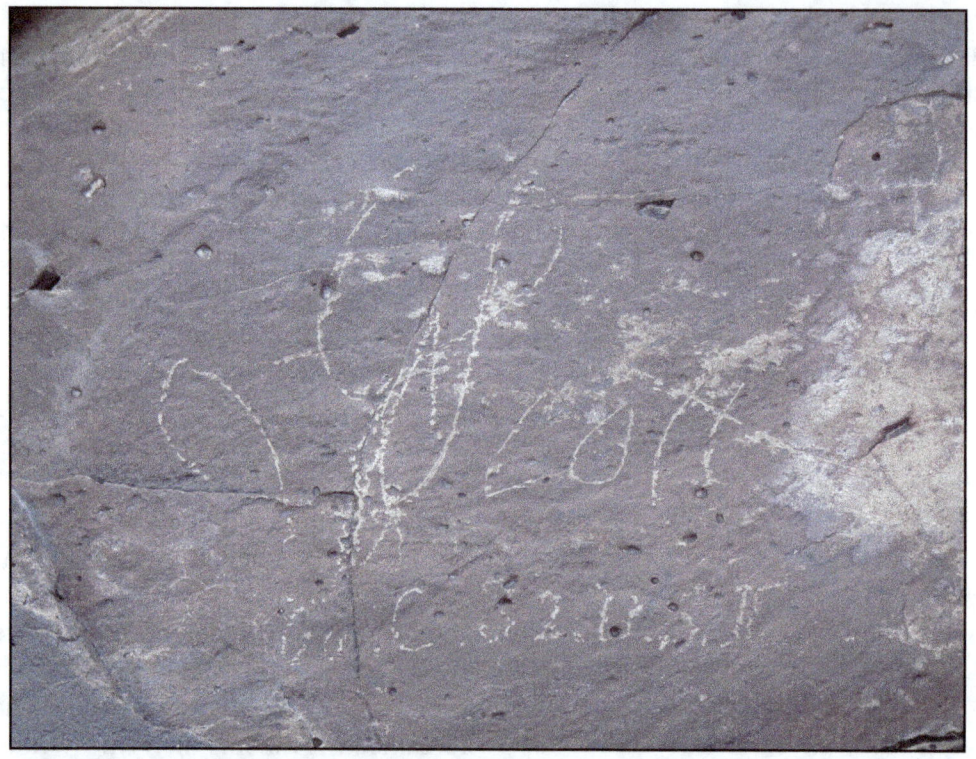

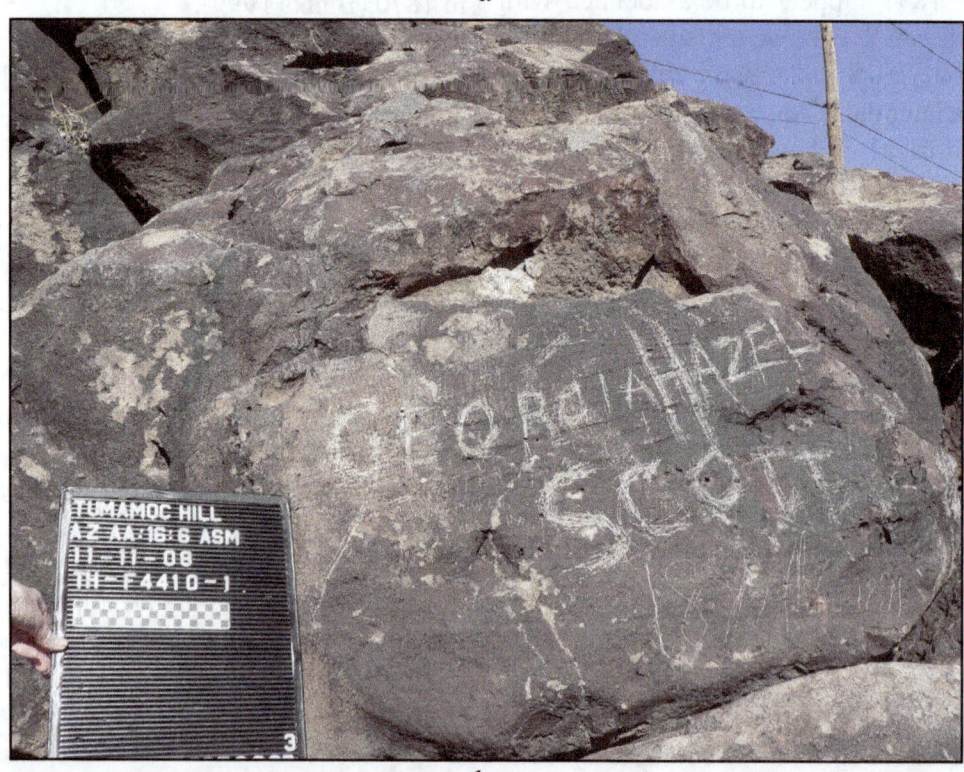

Figure II.28. Two graffiti with potential historical significance. a, J. Scott Co. C. 32 U.S.I (TH-F4452); b, Georgia Hazel Scott (TH-F4410, TH-F4413). (Photos by Janine Hernbrode, upper photo 6 January 2009)

Tohono O'odham companion, Lorenzo Montoya, reached the peak in 1898. Forbes was apparently the first white man to do so, and he climbed the peak several more times during his life. The route he pioneered, now called the "Forbes Route," remains the most popular climbing route to the peak.

The couple settled into a two-story territorial house at 105 Olive Road, adjacent to the U of A campus. There Georgie Forbes, known as "the duchess" to her friends because of her natural dignity and aristocratic bearing, became prominent in early Tucson society. The couple had no children.

In 1918, Georgie and Robert began a 15-year period of living abroad. Forbes acknowledged that the years abroad were partially to escape "the UA's meager salaries and desolate location" (*Arizona Daily Star* 1968). Dr. Forbes' work directing agricultural projects for the Egyptian, French, and Haitian governments, took them first to Egypt, then to Haiti and Paris. Charles Colley's (1977:46) biography of Forbes, *The Century of Robert H. Forbes*, includes a photo of Georgie astride a camel in front of the Great Sphinx in the Valley of the Kings. In 1931, they returned to Tucson.

From 1937 to 1939, Georgie served as the first female president of the Arizona Pioneers' Historical Society (now the Arizona Historical Society) for which her husband had secured funding during his tenure as a state representative. Georgie died in 1946 at the age of 73, reportedly while reading a good book.

As Katherine Cerino wrote in her article about Georgia Hazel Scott in *Glyphs* (2009:4-6), we implore all readers not to emulate Georgie's actions. Do not add your inscription to the collection of glyphs on Tumamoc Hill in the hope that it will, someday, be of historic value.

In addition to the two inscriptions just discussed, 18 others provide full names, surnames with dates, or in one case, an unusual surname. Katherine Cerino searched local historical records and was able to identify eight individuals. These are discussed briefly in Appendix VII. One name consisted of a surname with a single initial and another consisted of only a first name; both were from 1923 and were associated with "THS" as were initials from 1951. We assume these initials refer to Tucson High School, but individuals with these names or initials were not listed in the high school yearbooks. Most, but not all, of these early names are carefully executed, often with flowing script or clear printing with serifs. The individuals whose ages we could ascertain had only one thing in common: they were young when they inscribed their names, similar to the age distribution of graffiti "artists" today.

We did note that a few individuals, both pre-1959 and post-1959, were "repeat offenders" or perhaps the penchant to scratch their names on Tumamoc runs in families. In other words, names appear more than once, sometimes many years apart. For example, Albert Urbina appears with 1903 and 1957; Frank Wood appears with 19 (presumably an incomplete date), with 2004, and again with 2007; and Frank Wood, Jr., appears twice with 2000.

Of the historical inscriptions, just over half are located on the summit. One of these of particular interest is TH-F458, prominently located on a flat-lying bedrock slab on the southeast portion of the summit. The historical inscription shares the slab with a faint prehistoric anthropomorph, but does not impact it. The inscription consists of two sets of large, neatly pecked and incised initials with serifs, "W.D." and "F.H.," the date "A.D. 1891," and two enigmatic characters that appear to be a backward "P" and a cross or plus sign (Figure II.29). Many visitors to the hill over the years have noticed this inscription and commented on it. For example, a popular idea was that it might be a reference to a military company

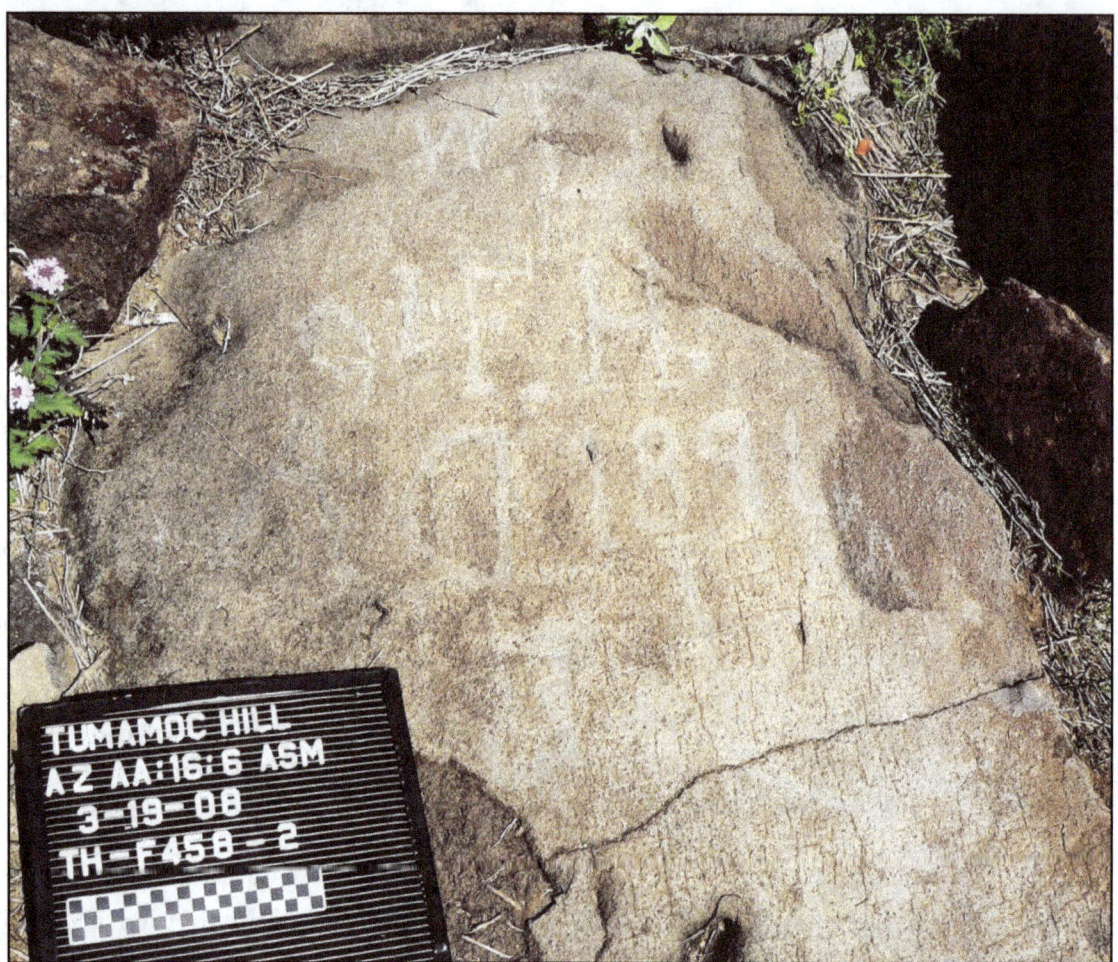

Figure II.29. Enigmatic historical inscription on southeast corner of summit (TH-F458). (Photo by Janine Hernbrode)

(perhaps from Fort Huachuca), much like TH-F4452 on the west side of the hill. However, discussions with military historians did not provide any corroboration to this theory. In researching this inscription further, we contacted El Morro National Monument to see if any of their historic inscriptions included these symbols. None did; thus, the inscription may represent nothing more than a typical "John loves Mary" expression, consisting of two sets of well-printed initials and two undecipherable characters created in 1891, a popular year for historic inscriptions.

Finally, we note that there is a tendency on Tumamoc Hill for multiple inscriptions, sometimes many years apart, to be on the same boulder or outcrop. One example, a small flat-lying slab that is cracked into two pieces, is near the road a little below the summit (TH-F189). It exhibits six inscriptions ranging from 14 April 1880 to 1970. Four are from midwestern states—two from Ohio, one from Kansas, and one from Indiana. We wondered whether some of these individuals might have had some connection with the Desert Laboratory, although the earliest would have predated the founding of the laboratory. However, after checking several publications that reference the history of the Desert Laboratory and talking with retired staff we were not able to corroborate this theory. The smooth surface of the slab may have attracted the initial inscription, with later individuals attracted by the earlier graffiti. It is definitely the case that graffiti attracts graffiti and quick removal, where possible, is important.

MANAGEMENT ISSUES

In considering our management recommendations, we note that Tumamoc Hill is not alone in trying to resolve the challenges of large numbers of unsupervised visitors. Managing a site with rock imagery in an urban setting is not an easy task, especially in a location with the limited staff resources of Tumamoc Hill. Former Phoenix city archaeologist Todd Bostwick (1998:120) notes in his discussion of management of the rock art within South Mountain Park in Phoenix, that "there are many examples of poorly managed rock art sites, either through neglect or improper use." At the same time it is heartening that in recent years, archaeologists and other rock art experts have begun to pay more attention to good management policies and techniques, and examples of well-managed sites do exist. Bostwick (1998:120) cites several examples of well-managed programs from around the world, including the Coconino National Forest in Arizona (Pilles 1989) and Petroglyph National Monument in New Mexico (Schmader 1995).

When Tumamoc Hill was first set aside at the turn of the twentieth century as a botanical preserve, it was essentially in a rural setting. It was located a few miles from the edge of the small town of Tucson, which then boasted a population of 7,000. Now the hill sits within a metropolitan area that is approaching one million residents; it is surrounded by residential neighborhoods, businesses, a high school, a hospital, and busy streets. The Tumamoc property is enclosed by a fence and a gate, but the fence is easily climbable, and the gate is open during the day and easily bypassed at night.

Partly because of ease of access and for other reasons cited below, Tumamoc is visited by a wide variety of individuals. Some visit for work-related reasons, such as employees of the Desert Laboratory and workers who maintain the various facilities on the hill. However, because the hill provides a large, and mainly unsupervised park-like area close to neighborhoods, it is also visited by many individuals who do not work on the hill.

For years, the hill was officially posted as closed to public use and most members of the public who lived nearby recognized that status. Visitation to the hill for unofficial purposes was infrequent and generally conducted in a clandestine manner. As the population of Tucson increased and more people became interested in aerobic exercise, however, it apparently seemed to many that the road should not be off-limits to walkers. Large numbers of people started to climb the hill on a daily basis. The University of Arizona finally had to acknowledge that it could not prohibit this use, even though it interfered with vehicular traffic and caused other problems for employees on the hill. Thus, the university and the City of Tucson worked to accommodate recreational walking before and after work hours. They provided parking along the road at the base of the hill to prevent walkers' use of the St. Mary's Hospital lot. Signs have been posted along the road limiting hours of walking, asking walkers to stay on the road, and prohibiting access to the summit, although these warnings are not always followed. Bicycles, skateboards, and inline skates are prohibited and pets are not allowed. The signs also point out that the hill is a research station, not a public park and that walking off-road can destroy a century worth of botanical research.

Undoubtedly, the "hill walkers" constitute the largest user group—they walk the paved road from the bottom of the hill to the summit as a way to get an aerobic workout. In recent years, this has become a very popular activity. From essentially no walkers up through the early to mid-1990s, numbers have increased exponentially (Julio Betancourt, former director, Desert Laboratory, personal communication, 2008). Former Arizona State Museum archaeologist John Madsen [now emeritus] (personal communication, 2008), who was for many years responsible for monitoring archaeological activities on the hill, estimates that on winter weekends as many as 1,000 walkers may ascend the hill. Although careful counts have not been made, it is clear that tens of thousands of ascents are made annually of the approximately one mile-long road, which rises 226 m (745 feet) from the valley floor.

A few local individuals have created new trails on the hill either through repeated use or by actual construction with pick and shovel (Richard Barber, Desert Laboratory staff member and John Madsen, former Arizona State Museum archaeologist [now emeritus], personal communication, 2008). Although Barber and volunteers have repeatedly tried to erase these trails, their locations are known to some recreational users of the hill who continue to use them, thus gaining access to locations not frequently visited in the past. In addition, the trail along the lower east slope of Tumamoc Hill created by the City of Tucson in "A" Mountain Park has made it easier for walkers to cross the fence onto the Tumamoc property.

Residents who live in nearby neighborhoods, especially along the west boundary of the hill, use the flat and nearly flat lower bajadas for recreational walking for themselves and their dogs. A gas line easement below the hill on its east side also attracts a small number of walkers and runners. Homeless individuals make camps in the washes and bajada areas that ring the hill, especially on the north and west sides. And high school students from Cholla High School have arranged rocks on the upper south side of the hill and painted them white.

At one time, these rocks spelled "C H," but at the request of the Arizona State Museum, they have been somewhat dispersed. Finally, the scratched initials "THS" on several boulders indicate that Tucson High School students have been responsible, over the years, for their share of vandalism.

Although almost certainly only a small fraction of the large number of hill visitors disturbs or defaces rock art on the hill, the result is clear. Graffiti is prevalent and continues to be created, with 36 examples defacing prehistoric rock art elements and 17 examples with post-2000 dates. Such activity, unless curtailed, will eventually degrade a significant portion of the prehistoric rock art record.

Such degradation is well known in other popular rock art locations. For example, Hueco Tanks State Historical Park in west Texas receives more than 65,000 visitors annually (Harry et al. 2001:153) while South Mountain Park receives an estimated 2.5 million visitors annually (Bostwick 1998:119). Both sites have suffered from extensive vandalism, and management staffs are working diligently toward solutions that they hope will reduce this problem.

Management Recommendations

In his excellent discussion of the management of rock art on South Mountain in Phoenix, Bostwick (1998) provides a helpful approach to management taken from rock art expert Georgia Lee (1991). This approach, somewhat modified here, consists of four steps: (1) development of a management policy, (2) assessment of the significance of the site, (3) documentation of the site, and (4) development of a management plan (Lee 1991:8 in Bostwick 1998:120). Because Tumamoc Hill is not the usual rock art locale that is managed primarily for public visitation, our management discussion focuses on the fourth step, development of a management plan specifically for rock art. We begin with a brief discussion of what has already been accomplished for Tumamoc rock art, that is, development of a management policy, assessment of significance, and documentation (Madsen 2008).

Management Policy

The recently completed cultural resources policy and management plan for Tumamoc (Madsen 2008) provides an overview of policies already in place, relating to cultural resources. The most general is part of the University of Arizona administrative policy relating to historic preservation activities. It was adopted on 1 May 2006 and states, in part, that "cultural resources will be considered in all phases of planning for land and facility use and development. The policy reaffirms the university's accord with the state's historic preservation acts and its willingness to document professionally the cultural resources it owns or controls and to consult with the SHPO [State Historic Preservation Office]. . . . It enjoins the University to encourage public appreciation of all Arizona's cultural resources through education, study, and interpretation." (Madsen 2008:44).

Specifically, in relation to Tumamoc Hill, the management plan states, "It is the goal of the ABOR [Arizona Board of Regents] and the University to maintain the Desert Laboratory as a premiere ecological research and education center and to promote research and education in a manner that protects the historical integrity of Tumamoc Hill" (Madsen 2008:49).

Assessment of Significance and Documentation of Rock Art

The Madsen (2008) policy and management plan provides details regarding the significance of Tumamoc and nominates the entire hill to the National Register of Historic Places. In the report, Tumamoc is defined as a "world-renowned center...that attracts leading researchers on desert ecosystems and archaeology" (Madsen 2008:1). In specific relation to rock art, the report refers to Ferg's (1979) study and notes that "petroglyphs appear to corroborate the long-term use of the hill. Different degrees of patina and the superposing of elements indicate time depth" (Madsen 2008:12). The report also notes the large number of petroglyphs recorded by Ferg, the identification of both a pecked and a scratched style, the fact that many of the pecked designs "appear to be consistent with petroglyphs defined as Hohokam elsewhere," and the important fact that Ferg's report was one of the first systematic studies of petroglyphs in the Tucson Basin (Madsen 2008:15). This study, of course, updates Ferg's work and provides considerable new information about the rock art on the hill. All of these statements underscore the significance of the rock art on Tumamoc. In addition, it is worth noting that Tumamoc Hill hosts more rock art than other known and quantified sites in the Tucson Basin, with Rillito Peak at Los Morteros (AZ AA:12:57[ASM]) coming in a distant second. Only the Sutherland Wash site, on the northwest side of the Santa Catalina Mountains, is known to have a larger quantity of rock art.

As to documentation, we relocated the rock art documented by Ferg (1979), including examples recorded by the student field school (University of Arizona Archaeological Field School on Tumamoc Hill 2005-2006), as well as a few glyphs recorded by small monitoring projects over the years (Estes et al. 2005; Whitney 2005), and, finally, we recorded a considerable amount of rock art not recorded previously. As part of this effort we also documented all graffiti that we observed. Although some rock art and some graffiti almost surely remain unrecorded, we believe that well over 95 percent is now recorded in sufficient detail that it can be easily located and assessed in the future.

Management Plan for Rock Art

The cultural resource policy and management plan provides some specific recommendations for the management of the archaeological resources of the hill in addition to the general goal of promoting research and education in a manner that protects historical integrity (Madsen 2008:51-60). We agree with all the recommendations outlined in that plan and we expand on some of them, emphasizing staffing, education, and reevaluation.

In addition, we strongly agree that research on the rock imagery, as well as the other archaeological resources, should continue. Over the three-plus decades that systematic archaeological research has been conducted on the hill, significant progress has been made on understanding the extent and temporal range of prehistoric and early historic activities on the hill. Examples include initial mapping and analysis of the trincheras, trails, and dry farming systems, among other features (Wilcox 1979; Hartmann and Hartmann 1979; Masse 1979; Wilcox et al. 1979); initial recording of prehistoric rock art (Ferg 1979); dating of corn cupules indicating that at least some of the trincheras were constructed as early as 500 B.C. (Fish et al. 1986); discovery and excavation of a large pit structure in the center of the summit (Fish et al. 2011); a report on early historic use of the hill (Howell 2006); and comprehensive recording of rock art including both prehistoric imagery and graffiti (this study). Thus, it seems virtually certain that the research promise of Tumamoc Hill has not been exhausted. In this report we have addressed only a few research questions, such as temporal affiliation and locational preference with very preliminary results. Continued research is likely to provide significant new and augmented findings.

Staffing. The need for a full-time manager for the hill has been recognized since at least 1982 when the *Tumamoc Hill Policy Plan* (Elkins et al. 1982) was submitted to the president of the University of Arizona. That position has not yet been filled, and the need is even greater 30 years later. The policy and management plan for the hill (Madsen 2008:58) notes that "The weakest link in the protection and preservation of cultural and ecological resources at the Desert Laboratory is the absence of a full-time manager." The plan goes on to recommend that the manager should reside on the property in the residence at the base of the hill and report to the Desert Laboratory Director. We heartily endorse this recommendation. It is time for the University of Arizona not only to recognize the cultural and ecological significance of Tumamoc Hill, but to take the necessary action to protect its world class resources. A full-time, resident manager is unquestionably the most important step toward achieving that goal. In addition, to address clandestine visits to rock art locations, security personnel are also essential. As an alternative and more cost effective approach, surveillance cameras could be used.

Education. Since the creation of the Desert Laboratory early in the twentieth century (Coville and MacDougal 1903), the primary function of Tumamoc Hill has been as a research site, first under the auspices of the Carnegie Institution, and now the University of Arizona and Pima County. Unfortunately, because there has never been a strong management presence on the hill, and access from surrounding areas is easy, vandalism of the site is common and ongoing. Education is a key to improving this situation. Peter Pilles (1988a:11), an archaeologist with a long history of dealing with site vandalism on institutional properties, concludes an article on Arizona's response to site vandalism by noting, "Public involvement and the development of partnerships is the final key for promoting public responsibility and help in the protection of public resources."

This is not the place to provide a detailed interpretive program, but we note a few ideas that have been employed at other rock art sites and that we recommend for Tumamoc.

• Positive signage that explains the significance of the cultural resources on the hill, emphasizes that the resources are part of our local cultural heritage, and encourages respectful behavior on the part of visitors. At the same time, specifically mentioning the rock art may not be wise, especially as long as there is no staff present on the hill. As Bostwick (1998:125) notes in regard to South Mountain Park in Phoenix, "park managers have concerns that putting signage at petroglyph sites will bring too much attention to the sites, increasing the chance of vandalism."

• Educational activities that explain the significance of the hill to the general public especially neighbors and those who regularly walk the road to the summit. Again, in his article about managing the rock art at South Mountain Park, Bostwick (1998:124) notes, "Educating the public about the preservation of rock art is an important component in a successful management strategy." Well-trained guides who can offer carefully planned tours of some of the more accessible rock art could be part of such an effort. At the same time, as archaeologist Johannes Loubser (2001:101) comments in an article on management, "Great care should be taken to ensure that training is thorough…as bad guides are often worse than no guides at all."

• Creating public support by forming a "Friends" group. At present, Tumamoc Hill is a bit of an institutional orphan. Although it is now owned by the University of Arizona and Pima County, for decades it has lacked both financial and management resources. A well-organized "Friends of Tumamoc" could not only contribute some of the needed financial resources, but should also encourage a better understanding within the community of the ecological and archaeological legacy of the hill.

Re-evaluation. In 1985, then governor, Bruce Babbitt, encouraged the creation of a volunteer program to monitor and record archaeological sites. Endorsed enthusiastically by Arizona's Archaeology Advisory Commission, this idea developed into the Arizona Site Steward Program administered by the State Historic Preservation Office (Pilles 1988b:42-43). This program has been quite successful by providing systematic visitation and monitoring of many of Arizona's numerous and remote archaeological sites including those exhibiting rock art.

Here we recommend a very specific approach utilizing site stewards, who can document and evaluate future change to the rock art on Tumamoc Hill.

We want to re-emphasize that although the vast majority of the rock art, both prehistoric and modern elements on Tumamoc are on the summit and north slope, all are not easily accessible either to researchers or members of the public who might be hiking along the road. Some are on steep, unstable slopes while others are in locations that take some time to reach on foot. To re-visit all the rock art on the hill each time an evaluation is deemed necessary is not feasible. As we noted earlier, our documentation effort required about 2,000 person-hours of field time. We recommend that only a sample of the rock images be evaluated frequently and suggest that this occur every three to five years. At the same time, all rock art features should be visited on occasion; we suggest every 10 years. To make a complete re-evaluation as simple as possible we encourage the use of a small, portable computer, tablet, or smart-phone that can be taken into the field. It would contain all recorded information about each rock art feature including the location, a drawing, and a photograph. Because the basic data for each rock art feature would already be in the data base, a comparison with previous evaluations could be made fairly quickly. The scientific goal will be not only to monitor human-caused changes such as damage caused by graffiti or construction activities, but also to record natural changes such as exfoliation and lichen growth. Understanding the rate of natural changes may ultimately lead to ways to better estimate the age of some of the rock art features.

Also, our documentation to date strongly suggests that certain areas are more prone to damage from vandalism than others. As we have discussed, vandalism on Tumamoc consists almost exclusively of scratched names and dates (sometimes superimposed over prehistoric rock art); we also documented examples of rock art removal and vandalism at two locations (see Figures II.10 and II.11). We documented no natural change in 34 years (with the possible exception of TH-F2912 that may have rolled down a short slope), and we have no evidence that natural change is occurring more rapidly in some areas as opposed to others. Thus, we recommend a sample approach that concentrates on areas where we have documented that vandalism is common and continuing; any naturally occurring changes can easily be measured as well. This approach would use the data on the computerized rock art recording forms as a basis for comparison. Thus, a quick look at variables such as presence/absence, description, condition, and disturbance, combined with a new photograph, would provide a new assessment of the feature.

We recommend that future evaluation concentrate on rock art in two types of locations: (1) one or more locations easily accessible to the public where there is significant prehistoric rock art and where considerable vandalism has occurred, and (2) one or more locations less accessible and less visible to public scrutiny, where there is significant rock art and vandalism has occurred. We suggest three specific locations, although others could be chosen as well. The important aspect of this approach is that these locations should be visited regularly and the same evaluation be conducted each time.

The first locale that we recommend for re-evaluation is the southeast corner of the summit where the large number and diversity of glyphs suggest considerable prehistoric significance. This location contains several one-of-a-kind glyphs; it has elaborated anthropomorphs; and it includes glyphs that may have functioned as solar markers. This cluster (Cluster Q) is easily accessible, it is commonly included as a destination for guided tours and classes, and some glyphs are on flat, ground-level boulders or slabs that frequently are walked on, an activity that presumably leads to erosion of the rock art. In addition, the largest amount of graffiti (92 elements) occurs here; one dramatic example is of the initials "HHH" immediately above prehistoric glyphs (TH-F695).

The second locale is an easily accessible rock art cluster (Cluster N) on a large outcrop approximately 50 meters west of the road on the upper north slope. The outcrop is a favorite location for hill visitors to sit and enjoy the view; unfortunately, it is also a favorite target for vandalism. This cluster has 70 graffiti elements, the second highest concentration on the hill, far outnumbering the 24 prehistoric elements. Dates as recent as 2005 indicate that vandalism on this cluster continues to occur.

The third locale is a feature consisting of 12 elements that is on the west slope and is not easily accessible from the road (TH-F4341). Presumably, modern visitors reach it by walking from Greasewood Road across the flats on the west side of the hill, and then climbing the slope to this outcrop. This feature contains an example of a glyph where removal was attempted but failed, a glyph on a large rock flake that was detached from the larger boulder but not taken away, and a glyph that was broken into pieces when removal was attempted.

In addition to monitoring changes over time, studies in these three areas may provide a better understanding of the rate of damage from modern graffiti producers, and whether such rates change from year to year or decade to decade, subject to mores of the time. Understanding the rates and variability of graffiti creation should be a factor in any discussions of access, education, and management on Tumamoc Hill.

Finally, in working toward a successful management strategy for rock art, it is important to remember that the education and involvement of the public is essential, especially in the case of Tumamoc, which is located in an urban setting and is visited by large numbers of recreational walkers each day. Trying to prevent damage to the rock art resource by keeping the location completely off-limits and/ or by trying to repair the damage is far less likely to be successful than creating strategies that explain the significance of the resource and its role in our local cultural heritage (Loubser 2001:108-109). At the same time, we strongly believe that the key to a successful management and conservation program is full-time staff augmented by security personnel. Without these we fear degradation to the prehistoric rock art will continue.

SUMMARY AND CONCLUDING THOUGHTS

Tumamoc Hill, a prominent landmark near the western edge of metropolitan Tucson, is unique in the Tucson Basin and beyond. It is significant as both a Sonoran Desert preserve where ecological research has been conducted since the first decade of the twentieth century and as the home of a wide variety of significant cultural resources. The earliest known Native American construction on the hill apparently dates to approximately 800 B.C. and rock art creation may have continued into early historic times.

In this paper we have reported on a re-evaluation of Tumamoc's prehistoric rock art that recorded 734 elements, a significant increase over previous recording efforts. In addition, we recorded the substantial and growing amount of graffiti in order to aid future management efforts. The principal rock art styles on the hill are the Hohokam Pecked style;

a Scratched style, probably also of Hohokam affinity; and, we believe, a small number of elements that belong to the Western Archaic Tradition. The rock art, including graffiti, is primarily on the gentler north slope, where both the prehistoric trail and modern road are located, and on the summit.

The Hohokam Pecked-style glyphs are dominantly abstract (geometric) motifs followed in frequency by anthropomorphs and then zoomorphs. The Hohokam Scratched-style glyphs are, with a single exception, abstract, with over half consisting of cross hatch and parallel line motifs. One aspect of the Hohokam style that we discussed is the number of elaborated anthropomorphs, which are more numerous on Tumamoc than at other Tucson Basin sites where rock art has been recorded, hinting at the importance of this location. We offer evidence that the Hohokam-style glyphs represent the entire local sequence from the Pioneer period into the historical era. And, we note that two glyphs, one probably from the Classic period and one possibly from historic times, may have been created by non-local individuals.

The enigmatic Scratched style differs from the Hohokam Pecked style in several intriguing ways. Perhaps the most noteworthy is the fact that it is composed of a small number of almost exclusively rectilinear elements. Also, the distribution of Scratched-style elements is heavily skewed toward a single rock outcrop on the west slope of the hill, and Scratched-style elements are superimposed on each other to a greater degree than the Hohokam pecked elements. We recorded a single Scratched-style anthropomorph, which also included a little pecking and abrading. This anthropomorph bears some similarity to Scratched-style figurative elements on South Mountain in Phoenix and is the first Scratched-style figurative element recorded in the Tucson Basin.

Because Tumamoc Hill was first used

extensively by humans during the Early Agricultural period when Western Archaic Tradition rock art was presumably being created elsewhere in the region, we would expect that some of the rock art on the hill should belong to this tradition. Unlike locations like the Picacho Mountains where Western Archaic Tradition motifs are common and are clearly different from Hohokam motifs, Tumamoc does not have any such examples. Nor does it have rock art with extremely heavy patination that is markedly different from the Hohokam examples. When, however, we combined five criteria with independent evaluation, the evidence supports the existence of a small amount of Western Archaic Tradition rock art on the hill. Why there is so little rock art during a time of considerable human activity is not at all clear. What this does suggest is that, during the Cienega and Tortolita phases when the Archaic Tradition rock art was presumably created, the activities on the hill differed in some qualitative way from those in subsequent times

On a related subject, it is worth re-emphasizing that (1) the creators of the rock art (both during Western Archaic Tradition and Hohokam times) apparently made conscious decisions not to create glyphs on human-built structures, and (2) since the few glyphs on human-built structures appear to be Hohokam rather than Archaic in age, they would have been created after the hill was basically abandoned as a Cienega and Tortolita phase agricultural and habitation site. It is also worth noting that since the majority of the rock art on the hill belongs to the Gila (Hohokam) style, the hill continued to be used through Hohokam times, even if there were no construction activities during that approximately 750-year period.

A part of the hill that appears to be of special significance from a rock art perspective is the southeast corner of the summit. Glyphs are abundant at this location; both one-of-a-kind and unusual motifs are present. In addition, the concentration of possible solar markers suggests that observers may have been recording important dates related to agricultural or ceremonial activities during the annual calendrical cycle.

Turning to modern activities on the hill that are related to rock art, we recorded graffiti as well as missing and disturbed glyphs. We noted that one previously recorded prehistoric glyph (an anthropomorph) could not be found, although we did ascertain where it had been. In addition we recorded three instances of serious vandalism within a single feature. One glyph, a two-ring concentric circle, had been removed (some of the rock pieces were found nearby). Another glyph, a geometric indeterminate, and the rock flake into which it was pecked, had been detached but left nearby. And an attempt had been made to chisel out a foot/bear paw. We were interested in the impact of graffiti on prehistoric rock art and were pleasantly surprised to find that only 5 percent have been defaced by graffiti.

Although 75 examples of graffiti could be dated as older than 50 years and, thus, potentially of historic interest, we could connect only eight historical inscriptions with known or probably known individuals. The two we considered to be of the greatest historical interest are described in the text while the others are briefly described in Appendix VII. The oldest inscription on the hill was the name of a soldier (J. Scott) attached to an infantry company that was stationed at Camp Lowell in 1867 and 1868; at that time Camp Lowell was located in downtown Tucson. The second inscription of interest, dated 1891, was the name of a young woman, Georgia Hazel Scott. She was the daughter of prominent Tucsonans Larcena Pennington and William Scott. She later married Robert Forbes, a professor at the University of Arizona, and served as the first female president of the Arizona Pioneers' Historical Society (now the Arizona Historical Society). We remind readers not to add their names to the glyphs on the hill in the hope that they may, one day, be of historic interest.

We were also interested in the temporal range and changes over time of graffiti production. Dated graffiti range from 1867-1868 to 2010 and, unfortunately, after three decades of relatively low graffiti creation, the most intense period of production occurred in the most recent decade.

Finally, our management discussion is intended to assist future staff in understanding the cultural values of the hill as well as providing specific management suggestions. We emphasize that an existing cultural resources policy and management plan for the hill makes it very clear that it is the goal of the University of Arizona to "promote research and education in a manner that protects the historical integrity of Tumamoc Hill" (Madsen 2008:49). To achieve that end we emphasize the need for a full-time manager and a comprehensive education program. In relation to the rock art itself, there is a need for periodic re-evaluation to check for natural and human-caused change over time. We provide specific suggestions for such a program, recommending certain locales in relation to their accessibility, their cultural significance, and the likelihood of vandalism.

In sum, since serious archaeological study began on Tumamoc Hill in the early 1970s, much has been learned both about the hill's rock art, as well as the role the hill played in local prehistory. At the same time, this study and other recent work reinforce our sense that much remains to be learned, and that Tumamoc Hill merits continued archaeological research as well as serious and sustained efforts to preserve existing cultural resources and effectively manage them for the future.

Acknowledgments. We wish to extend sincere thanks to Alan Ferg for his initial recording of the rock art on Tumamoc Hill in 1974-1975; his records and maps have withstood the test of time and were invaluable to us. In addition, we thank Steve Larson, astronomer and photographer, for providing us with his original photographs from the 1974-1975 survey.

We thank Suzanne Fish and Paul Fish for encouraging us to take on this task, which, of course, turned out to be much larger and more complex than we imagined. We thank John Madsen for his work on the resources policy and management plan of the hill, which was completed just in time to be very helpful to us; we also thank John for helping us locate two glyphs on the western bajada that had been recorded since Ferg's survey. Todd Pitezel gave us very helpful advice throughout the project; we extend our sincere thanks to him.

We are very grateful to Henry Wallace and Todd Bostwick for providing us with their evaluation of the cultural and temporal affiliation of some of the rock art; we appreciate their time and expertise. We also thank Suzanne Fish, Linda Gregonis, and Mike Jacobs for their evaluation of some of the rock art; Chuck Adams for sharing his expertise on late prehistoric design motifs in the Southwest; Homer Thiel for identifying Georgia Scott; astronomer John Fountain for visiting the hill on numerous occasions with members of our crew in his successful search for solar interactions; Matt Pailes for his expertise with the Trimble GPS; and Sharon Urban for the loan of numerous books and periodicals from her excellent rock art library. We also appreciate the assistance of Rebecca Donnelly, former Curator of Photographic Collections at the Arizona State Museum for providing access to photographs from the 1974-1975 survey. We would also like to extend our thanks to visiting rock art "gurus" Ken Hedges and Steve Freers for their thoughtful comments.

We are especially grateful to the core "gang of six," AAHS members who persevered through three winters of recording: Katherine Cerino, Valerie Davison, Janine Hernbrode, David McLean, Irma Moreno, and Donna Yoder. In addition we are grateful to those who tried their hand at rock art recording, primarily during the first season: Mel Copeland, Ken Fleshman, Cherie Freeman, Victoria Mattox, Jill May, Judy Oyen, Steve Rathman, Dwight Riggs, and Larry Todd.

We also want to express our appreciation to our photographer Janine Hernbrode and her able assistants, Valerie Davison and Dwight Riggs. Valerie Davison also put her drawing skill to good use by illustrating the elaborated anthropomorphs, and Bill Hartmann provided the sketches to augment two illustrations. We also thank Todd Pitezel for his expertise in creating the maps. Finally, we thank Amy Hartmann-Gordon, Bill Hartmann, and especially Kelly Rehm for providing expertise with the formatting of photographs, tables, and figures. Their skill level far exceeds ours, and we could not have created the finished product without them.

Publication of this report was financed by the Arizona Archaeological and Historical Society; we are most grateful for their support.

REFERENCES CITED

Arizona Daily Star
1946 *Pioneer Dies; Rites Friday.* Nov. 27. Tucson, AZ.
2008 *When Graffiti Is Cleaned Up, Vandals Often Strike Again.* Jan. 7. Tucson, AZ.

Banks, Leo W.
1999 Stalwart Women: Frontier Stories of Indomitable Spirit. *Arizona Highways*, Phoenix.

Bernardini, Wesley
2009 *Hopi History in Stone: The Tutuveni Petroglyph Site.* Arizona State Museum Archaeological Series 200. Arizona State Museum, University of Arizona, Tucson.

Bostwick, Todd W.
1998 Managing Rock Art in an Urban Setting: The Challenge of South Mountain Park. *American Indian Rock Art* 22:119-128, edited by Steven M. Freers.
1999 Hourglass Anthropomorph Petroglyphs in the South Mountains, Arizona. *American Indian Rock Art* 25:121-132, edited by Steven M. Freers.
2002 *Landscape of the Spirits: Hohokam Rock Art at South Mountain Park.* University of Arizona Press, Tucson.

Cerino, Katherine
2009 On the Trail of Tumamoc Graffiti: Georgie Hazel Scott. *Glyphs: The Monthly Newsletter of the Arizona Archaeological and Historical Society* 60(2):4-6.

Christensen, Don D.
1992 Scratched Glyphs in Arizona: A Reevaluation. *Rock Art Papers* 9:101-110, edited by Ken Hedges. San Diego Museum Papers No. 28. San Diego.

Colley, Charles C.
1977 *The Century of Robert H. Forbes: The Career of a Pioneer Agriculturalist, Agronomist, Environmentalist, Conservationist and Water Specialist in Arizona and Abroad.* Arizona Historical Society, Tucson.

Coville, Frederick V., and Daniel T. MacDougal
1903 Desert Botanical Laboratory of the Carnegie Institution. *Carnegie Institution of Washington Publication 6.*

Dutton, Bertha
1963 *Sun Father's Way: The Kiva Murals of Kuaua, a Pueblo Ruin, Coronado State Monument, New Mexico.* University of New Mexico Press, Albuquerque.

Elkins, Rosemary, Gayle H. Hartmann, Robert C. Johnson, Thomas Saarinen, Terah L. Smiley, Brock Tunnicliff, and Stanley K. Brickler
1982 *Tumamoc Hill Policy Plan.* Prepared for the Tumamoc Hill Advisory Committee, University of Arizona, Tucson.

Estes, Allen, Morgan Reider, Kyle Brown, Kyle Kearney, Aimee Arrigoni, Tom Young, Adam Marlow, James Allan, and William Self
2005 *Final Data Recovery and Monitoring Report: KMEP Tucson Pipeline Replacement Project, Phases III and IV, Pima County, Arizona.* William Self Associates, Orinda, CA.

Ferg, Alan
1979 The Petroglyphs of Tumamoc Hill. In "The Tumamoc Hill Survey: An Intensive Study of a *Cerro de Trincheras* in Tucson, Arizona." *The Kiva* 45(1-2):95-118.

Fish, Paul R., Suzanne K. Fish, Austin Long, and Charles Miksicek
1986 Early Corn Remains from Tumamoc Hill, Southern Arizona. *American Antiquity* 51:563-572.

Fish, Suzanne K., Paul R. Fish, Gary Christopherson, Todd A. Pitezel, and James T. Watson
2011 Two Villages on Tumamoc Hill. *Journal of Arizona Archaeology* 1(2):185-196. Arizona Archaeological Council.

Fountain, John, and Janine Hernbrode
2008 Marking the Sun on Tumamoc Hill. Paper presented at the 33rd Annual Rock Art Symposium of the San Diego Museum of Man, San Diego, 1 Nov. 2008.

Golio, J. J., Susie Bradshaw, Ernest Snyder, and Mike Golio
1995 An Analysis of the Pipette Element in Hohokam Rock Art. *Rock Art Papers* 12:95-106, edited by Ken Hedges. San Diego Museum Papers 33.

Harry, Karen G., Evelyn Billo, and Robert Mark
2001 The Challenge of Long-Term Preservation: Managing Impacts to Rock Art at Hueco Tanks State Historical Park. *American Indian Rock Art* 27:151-159, edited by Steven M. Freers and Alanah Woody.

Hartmann, Gayle Harrison, and William K. Hartmann
  1979   Prehistoric Trail Systems and Related Features on the Slopes of Tumamoc Hill. In "The Tumamoc Hill Survey: An Intensive Study of a *Cerro de Trincheras* in Tucson, Arizona." *The Kiva* 45 (1-2):39-69.

Haury, Emil W.
  1976   *The Hohokam: Desert Farmers & Craftsmen.* University of Arizona Press, Tucson.

Hayden, Julian D.
  1972   Hohokam Petroglyphs of the Sierra Pinacate, Sonora, and the Hohokam Shell Expeditions. *The Kiva* 37(2):74-83.

Hedges, Ken
  1973   Rock Art in Southern California. *Pacific Coast Archaeological Society Quarterly* 9:1-28.
  1982   Great Basin Rock Art Styles: A Revisionist View. *American Indian Rock Art* 7:205-211, edited by Frank G. Bock.

Heizer, Robert F., and Martin A. Baumhoff
  1962   *Prehistoric Rock Art of Nevada and Eastern California.* University of California Press, Berkeley.

Hoover, J. W.
  1941   Cerros de Trincheras of the Arizona Papaguería. *The Geographical Review* 31:228-239

Howell, R. Emerson
  2006   The Historic Use of Tumamoc Hill: Landownership, Quarrying, and Talus Pits. MS on file, Borderlands Laboratory, Arizona State Museum, University of Arizona, Tucson.

Larson, Stephen M.
  1972   The Tumamoc Hill site near Tucson, Arizona. *The Kiva* 38:95-102.

Lee, Georgia
  1991   *Rock Art and Cultural Resource Management.* Wormwood Press, Calabasas, CA.

Lindsay, Alexander J., Jr., and Michael D. Metcalf
  1973   *Archaeological Clearance Investigations, Mountain States Telephone and Telegraph Company 1973 Kitt Peak-Tucson Radio Project, Arizona State Land-University of Arizona, Pima County, Arizona: Final Report for Archaeological Investigations, Tumamoc Hill Proposed Service Facility Installations on Existing Lease Lot and Power Line Modifications on Existing Pole Line Right-of-Way.* Department of Anthropology, Museum of Northern Arizona, Flagstaff.

Lipman, Peter W.
  1993   *Geologic Map of the Tucson Mountains Caldera, Southern Arizona.* Miscellaneous Investigations Series, Map I-2205, U.S. Geological Survey. U.S. Department of the Interior, Washington, D.C.

Loubser, Johannes
  2001   Management Planning for Conservation in *Handbook of Rock Art Research*, edited by David S. Whitley, pp. 80-115. AltaMira Press, Walnut Creek, CA.

Madsen, John H. (Editor)
  2008   *Tumamoc Hill Cultural Resources Policy and Management Plan.* University of Arizona, Campus and Facility Planning, printed by SWCA Environmental Consultants, Inc., Tucson.

Martineau, LaVan
  1976   *The Rocks Begin to Speak.* KC Publications, Las Vegas, NV.

Masse, W. Bruce
  1979   An Intensive Survey of Prehistoric Dry Farming Systems near Tumamoc Hill in Tucson, Arizona. In "The Tumamoc Hill Survey: An Intensive Study of a *Cerro de Trincheras* in Tucson, Arizona." *The Kiva* 45 (1-2):141-186.

McCreery, Patricia, and Ekkehart Malotki
  1994   *Tapamveni: The Rock Art Galleries of Petrified Forest and Beyond.* Petrified Forest Museum Association, Petrified Forest, AZ.

Pilles, Peter J., Jr.
  1988a *Archaeological Site Vandalism and the Arizona Response.* Presented at the International Symposium on Vandalism: Research, Prevention, andSocial Policy, April 20-23, Seattle. In *A Workshop on Rock Art Site Management and Protection*, presented by the American Rock Art Research Association, May 23, 24, 25, 1990, pp. 1-17. Tucson.
  1988b The Arizona Archaeology Advisory Commission and the Site Stewards Program. In *Fighting Indiana Jones in Arizona*, edited by A.E. Rogge, pp. 39-44. 1988 Proceedings American Society for Conservation Archaeology, papers from a Symposium held at the 53rd Annual Meeting of the Society for American Archaeology, Phoenix.
  1989   Public Education and the Management of Rock Art Sites on the Coconino National Forest. In *Preserving our Rock Art Heritage: Proceedings from the Symposium on Rock Art Conservation and Protection*, edited by H.K. Crotty, pp. 23-44. American Rock Art Research Association Occasional Paper No. 1. San Miguel, CA.

Randall, Kenneth A.
  1991   *Haven in a Hostile Land, Fort Lowell, A.T. 1866-1891, A Chronicle.* Arizona Historical Society, Tucson.

Sauer, Carl, and Donald Brand
  1931   Prehistoric Settlements of Sonora, with Special Reference to Cerros de Trincheras. *University of California Publications in Geography* 5(3):67-148.

Schaafsma, Polly
1997   *Rock Art Sites in Chihuahua, Mexico.* Archaeology Notes 171. Office of Archaeological Studies, Museum of New Mexico.
1980   *Indian Rock Art of the Southwest.* University of New Mexico Press, Albuquerque.
1992   *Rock Art in New Mexico.* Museum of New Mexico Press, Santa Fe, NM.
1994   Trance and Transformation in the Canyons: Shamanism and Early Rock Art on the Colorado Plateau. *In Shamanism and Rock Art in North America,* edited by S. Turpin, pp. 45-71. Rock Art Foundation, Inc., San Antonio, Texas.

Schaafsma, Polly, and Patricia Vivian
1975   *The Malapais Hill Pictograph Site (Ariz. BB:2:16).* Archaeological Series No. 74. Arizona State Museum, University of Arizona, Tucson.

Schmader, Matthew
1995   Conservation and Management at Petroglyph National Monument. Paper presented at the Symposium on Conservation and Management, 22nd annual meeting of the American Rock Art Research Association, Albuquerque.

Snyder, Ernest E.
1966   Petroglyphs of the South Mountains of Arizona. *American Antiquity* 31:701-709.

Spalding, Volney M.
1909   Distribution and movements of desert plants. *Carnegie Institution of Washington Publication* 113.

Stacy, V. K. P.
1974   *Cerros de Trincheras in the Arizona Papagueria.* Ph.D. dissertation, Department of Anthropology, University of Arizona. MS on file, Arizona State Museum Library, University of Arizona. University Microfilms, Ann Arbor.

Steward, Julian
1929   Petroglyphs of California and Adjoining States. *University of California Publications in American Archaeology and Ethnology,* vol. 24(2):47-238.

Thiel, J. Homer
1995   *Rock Art in Arizona.* Arizona State Historic Preservation Office, Phoenix.

Turner, Christy G., II
1963   *Petroglyphs of the Glen Canyon Region.* Bulletin No. 38. Museum of Northern Arizona, Flagstaff.

Turpin, Solveig
2001   Archaic North American. In *Handbook of Rock Art Research,* edited by David S. Whitley, pp. 361-413. AltaMira Press, Walnut Creek, CA. University of Arizona Archaeological Field School at Tumamoc Hill

University of Arizona Archaeological Field School at Tumamoc Hill
2005-06   University of Arizona Archaeological Field School at Tumamoc Hill. Arizona State Museum, University of Arizona, Tucson.

Vastokas, Joan M., and R. K. Vastokas
1973   *Sacred Art of the Algonkians; A Study of the Peterborough Petroglyphs.* Mansard, Peterborough, Ontario, Canada.

Wade, Edwin L., and Lea S. McChesney, editors
1981   *Historic Hopi Ceramics.* Peabody Museum Press, Cambridge, MA.

Wallace, Henry D.
1983   The Mortars, Petroglyphs, and Trincheras on Rillito Peak. *The Kiva* 48(3):137-246.
1989   *Archaeological Investigations at Petroglyph Sites in the Painted Rock Reservoir Area, Southwestern Arizona.* Contributions by Allen Dart and James P. Holmlund. Institute for American Research, Technical Report No. 89-5. Tucson, AZ.
2001   Middle Gila Buffware Ceramic Illustrations. In *Grewe Archaeological Project: Vol. 2. Material Culture, Part I: Ceramic Studies,* edited by D. R. Abbott, pp. 417-439. Anthropological Papers No. 99-1. Northland Research, Inc., Flagstaff and Tempe, Arizona.
2004   Update to the Middle Gila Buff Ware Ceramic Sequence. Chapter 3 in *Hohokam Farming on the Salt River Floodplain: Refining Models and Analytical Methods,* edited by T. Kathleen Henderson, pp. 45-124. Anthropological Papers No. 43, Center for Desert Archaeology, Tucson, and Anthropological Papers No. 10, Pueblo Grande Museum, Phoenix.
2008   The Petroglyphs of Atlatl Ridge, Tortolita Mountains, Pima County, Arizona. Chapter 4 in *Life in the Foothills: Archaeological Investigations in the Tortolita Mountains of Southern Arizona,* edited by Deborah L. Swartz, pp. 159-231. Anthropological Papers No. 46, Center for Desert Archaeology, Tucson.

Wallace, Henry D., and James P. Holmlund
1986   *Petroglyphs of the Picacho Mountains, South Central Arizona.* Anthropological Papers No. 6, Institute for American Research, Tucson.

Wallace, Henry D., Paul R. Fish, and Suzanne K. Fish
2007   Tumamoc Hill and the Early Pioneer Period Occupation of the Tucson Basin. In *Trincheras Sites in Time, Space, and Society,* edited by Suzanne K. Fish, Paul R. Fish, and M. Elisa Villalpando, pp. 53-99. University of Arizona Press, Tucson.

Wasley, William W., and Alfred E. Johnson
1965   *Salvage Archaeology in Painted Rocks Reservoir, Western Arizona.* Anthropological Papers No. 9. University of Arizona Press, Tucson.

Weaver, Donald, E., Jr., and Bettina H. Rosenberg
1978   Petroglyphs of the Southern Estrella: A Locational Interpretation. *American Indian Rock Art* 4:108-123, edited by Ernest Snyder, A.J. Bock and Frank G. Bock.

Wellman, Klaus F.
1979   *A Survey of North American Indian Rock Art.* Akademiche Drucke und Verlagsanstalt, Graz, Austria.

Welsh, Liz, and Peter Welsh
2004   *Rock-Art of the Southwest: A Visitor's Companion.* Wilderness Press, Berkeley, CA.

White, Cheryl Ann
1965   *The Petroglyphs of Saguaro National Monument, Tucson, Arizona.* Senior Honor's Thesis, on file, Arizona State Museum Library, University of Arizona.

Whitley, David S.
2000   *The Art of the Shaman: Rock Art of California.* University of Utah Press, Salt Lake City.

Whitney, Gregory
2005   *Cultural Resources Survey of a Proposed Overhead Fiber Optic Line along the Northern Slope and Summit of Tumamoc Hill, Tucson, Arizona.* Project Report 05-144. Desert Archaeology, Inc., Tucson.

Wilcox, David R.
1979   Warfare Implications of Dry-Laid Masonry Walls on Tumamoc Hill. In "The Tumamoc Hill Survey: An Intensive Study of a *Cerro de Trincheras* in Tucson, Arizona." *The Kiva* 45 (1-2):15-38.

Wilcox, David R., Stephen Larson, W. Bruce Masse, Gayle H. Hartmann, and Alan Ferg
1979   A Summary of Conclusions and Recommendations of the Tumamoc Hill Survey. In "The Tumamoc Hill Survey: An Intensive Study of a *Cerro de Trincheras* in Tucson, Arizona." *The Kiva* 45(1-2):187-195.

Wright, Aaron M., and Todd W. Bostwick
2009   Technological Styles of Hohokam Rock Art Production in the South Mountains, South-Central Arizona. *American Rock Art Research Association* 35:61-78, edited by James D. Keyser, David Kaiser, George Poetschat, and Michael W. Taylor.

Wright, Barton
1977   *Hopi Kachinas: The Complete Guide to Collecting Kachina Dolls.* Northland Press, Flagstaff.

Appendix I

Tumamoc Hill Mapping Project (AZ AA:16:6) Rock Art Recording Form

Tumamoc Hill Mapping Project (AZ AA:16:6) Rock Art Recording Form

1. Feature Identification

Feature ID: _____   Ferg ID: _____

Recorders: _____

Date: _____   Time: _____   Easting: _____   Northing: _____

_____

2. Feature Description

Number of Individual Glyphs: _____

Feature Type (circle one):   Isolate   Panel   Other

Feature Location (circle one):   Bedrock   Boulder   Cliff Face   Other

Panel Angle: _____   Panel Aspect: _____   Panel Height: _____ - _____

Patination: _____

_____

_____

_____

Condition: _____

_____

_____

_____

Disturbance: _____

_____

_____

_____

Description: _____

_____

_____

_____

Tumamoc Hill Mapping Project (AZ AA:16:6) Rock Art Recording Form

Feature ID

3. Design Elements:

	Element Number	Element Name	Technique	Width of "lines"	Max. Dim.	Min. Dim.	Over	Under
1								
2								
3								
4								
5								
6								
7								
8								
9								
10								

4. Comments:

_____

_____

_____

_____

_____

_____

_____

5. Photo ID Number(s) and dates:

_____

_____

_____

Revised 1/3/07

Appendix II

Rock Art Recording Manual for Tumamoc Hill Mapping Project

TUMAMOC HILL MAPPING PROJECT
Arizona Archaeological and Historical Society
Rock Art Recording Manual

All information should be recorded on the addendum form; please do not make corrections directly on the existing form.

1. Feature Identification:
> **Feature ID:** Record from existing form.
> **Ferg ID:** Record from existing form if it is written on top of first page
> **Recorders:** first and last names of the people filling out the form.
> **Date:** the current date; please use the format mm/dd/yyyy.
> **Time:** the current time.
> **Easting and Northing:** Record from existing form

2. Feature Description: Record complete information on the following; the original form is provided for reference, but you should complete each section fully even if you agree with the earlier observations.
> **Number of Individual Glyphs:** an individual glyph is defined as a design that is not connected to any others or represents an individual shape or animal.
> **Feature Type:** circle the appropriate listing.
>> Isolate – an individual glyph.
>> Panel – a number of glyphs in the same location.
>> Other – something that does not fall into the other categories, (EXPLAIN).
> **Feature Location:** circle the appropriate listing.
>> Bedrock – expanse of rock protruding from the ground.
>> Boulder – a loose rock.
>> Cliff Face – an expanse of rock with significant vertical exposure.
>> Other – something that does not fall into the other categories, (EXPLAIN).
> **Angle of Panel:** from base of rock face to the top; use 0, 45, 90, 135 (0 degrees equals horizontal, 90 degrees equals vertical).
> **Panel Aspect:** compass direction the panel faces (if one imagined oneself to be the rock art). Compass readings should be corrected for declination of 11 degrees Eastern.
> **Panel Height:** distance (cm) from ground surface to lowest and highest point of panel.
> **Patination:** the chemical weathering of rock through exposure, generally resulting in a darkening of the rock surface (to brown, gray, or black). Please record patination of the rock art specifically, using none, light, moderate, or heavy. Broken, pecked areas, or portions of the rock not exposed to sun, wind, and water tend to represent the original color of the rock. You may also include distribution of patination across the rock (even, speckled, etc.).

Condition: describe the condition of the rock art and the rock upon with it is located, noting such characteristics as weathering, splits in the rock, lichen growth, etc.

Disturbance: describe any visible vandalism to the rock art since it was created, this includes breakage of the rock. Also note any disturbance in terms of movement of the rock or other rocks on top of it. Consult Ferg research and Larson photos if available.

Description: describe the rock art, noting salient features such as the major design elements used, its location and visibility, relationship to prominent, nearby features, landmarks etc.

3. Design Elements:

Element Type: Refer to and use the numbers and names in **Design Element Reference** appended to the end of the manual (from Ferg 1979; Wallace and Holmlund (1986).

Technique (Marking Type): enter the appropriate listing: Pecked, Scratched, Incised, Abraded, Other

Width of marking: enter the approximate width of the pecked, scratched, etc. "line"; record in tenths of centimeters (e.g. 0.5 cm).

Dimensions, maximum and minimum: record in centimeters (e.g., 45 cm).

Over/Under: list the number of elements superimposed over or under the element.

4. Comments:

Record any observations here that you feel have not been adequately addressed.

5. Sketch:

Sketch the rock art on the graph paper provided; the idea is to sketch the rock art, not to attempt a full artistic representation. Provide a scale for the sketch and record Feature ID, date, and time of the drawing.

6. Photo ID Number(s) and date:

Photography will be done separately from items 1-5 above. Photo numbers are represented tri-nomially, separated by a dash, e.g., TH-F102-1 where TH refers to Tumamoc Hill, F102 refers to the feature number, and 1 refers to the frame number for this feature. The second frame for Feature 102, then, is numbered 102-2. Record the date(s) the photos are taken.

Revised 10/6/08

Design Element Reference

Anthropomorphic

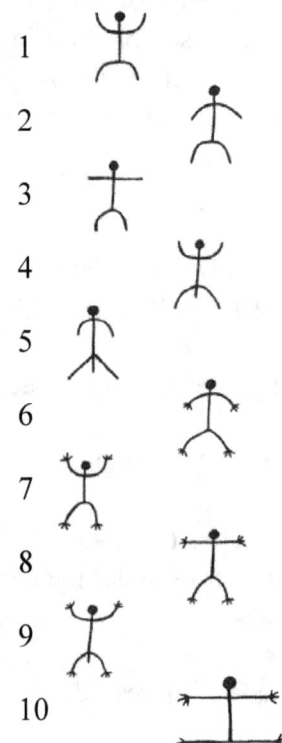

1

2

3

4

5

6

7

8

9

10

11 – Any stickperson with incised digits

12 – Any stickperson holding material culture (BUT NOT 14)

13 – Anthromorphic other than a stickfigure

14 – Person (not a stickperson) with staff

15 – Foot

16 – Anthropomorphic indeterminate

17 – Anthropomorphic other

Zoomorphic

18 – Bird foot

19 – Centipede

20 – Insect

21 – Lizard with toes

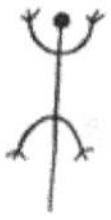

22 – Lizard without toes

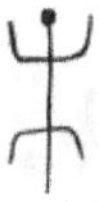

23 – Quadruped, horned

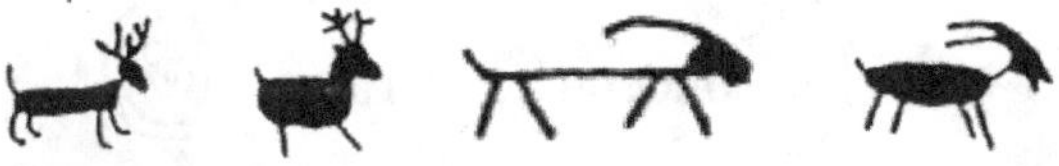

24 – Quadruped without horns

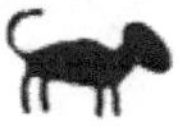

25 – Tortoise

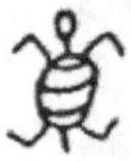

26 – Zoomorphic indeterminate

27 – Zoomorphic other

Geometric

28 – Arc with dot

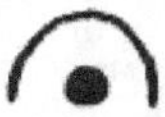

29 – Arcs, concentric

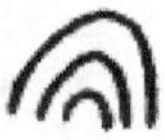

30 – Arcs, concentric, spoked: One of the above with the addition of spokes.

31 – Asterisk

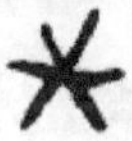

32 – Bull's eye, 1 ring

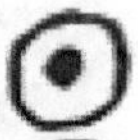

33 – Bull's eye, 2 rings

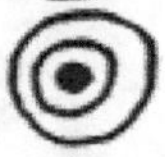

34 – Bull's eye 3+ rings

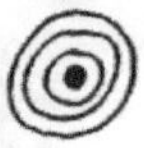

35 – Chevron ladder

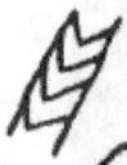

36 – Chevron nested

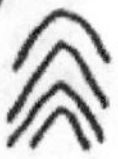

37 – Circle

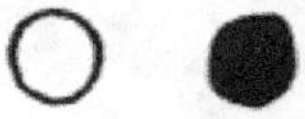

38 – Circle chain

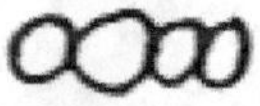

39 – Circle cluster

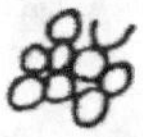

40 – Circle pattern

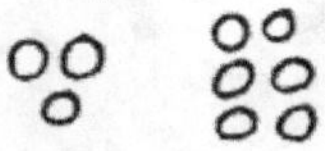

41 – Circle tailed

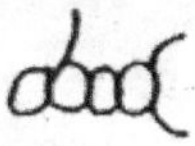

42 – Circles, concentric, 2 rings

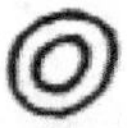

43 – Circles, concentric, 3 rings

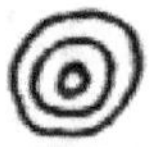

44 – Circles, concentric, 4 rings

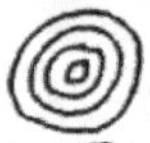

45 – Circles, concentric, 5+ rings

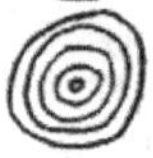

46 – Circles, line connected

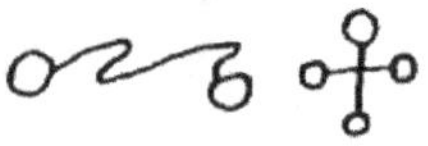

47 – Circles, sectioned

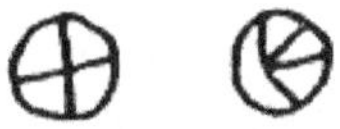

48 – Circles with arc

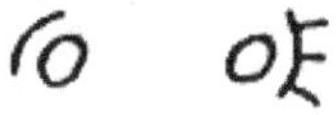

49 – Cross

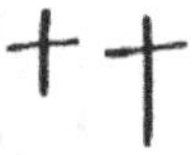

50 – Cross hatch, band

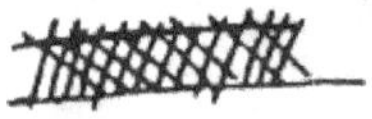

51 – Cross hatch, diamond

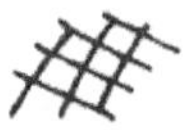

52 – Cross hatch, grid

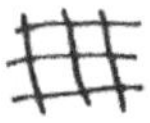

53 – Curvilinear abstract

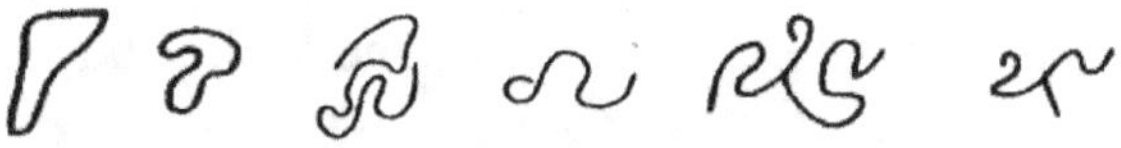

54 – Diamond

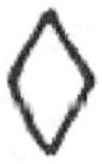

55 – Dot framing

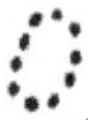

56 – Dot meander

57 – Dot pattern

58 – Dot undefined pattern

59 – Indeterminate geometric

60 – Ladder

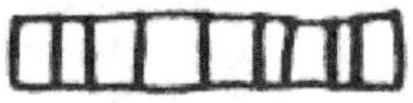

61 – Line, curved

62 – Line, straight

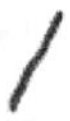

63 – Line, parallel

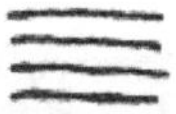

64 – Line, zigzag or wavy

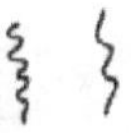

66 – Pipette

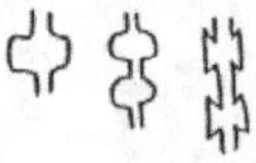

67 – Pipette with dots

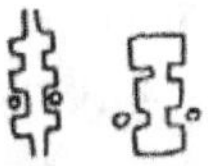

68 – Rain cloud

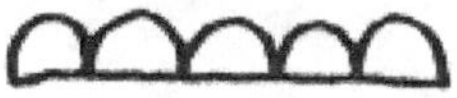

69 – Rake

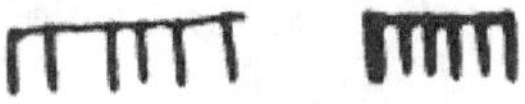

70 – Rake, double

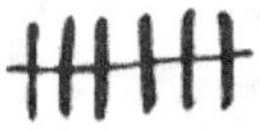

71 – Reticulate

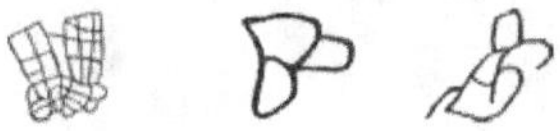

72 – Rectilinear abstract

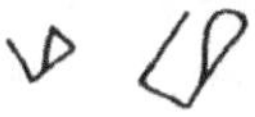

73 – Rectilinear meander

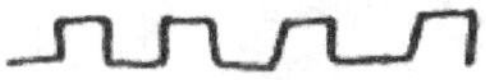

74 – Scroll, curvilinear clockwise

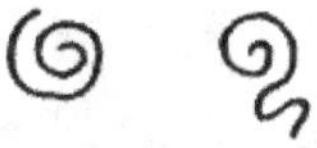

75 – Scroll, curvilinear connected

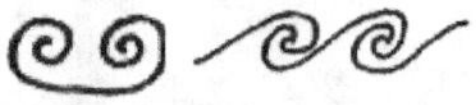

76 – Scroll, curvilinear counterclockwise

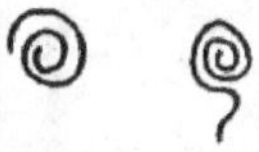

77 – Scroll, curvilinear interlocking

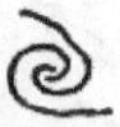

78 – Scroll, rectilinear clockwise

79 – Scroll, rectilinear connected

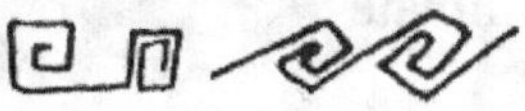

80 – Scroll, rectilinear counterclockwise

81 – Scroll, rectilinear interlocking

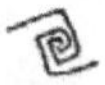

82 – Shell

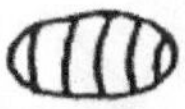

83 – Snake

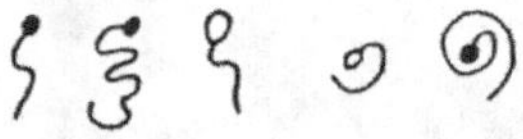

84 – Square

85 – Square with dot

86 – Sun disc

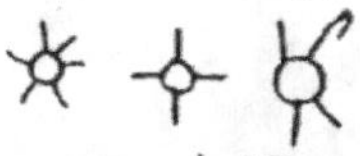

87 – Swastika

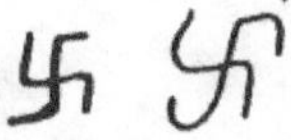

88 – Terraced element

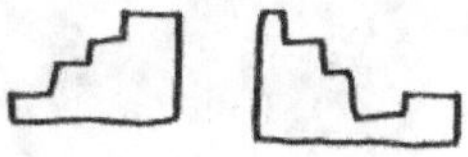

89 – Triangle

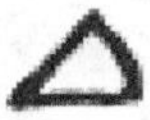

90 – Geometric indeterminate: a geometric element with no recognizable shape; this may be because the element was ambiguous when created or because it has become obscure over time from weathering, vandalism, etc.

91 – Geometric other: a geometric element with a recognizable shape, but the shape is not included in the element list used in this study.

Not listed above

100 – Not listed above indeterminate

101 – Not listed above other

Modern

200 - Letter

201 - Number

202 - Letter & Number

250 - Modern Other   (includes scratched lines)

290 - Modern Indeterminate

Appendix III

Photographing Tumamoc Rock Art
by Janine Hernbrode

Photographing Tumamoc Rock Art
Janine Hernbrode

The photographic team consisted of a photographer, Janine Hernbrode and a recorder, Valerie Davison and/or Dwight Riggs. A photo log was created consisting of the date, feature number, and photographer. The recorder kept the photo log and transferred the photo numbers to the recording forms. The recorder was also often pressed into service to locate glyphs using the locational information available to us (GPS readings or Ferg's map locations), shade the glyphs for the photo (using a car windshield shade), hold bushes out of the camera view, change the numbers or letters on the board, hold the board when no natural perch could be found, carry equipment from place to place, and, on a precarious perch, stabilize the photographer to keep her from falling. Shading the glyphs with a car windshield shade seemed a simple task until it was tried on a windy day (see Figure II.3).

The photographer set up the appropriate location, changed numbers or letters on the board, positioned the board for the photos (sometimes holding the board with a foot or knee), and took the photos. She later downloaded the images onto a computer, labeled the photos with the ASM feature number, checked the photos against the photo log, made computer back-ups of the photos, and printed or electronically copied images as needed.

Two different digital cameras were used. The primary camera was a Panasonic Lumix 6.1 megapixel (DMC-FZ20) with a Leica 1:2.8/6 lens and a 12X optical zoom capability (35 mm equivalent 36-432). The camera contained an image stabilization feature, but generally was used with either a tripod or monopod, depending on the terrain. No filtering or editing was done to the images to ensure they were as natural as possible, reflecting the rock art and the surrounding rock at the time the photos were taken.

A secondary camera was used for close-ups, as some close-ups were more distinct with a smaller camera. This camera was also a Panasonic Lumix (DMC-FX12) with a Leica 1:2.8 lens and image stabilization. The 7.2 megapixel camera allows images to be enlarged to show greater detail.

The 12 x 16 inch letter board (with feature number, ASM site number, date, a centimeter scale and photo number) appears in all photos except close-ups. The outer aluminum frame of the board was covered with black electrical tape to reduce glare. In many cases, only the top section of the board appears in photos. Extra numbers and letters were stored on the bottom of the board.

To simplify printing and eliminate confusion regarding orientation, all images were taken in a horizontal format. At least two images were taken of each feature: a "panel" photo and a "context" photo. The panel photo was taken as near to 90 degrees from the rock face as the terrain would allow and encompassed as much of the rock face as possible. To obtain the best photo (minimizing glare and providing even lighting), shading was sometimes necessary. Images were taken with as high a resolution as the camera would allow, so enlargement was possible.

The context photo was intended to aid researchers in locating the feature. Images were taken with the board close to the rock face, but showing the relationship of the location to other Tucson landmarks or buildings and to landmarks on Tumamoc Hill itself. Under favorable lighting conditions, the glyphs are clearly visible in the context photos. Conversely, if the lighting conditions were unfavorable the glyphs may not be clearly visible, but the relationship of the glyphs to another recognizable landmark is shown. The volume of features to be photographed and our own work schedule sometimes did not allow us to photograph a given feature under the best lighting conditions. We photographed all features after the recording teams had completed their work so we could be sure to include in the photographs all elements indicated on the recording forms.

The following locations appear as part of the photo log and in the background of the context photos: Saint Mary's Hospital (north of Tumamoc Hill), Pima Community College West Campus (northwest), the Santa Catalina Mountains (northeast), downtown Tucson (east), "A" Mountain (east, but south of downtown), the Santa Rita Mountains (southeast), Baboquivari Peak (southwest), the Tucson Mountains and the Starr Pass Resort (west). Also used as background of the context photos were the Main Building containing administration and the library (Bldg. 801), the Chemistry/Paleobotany building (Bldg. 802), and the tower structure (fire lookout frame on the southeast edge of the summit). Many features were clustered near Feature 436 (sun disk) on the southeast summit, so we used this feature as context in some photos. Figures II.7 and II.24 illustrate the general location of all rock art features, both prehistoric and graffiti.

Occasionally, when the elements of a particular feature were widely separated or exceptionally complex, additional photos were taken. Close-ups of elements often included the board with the photo number, thus providing scale, except in the most detailed photos where this was not possible.

The photo identification numbers are defined as follows, using TH-F436-2 as an example: TH = Tumamoc Hill, F = feature, 436 is the feature number assigned either by this project or previous projects, and the digit 2 indicates this is the second photo of this feature.

Appendix IV

Prehistoric Rock Art Data from Tumamoc Hill

Appendix IV. Prehistoric Rock Art Data from Tumamoc Hill

Feature ID	Ferg ID	Element Code	Element Name	Primary Technique
4	S-New	36	Chevron nested	Pecked
14	N-4, Map 10	4	Anthro. arms up with phallus (None 4)	Pecked
15	N-7, Map 10	90	Geometric indeterminate	Pecked
16	N-New	16	Anthropomorphic indeterminate	Pecked
18	N-New	90	Geometric indeterminate	Pecked
20	N-6, Map 10	42	Circles, concentric, 2 rings	Pecked
20	N-6, Map 10	53	Curvilinear abstract	Pecked
20	N-6, Map 10	53	Curvilinear abstract	Pecked
20	N-6, Map 10	64	Line, zigzag or wavy	Pecked
20	N-6, Map 10	79	Scroll, rectilinear connected	Pecked
22	N-New	62	Line, straight	Pecked
22	N-New	90	Geometric indeterminate	Pecked
30	N-New	90	Geometric indeterminate	Pecked
35	N-New-Near	82	Shell	Pecked
102	R-1, Map 13	7	Anthro. arms up with digits (None 7)	Pecked
102	R-1, Map 13	26	Zoomorphic indeterminate	Pecked
102	R-1, Map 13	90	Geometric indeterminate	Pecked
103	R-2, Map 13	17	Anthropomorphic other	Pecked
103	R-2, Map 13	45	Circles, concentric, 5+ rings	Pecked
103	R-2, Map 13	86	Sun disk	Pecked
104	R-3, Map 13	37	Circle	Pecked
104	R-3, Map 13	37	Circle	Pecked
104	R-3, Map 13	37	Circle	Pecked
104	R-3, Map 13	42	Circles, concentric, 2 rings	Pecked
104	R-3, Map 13	43	Circles, concentric, 3 rings	Pecked
104	R-3, Map 13	52	Cross hatch, grid	Scratched
104	R-3, Map 13	52	Cross hatch, grid	Scratched
104	R-3, Map 13	63	Line, parallel	Pecked
106	S-New	63	Line, parallel	Pecked
106	S-New	90	Geometric indeterminate	Pecked
108	S-New	38	Circle chain	Pecked
136	S-11, Map 14	53	Curvilinear abstract	Pecked
136	S-11, Map 14	64	Line, zigzag or wavy	Pecked
157	R-New-Near	1	Anthro. arms up (None 1)	Pecked
157	R-New-Near	1	Anthro. arms up (None 1)	Pecked
157	R-New-Near	1	Anthro. arms up (None 1)	Pecked
157	R-New-Near	9	Anthro. arms up with digits and phallus (None 9)	Pecked
168	M-2, Master Topo Map	2	Anthro. arms down (None 2)	Pecked
168	M-2, Master Topo Map	14	Person (not a stickperson) with a staff	Pecked

Appendix IV. Prehistoric Rock Art Data from Tumamoc Hill

Feature ID	Ferg ID	Element Code	Element Name	Primary Technique
168	M-2, Master Topo Map	16	Anthropomorphic indeterminate	Pecked
168	M-2, Master Topo Map	26	Zoomorphic indeterminate	Pecked
168	M-2, Master Topo Map	90	Geometric indeterminate	Pecked
192	O-2, Map 11	33	Bull's eye, 2 rings	Pecked
193	O-3, Map 11	66	Pipette	Pecked
193	O-3, Map 11	90	Geometric indeterminate	Pecked
194	O-7, Map 11	38	Circle chain	Pecked
195	O-6, Map 11	3	Anthro. arms straight out (None 3)	Pecked
197	O-8 & 9, Map 11	40	Circle pattern	Pecked
197	O-8 & 9, Map 11	51	Cross hatch, diamond	Pecked
197	O-8 & 9, Map 11	87	Swastika	Pecked
318	L-2, Master Topo Map	72	Rectilinear abstract	Pecked
319	L-1, Master Topo Map	32	Bull's eye, 1 ring	Pecked
319	L-1, Master Topo Map	37	Circle	Pecked
319	L-1, Master Topo Map	42	Circles, concentric, 2 rings	Pecked
402	S-New	63	Line, parallel	Pecked
403	S-5, Map 14	16	Anthropomorphic indeterminate	Pecked
403	S-5, Map 14	27	Zoomorphic other	Pecked
403	S-5, Map 14	36	Chevron nested	Pecked
403	S-5, Map 14	51	Cross hatch, diamond	Pecked
403	S-5, Map 14	51	Cross hatch, diamond	Pecked
403	S-5, Map 14	53	Curvilinear abstract	Pecked
403	S-5, Map 14	53	Curvilinear abstract	Pecked
403	S-5, Map 14	53	Curvilinear abstract	Pecked
403	S-5, Map 14	53	Curvilinear abstract	Pecked
403	S-5, Map 14	53	Curvilinear abstract	Pecked
403	S-5, Map 14	64	Line, zigzag or wavy	Pecked
403	S-5, Map 14	64	Line, zigzag or wavy	Pecked
403	S-5, Map 14	64	Line, zigzag or wavy	Pecked
403	S-5, Map 14	90	Geometric indeterminate	Pecked
403	S-5, Map 14	90	Geometric indeterminate	Pecked
403	S-5, Map 14	90	Geometric indeterminate	Pecked
403	S-5, Map 14	90	Geometric indeterminate	Pecked
403	S-5, Map 14	91	Geometric other	Pecked
406	Q-New	43	Circles, concentric, 3 rings	Pecked
408	Q-New	72	Rectilinear abstract	Pecked
412	Q-26, Map 12	1	Anthro. arms up (None 1)	Pecked
412	Q-26, Map 12	1	Anthro. arms up (None 1)	Pecked
412	Q-26, Map 12	1	Anthro. arms up (None 1)	Pecked
412	Q-26, Map 12	1	Anthro. arms up (None 1)	Pecked
412	Q-26, Map 12	1	Anthro. arms up (None 1)	Pecked

	Appendix IV. Prehistoric Rock Art Data from Tumamoc Hill			
Feature ID	Ferg ID	Element Code	Element Name	Primary Technique
412	Q-26, Map 12	62	Line, straight	Pecked
412	Q-26, Map 12	90	Geometric indeterminate	Pecked
413	Q-New	12	Any stickperson holding material culture (NOT 14)	Pecked
422	Q-New	51	Cross hatch, diamond	Scratched
422	Q-New	60	Ladder	Pecked
427	Q-17, Map 12	19	Centipede	Pecked
428	Q-16, Map 12	4	Anthro. arms up with phallus (None 4)	Pecked
428	Q-16, Map 12	90	Geometric indeterminate	Pecked
429	Q-New	91	Geometric other	Pecked
431	Q-15, Map 12	49	Cross	Pecked
431	Q-15, Map 12	90	Geometric indeterminate	Pecked
432	Q-21, Map 12	74	Scroll, curvilinear clockwise	Pecked
434	Q-New	27	Zoomorphic other	Pecked
434	Q-New	41	Circle tailed	Pecked
434	Q-New	44	Circles, concentric, 4 rings	Pecked
436	Q-3, Map 12	86	Sun disk	Pecked
437	Q-4, Q-7, Map 12	16	Anthropomorphic indeterminate	Pecked
437	Q-4, Q-7, Map 12	39	Circle cluster	Pecked
437	Q-4, Q-7, Map 12	43	Circles, concentric, 3 rings	Pecked
437	Q-4, Q-7, Map 12	45	Circles, concentric, 5 rings	Pecked
442	S-New	7	Anthro. arms up with digits (None 7)	Pecked
444	S-6	37	Circle	Pecked
444	S-6	62	Line, straight	Pecked
452	Q-8, Map 12	23	Quadruped with horns	Pecked
452	Q-8, Map 12	23	Quadruped with horns	Pecked
452	Q-8, Map 12	32	Bull's eye, 1 ring	Pecked
453	Q-New	13	Anthropomorphic other than a stick figure	Pecked
453	Q-New	37	Circle	Pecked
455	Q-14, Map 12	42	Circles, concentric, 2 rings	Pecked
458	Q-New	16	Anthropomorphic indeterminate	Pecked
459	Q-11, Q-12, Q-13, Map 12	13	Anthropomorphic other than a stick figure	Pecked
459	Q-11, Q-12, Q-13, Map 12	19	Centipede	Pecked
459	Q-11, Q-12, Q-13, Map 12	27	Zoomorphic other	Pecked
459	Q-11, Q-12, Q-13, Map 12	52	Cross hatch, grid	Pecked
461	Q-23, Map 12	4	Anthro. arms up with phallus (None 4)	Pecked
461	Q-23, Map 12	90	Geometric indeterminate	Pecked
462	Q-New	90	Geometric indeterminate	Pecked
463	Q-22, Map 12	17	Anthropomorphic other	Pecked

Feature ID	Ferg ID	Element Code	Element Name	Primary Technique
		Appendix IV. Prehistoric Rock Art Data from Tumamoc Hill		
463	Q-22, Map 12	63	Line, parallel	Pecked
464	Q-24, Map 12	38	Circle chain	Pecked
466	Q-New	90	Geometric indeterminate	Pecked
468	IS-10, Master Topo	41	Circle tailed	Pecked
468	IS-10, Master Topo	41	Circle tailed	Pecked
468	IS-10, Master Topo	42	Circles, concentric, 2 rings	Pecked
468	IS-10, Master Topo	53	Curvilinear abstract	Pecked
468	IS-10, Master Topo	88	Terraced element	Pecked
470	IS-10-New-Near	40	Circle pattern	Pecked
483	S-New	53	Curvilinear abstract	Pecked
485	S-New	31	Asterisk	Pecked
485	S-New	41	Circle tailed	Pecked
494	S-10, Map 14	38	Circle chain	Pecked
494	S-10, Map 14	70	Rake, double	Pecked
494	S-10, Map 14	70	Rake, double	Pecked
495	S-8, Map 14	1	Anthro. arms up (None 1)	Pecked
495	S-8, Map 14	1	Anthro. arms up (None 1)	Pecked
495	S-8, Map 14	1	Anthro. arms up (None 1)	Pecked
495	S-8, Map 14	1	Anthro. arms up (None 1)	Pecked
495	S-8, Map 14	1	Anthro. arms up (None 1)	Pecked
495	S-8, Map 14	17	Anthropomorphic other	Pecked
495	S-8, Map 14	36	Chevron nested	Pecked
495	S-8, Map 14	61	Line, curved	Pecked
496	S-New	91	Geometric other	Pecked
501	S-New	32	Bull's eye, 1 ring	Pecked
502	S-New	64	Line, zigzag or wavy	Pecked
509	S-12, Map 14	26	Zoomorphic indeterminate	Pecked
509	S-12, Map 14	38	Circle chain	Pecked
512	S-13, Map 14	1	Anthro. arms up (None 1)	Pecked
512	S-13, Map 14	3	Anthro. arms straight out (None 3)	Pecked
512	S-13, Map 14	13	Anthropomorphic other than a stick figure	Pecked
512	S-13, Map 14	13	Anthropomorphic other than a stick figure	Pecked
512	S-13, Map 14	13	Anthropomorphic other than a stick figure	Pecked
512	S-13, Map 14	13	Anthropomorphic other than a stick figure	Pecked
513	S-New	62	Line, straight	Pecked
513	S-New	62	Line, straight	Pecked
513	S-New	69	Rake	Pecked
515	S-New	72	Rectilinear abstract	Pecked
516	P-2, Map 11	38	Circle chain	Pecked
516	P-2, Map 11	38	Circle chain	Pecked

Feature ID	Ferg ID	Element Code	Element Name	Primary Technique
		Appendix IV. Prehistoric Rock Art Data from Tumamoc Hill		
516	P-2, Map 11	49	Cross	Pecked
516	P-2, Map 11	76	Scroll, curvilinear clockwise	Pecked
516	P-2, Map 11	90	Geometric indeterminate	Pecked
517	P-3, Map 11	13	Anthropomorphic other than a stick figure	Pecked
517	P-3, Map 11	25	Tortoise	Pecked
517	P-3, Map 11	42	Circles, concentric, 2 rings	Pecked
519	P-4, Map 11	12	Any stickperson holding material culture (NOT 14)	Abraded
520	P-1, Map 11	52	Cross hatch, grid	Pecked
520	P-1, Map 11	90	Geometric indeterminate	Scratched
521	S-7, Map14	90	Geometric indeterminate	Pecked
522	S-New	90	Geometric indeterminate	Pecked
534	S-2, Map 14	17	Anthropomorphic other	Pecked
534	S-2, Map 14	42	Circles, concentric, 2 rings	Pecked
587	K-New-Near	76	Scroll, curvilinear counterclockwise	Pecked
588	H-4, Map 8	76	Scroll, curvilinear counterclockwise	Pecked
589	H-5, Map 8	24	Quadruped without horns	Pecked
589	H-5, Map 8	33	Bull's eye, 2 rings	Pecked
590	I-2, Map 8	34	Bull's eye, 3+ rings	Pecked
590	I-2, Map 8	42	Circles, concentric, 2 rings	Pecked
591	I-1, Map 8	33	Bull's eye, 2 rings	Pecked
592	I-3, Map 8	24	Quadruped without horns	Pecked
592	I-3, Map 8	33	Bull's eye, 2 rings	Pecked
592	I-3, Map 8	42	Circles, concentric, 2 rings	Pecked
594	H-3, Map 8	4	Anthro. arms up with phallus (None 4)	Pecked
594	H-3, Map 8	4	Anthro. arms up with phallus (None 4)	Pecked
594	H-3, Map 8	23	Quadruped with horns	Pecked
594	H-3, Map 8	23	Quadruped with horns	Pecked
594	H-3, Map 8	90	Geometric indeterminate	Pecked
594	H-3, Map 8	90	Geometric indeterminate	Pecked
595	H-2, Map 8	23	Quadruped with horns	Pecked
596	H-1, Map 8	3	Anthro. arms straight out (None 3)	Pecked
596	H-1, Map 8	4	Anthro. arms up with phallus (None 4)	Pecked
596	H-1, Map 8	32	Bull's eye, 1 ring	Pecked
596	H-1, Map 8	38	Circle chain	Pecked
596	H-1, Map 8	53	Curvilinear abstract	Pecked
596	H-1, Map 8	90	Geometric indeterminate	Scratched
653	IS-6, Master Topo Map	6	Anthro. arms down with digits (None 6)	Pecked
653	IS-6, Master Topo Map	13	Anthropomorphic other than a stick figure	Pecked
653	IS-6, Master Topo Map	90	Geometric indeterminate	Pecked
653	IS-6, Master Topo Map	90	Geometric indeterminate	Pecked

Feature ID	Ferg ID	Element Code	Element Name	Primary Technique
		Appendix IV. Prehistoric Rock Art Data from Tumamoc Hill		
679	IS-9, Master Topo	17	Anthropomorphic other	Pecked
679	IS-9, Master Topo	17	Anthropomorphic other	Pecked
689	R-New-Near	32	Bull's eye, 1 ring	Pecked
690	R-New-Near	29	Arcs, concentric	Pecked
690	R-New-Near	40	Circle pattern	Pecked
691	R-New-Near	1	Anthro. arms up (None 1)	Pecked
693	S-New	13	Anthropomorphic other than a stick figure	Pecked
694	Q-25, Map 12	90	Geometric indeterminate	Pecked
695	Q-1, Q-2, Map 12	12	Any stickperson holding material culture (NOT 14)	Pecked
695	Q-1, Q-2, Map 12	16	Anthropomorphic indeterminate	Pecked
695	Q-1, Q-2, Map 12	16	Anthropomorphic indeterminate	Pecked
695	Q-1, Q-2, Map 12	86	Sun disk	Pecked
695	Q-1, Q-2, Map 12	90	Geometric indeterminate	Pecked
696	Q-6, Map 12	19	Centipede	Pecked
697	Q-5, Map 12	91	Geometric other	Pecked
707	S-4	13	Anthropomorphic other than a stick figure	Pecked
707	S-4	13	Anthropomorphic other than a stick figure	Pecked
707	S-4	13	Anthropomorphic other than a stick figure	Pecked
800	P-New	25	Tortoise	Pecked
2375	R-4	90	Geometric indeterminate	Pecked
2376	R-New-Near	51	Cross hatch, diamond	Scratched
2377	S-New	16	Anthropomorphic indeterminate	Pecked
2378	R-New-Near	16	Anthropomorphic indeterminate	Pecked
2382	N-8, Map 10	86	Sun disk	Pecked
2387	N-New	90	Geometric indeterminate	Pecked
2389	M-1, Master Topo Map	31	Asterisk	Pecked
2911	A-1, Map 1	1	Anthro. arms up (None 1)	Pecked
2912	A-2, Map 1	76	Scroll, curvilinear counterclockwise	Pecked
2912	A-2, Map 1	90	Geometric indeterminate	Pecked
2913	A-3, Map 1	37	Circle	Pecked
2914	B-1, Map 2	4	Anthro arms up with phallus (None 4)	Pecked
2915	B-2, Map 2	53	Curvilinear abstract	Pecked
2916	B-3, Map 2	17	Anthropomorphic other	Pecked
2916	B-3, Map 2	90	Geometric indeterminate	Pecked
2916	B-3, Map 2	90	Geometric indeterminate	Pecked
2917	B-4, Map 2	7	Anthro. arms up with digits (None 7)	Pecked
2918	B-5, Map 2	12	Any stickperson holding material culture (NOT 14)	Pecked
2918	B-5, Map 2	42	Circles, concentric, 2 rings	Pecked
2918	B-5, Map 2	72	Rectilinear abstract	Pecked

Appendix IV. Prehistoric Rock Art Data from Tumamoc Hill

Feature ID	Ferg ID	Element Color	Element Name	Primary Technique
2919	B-6, Map 2	42	Circles, concentric, 2 rings	Pecked
2919	B-6, Map 2	90	Geometric indeterminate	Scratched
2920	B-7, Map 2	53	Curvilinear abstract	Pecked
2921	B-8, Map 2	2	Anthro. arms down (None 2)	Pecked
2921	B-8, Map 2	42	Circles, concentric, 2 rings	Pecked
2921	B-8, Map 2	76	Scroll, curvilinear counterclockwise	Pecked
2922	B-9, Map 2	4	Anthro. arms up with phallus (None 4)	Pecked
2922	B-9, Map 2	62	Line, straight	Pecked
2922	B-9, Map 2	90	Geometric indeterminate	Scratched
2923	B-10, Map 2	77	Scroll, curvilinear interlocking	Pecked
2924	B-11, Map 2	17	Anthropomorphic other	Pecked
2924	B-11, Map 2	76	Scroll, curvilinear counterclockwise	Pecked
2925	B-12, Map 2	4	Anthro. arms up with phallus (None 4)	Pecked
2925	B-12, Map 2	4	Anthro. arms up with phallus (None 4)	Pecked
2925	B-12, Map 2	5	Anthro.arms down with phallus (None 5)	Pecked
2925	B-12, Map 2	32	Bull's eye, 1 ring	Pecked
2925	B-12, Map 2	37	Circle	Pecked
2925	B-12, Map 2	90	Geometric indeterminate	Pecked
2925	B-12, Map 2	90	Geometric indeterminate	Pecked
2926	B-13, Map 2	26	Zoomorphic indeterminate	Pecked
2926	B-13, Map 2	37	Circle	Pecked
2926	B-13, Map 2	37	Circle	Pecked
2926	B-13, Map 2	42	Circles, concentric, 2 rings	Pecked
2926	B-13, Map 2	42	Circles, concentric, 2 rings	Pecked
2926	B-13, Map 2	49	Cross	Pecked
2926	B-13, Map 2	86	Sun disk	Pecked
2926	B-13, Map 2	90	Geometric indeterminate	Pecked
2926	B-13, Map 2	90	Geometric indeterminate	Scratched
2927	B-14, Map 2	72	Rectilinear abstract	Pecked
2928	B-15, Map 2	75	Scroll, curvilinear connected	Pecked
2929	B-16, Map 2	4	Anthro. arms up with phallus (None 4)	Pecked
2929	B-16, Map 2	66	Pipette	Pecked
2930	B-17, Map 2	4	Anthro. arms up with phallus (None 4)	Pecked
2930	B-17, Map 2	4	Anthro. arms up with phallus (None 4)	Pecked
2931	C-1, Map 3	25	Tortoise	Pecked
2931	C-1, Map 3	37	Circle	Pecked
2931	C-1, Map 3	37	Circle	Pecked
2931	C-1, Map 3	86	Sun disk	Pecked
2932	C-2, Map 3	41	Circle tailed	Pecked
2933	C-3, Map 3	38	Circle chain	Pecked
2934	C-4, Map3	12	Any stickperson holding material culture (NOT 14)	Pecked

Appendix IV. Prehistoric Rock Art Data from Tumamoc Hill

Feature ID	Ferg ID	Element Code	Element Name	Primary Technique
2934	C-4, Map3	62	Line, straight	Pecked
2935	C-5, Map 3	37	Circle	Pecked
2935	C-5, Map 3	37	Circle	Pecked
2935	C-5, Map 3	37	Circle	Pecked
2936	D-1, Map 4	37	Circle	Pecked
2936	D-1, Map 4	53	Curvilinear abstract	Pecked
2936	D-1, Map 4	53	Curvilinear abstract	Pecked
2937	D-2, Map 2	17	Anthropomorphic other	Pecked
2937	D-2, Map 2	32	Bull's eye, 1 ring	Pecked
2937	D-2, Map 2	49	Cross	Pecked
2937	D-2, Map 2	74	Scroll, curvilinear clockwise	Pecked
2938	D-3, Map 4	22	Lizard without toes	Pecked
2939	D-4, Map 4	5	Anthro. arms down with phallus (None 5)	Pecked
2939	D-4, Map 4	38	Circle chain	Pecked
2939	D-4, Map 4	46	Circles, line connected	Pecked
2939	D-4, Map 4	53	Curvilinear abstract	Pecked
2939	D-4, Map 4	62	Line, straight	Pecked
2939	D-4, Map 4	86	Sun disk	Pecked
2939	D-4, Map 4	91	Geometric other	Pecked
2940	D-5, Map 4	41	Circle tailed	Pecked
2940	D-5, Map 4	90	Geometric indeterminate	Pecked
2940	D-5, Map 4	90	Geometric indeterminate	Pecked
2941	D-6, Map 4	22	Lizard without toes	Pecked
2941	D-6, Map 4	22	Lizard without toes	Pecked
2941	D-6, Map 4	46	Circles, line connected	Pecked
2942	D-7, Map 4	39	Circle cluster	Pecked
2943	D-8, Map 4	1	Anthro. arms up (None 1)	Pecked
2943	D-8, Map 4	3	Anthro. arms straight out (None 3)	Pecked
2943	D-8, Map 4	38	Circle chain	Pecked
2943	D-8, Map 4	38	Circle chain	Pecked
2943	D-8, Map 4	90	Geometric indeterminate	Pecked
2943	D-8, Map 4	90	Geometric indeterminate	Pecked
2944	D-9, Map 4	53	Curvilinear abstract	Pecked
2944	D-9, Map 4	53	Curvilinear abstract	Pecked
2944	D-9, Map 4	62	Line, straight	Pecked
2945	D-10, Map 4	2	Anthro. arms down (None 2)	Pecked
2945	D-10, Map 4	21	Lizard with toes	Pecked
2945	D-10, Map 4	74	Scroll, curvilinear clockwise	Pecked
2945	D-10, Map 4	76	Scroll, curvilinear counterclockwise	Pecked
2946	D-11, Map 4	89	Triangle	Pecked
2947	D-12, Map 4	90	Geometric indeterminate	Pecked

Feature ID	Ferg ID	Element Code	Element Name	Primary Technique
			Appendix IV. Prehistoric Rock Art Data from Tumamoc Hill	
2948	D-13, Map 4	83	Snake	Pecked
2949	D-14, Map 4	40	Circle pattern	Pecked
2950	D-15, Map 4	38	Circle chain	Pecked
2951	D-16, Map 4	4	Anthro arms up with phallus (None 4)	Pecked
2951	D-16, Map 4	37	Circle	Pecked
2952	D-17, Map 4	37	Circle	Pecked
2952	D-17, Map 4	42	Circles, concentric, 2 rings	Pecked
2952	D-17, Map 4	42	Circles, concentric, 2 rings	Pecked
2953	D-18, Map 4	43	Circles, concentric, 3 rings	Pecked
2953	D-18, Map 4	90	Geometric indeterminate	Pecked
2954	D-19, Map 4	12	Any stickperson holding material culture (NOT 14)	Pecked
2954	D-19, Map 4	42	Circles, concentric, 2 rings	Pecked
2954	D-19, Map 4	53	Curvilinear abstract	Pecked
2954	D-19, Map 4	53	Curvilinear abstract	Pecked
2955	D-20, Map 4	42	Circles, concentric, 2 rings	Pecked
2956	D-21, Map 4	37	Circle	Pecked
2958	E-1, Map 5	37	Circle	Pecked
2958	E-1, Map 5	37	Circle	Pecked
2959	E-2, Map 5	13	Anthropomorphic other than a stick figure	Pecked
2959	E-2, Map 5	90	Geometric indeterminate	Scratched
2960	E-3, Map 5	37	Circle	Pecked
2961	E-4, Map 5	53	Curvilinear abstract	Pecked
2961	E-4, Map 5	76	Scroll, curvilinear counterclockwise	Pecked
2962	E-5, Map 5	33	Bull's eye, 2 rings	Pecked
2962	E-5, Map 5	37	Circle	Pecked
2962	E-5, Map 5	37	Circle	Pecked
2962	E-5, Map 5	49	Cross	Pecked
2962	E-5, Map 5	61	Line, curved	Pecked
2962	E-5, Map 5	84	Square	Pecked
2962	E-5, Map 5	90	Geometric indeterminate	Pecked
2963	E-6, Map 5	37	Circle	Pecked
2963	E-6, Map 5	42	Circles, concentric, 2 rings	Pecked
2964	E-7, Map 5	16	Anthropomorphic indeterminate	Pecked
2965	E-8, Map5	22	Lizard without toes	Pecked
2966	E-9, Map 5	4	Anthro. arms up with phallus (None 4)	Pecked
2967	E-10, Map 5	64	Line, zigzag or wavy	Pecked
2968	E-11, Map 5	7	Anthro. arms up with digits (None 7)	Pecked
2969	E-12, Map 5	4	Anthro. arms up with phallus (None 4)	Pecked
2969	E-12, Map 5	61	Line, curved	Pecked
2970	E-13, Map 5	16	Anthropomorphic indeterminate	Pecked
2970	E-13, Map 5	22	Lizard without toes	Pecked

Feature ID	Ferg ID	Element Code	Element Name	Primary Technique
2971	E-14, Map 5	1	Anthro. arms up (None 1)	Pecked
2971	E-14, Map 5	12	Any stickperson holding material culture (NOT 14)	Pecked
2971	E-14, Map 5	31	Asterisk	Pecked
2971	E-14, Map 5	72	Rectilinear abstract	Pecked
2971	E-14, Map 5	72	Rectilinear abstract	Pecked
2972	E-15, Map 5	37	Circle	Pecked
2972	E-15, Map 5	53	Curvilinear abstract	Pecked
2973	E-16, Map 5	2	Anthro. arms down (None 2)	Pecked
2974	E-17, Map 5	37	Circle	Pecked
2974	E-17, Map 5	61	Line, curved	Pecked
2975	E-18, Map 5	53	Curvilinear abstract	Pecked
2976	E-19, Map 5	36	Chevron nested	Scratched
2976	E-19, Map 5	41	Circle tailed	Pecked
2977	E-20, Map 5	5	Anthro. arms down with phallus (None 5)	Pecked
2977	E-20, Map 5	13	Anthropomorphic other than a stick figure	Pecked
2978	E-21, Map 5	23	Quadruped with horns	Pecked
2978	E-21, Map 5	37	Circle	Pecked
2978	E-21, Map 5	53	Curvilinear abstract	Pecked
2978	E-21, Map 5	72	Rectilinear abstract	Pecked
2978	E-21, Map 5	72	Rectilinear abstract	Pecked
2979	E-22, Map 5	90	Geometric indeterminate	Pecked
2980	E-23, Map 5	42	Circles, concentric, 2 rings	Pecked
2981	E-24, Map 5	23	Quadruped with horns	Pecked
2982	E-25, Map 5	72	Rectilinear abstract	Pecked
2983	F-1, Map 6	90	Geometric indeterminate	Pecked
2984	F-2, Map 6	76	Scroll, curvilinear counterclockwise	Pecked
2985	F-3, Map 6	51	Cross hatch, diamond	Scratched
2985	F-3, Map 6	51	Cross hatch, diamond	Scratched
2985	F-3, Map 6	52	Cross hatch, grid	Scratched
2986	F-4, Map 6	76	Scroll, curvilinear counterclockwise	Pecked
2987	F-5, Map 6	53	Curvilinear abstract	Pecked
2988	F-6, Map 6	13	Anthropomorphic other than a stick figure	Pecked
2989	F-7, Map 6	51	Cross hatch, diamond	Scratched
2989	F-7, Map 6	63	Line, parallel	Scratched
2989	F-7, Map 6	90	Geometric indeterminate	Scratched
2990	G-1, Map 7	23	Quadruped with horns	Pecked
2990	G-1, Map 7	84	Square	Pecked
2991	G-2, Map 7	37	Circle	Pecked
2991	G-2, Map 7	72	Rectilinear abstract	Scratched
2992	G-3, Map 7	75	Scroll, curvilinear connected	Pecked
2993	G-4, Map 7	30	Arcs, concentric, spoked	Pecked

			Appendix IV. Prehistoric Rock Art Data from Tumamoc Hill	
Feature ID	Ferg ID	Element Code	Element Name	Primary Technique
2993	G-4, Map 7	35	Chevron ladder	Pecked
2994	G-5, Map 7	69	Rake	Pecked
2995	G-6, Map 7	90	Geometric indeterminate	Pecked
2995	G-6, Map 7	90	Geometric indeterminate	Pecked
2996	G-7, Map 7	2	Anthro. arms down (None 2)	Pecked
2996	G-7, Map 7	74	Scroll, curvilinear clockwise	Pecked
2996	G-7, Map 7	90	Geometric indeterminate	Scratched
2997	IS-1, Map 8	12	Any stickperson holding material culture (NOT 14)	Pecked
2997	IS-1, Map 8	64	Line, zigzag or wavy	Pecked
2997	IS-1, Map 8	76	Scroll, curvilinear counterclockwise	Pecked
2998	IS-2, Master topo	72	Rectilinear abstract	Pecked
2999	J-1, Map 8	1	Anthro. arms up (None 1)	Pecked
2999	J-1, Map 8	2	Anthro. arms down (None 2)	Pecked
2999	J-1, Map 8	2	Anthro. arms down (None 2)	Pecked
2999	J-1, Map 8	12	Any stickperson holding material culture (NOT 14)	Pecked
2999	J-1, Map 8	23	Quadruped with horns	Pecked
2999	J-1, Map 8	53	Curvilinear abstract	Pecked
2999	J-1, Map 8	90	Geometric indeterminate	Pecked
3000	J-2, Map 8	37	Circle	Pecked
3001	J-3, Map 8	29	Arcs, concentric	Pecked
3001	J-3, Map 8	74	Scroll, curvilinear clockwise	Pecked
3002	J-4, Map 8	22	Lizard without toes	Pecked
3002	J-4, Map 8	23	Quadruped with horns	Pecked
3003	J-5, Map 8	76	Scroll, curvilinear counterclockwise	Pecked
3004	H-New	16	Anthropomorphic indeterminate	Pecked
3005	I-New	2	Anthro. arms down (None 2)	Abraded
3005	I-New	2	Anthro. arms down (None 2)	Abraded
3006	J-New	75	Scroll, curvilinear connected	Pecked
3009	J-New	37	Circle	Pecked
3010	KK-New	46	Circles, line connected	Pecked
3012	G-New	49	Cross	Pecked
3013	F-New	16	Anthropomorphic indeterminate	Pecked
3016	E-New	1	Anthro. arms up (None 1)	Pecked
3016	E-New	90	Geometric indeterminate	Pecked
3018	E-New	49	Cross	Pecked
3018	E-New	49	Cross	Pecked
3019	E-New	16	Anthropomorphic indeterminate	Pecked
3019	E-New	90	Geometric indeterminate	Pecked
3020	E-New	53	Curvilinear abstract	Pecked
3020	E-New	64	Line, zigzag or wavy	Pecked
3021	E-New	73	Rectilinear meander	Pecked

Feature ID	Ferg ID	Element Code	Element Name	Primary Technique
		Appendix IV. Prehistoric Rock Art Data from Tumamoc Hill		
3022	E-New	2	Anthro. arms down (None 2)	Pecked
3023	E-New	49	Cross	Pecked
3023	E-New	62	Line, straight	Pecked
3024	E-New	90	Geometric indeterminate	Pecked
3025	E-New	72	Rectilinear abstract	Incised
3026	D-New	4	Anthro. arms up with phallus (None 4)	Pecked
3026	D-New	23	Quadruped with horns	Pecked
3026	D-New	38	Circle chain	Pecked
3026	D-New	62	Line, straight	Scratched
3028	D-New	41	Circle tailed	Pecked
3029	D-New	12	Any stickperson holding material culture (NOT 14)	Pecked
3029	D-New	26	Zoomorphic indeterminate	Pecked
3030	D-New	5	Anthro. arms down with phallus (None 5)	Pecked
3241	D-New	42	Circles, concentric, 2 rings	Pecked
3242	D-New	84	Square	Scratched
3245	B-New	37	Circle	Pecked
3245	B-New	86	Sun disk	Pecked
3246	B-New	17	Anthropomorphic other	Pecked
3246	B-New	17	Anthropomorphic other	Pecked
3247	B-New	17	Anthropomorphic other	Pecked
3247	B-New	90	Geometric indeterminate	Pecked
3247	B-New	90	Geometric indeterminate	Pecked
3248	B-New	42	Circles, concentric, 2 rings	Pecked
3249	B-New	38	Circle chain	Pecked
3249	B-New	90	Geometric indeterminate	Pecked
3249	B-New	90	Geometric indeterminate	Pecked
3250	IS-13	42	Circles, concentric, 2 rings	Pecked
3250	IS-13	43	Circles, concentric, 3 rings	Pecked
3250	IS-13	43	Circles, concentric, 3 rings	Pecked
3250	IS-13	90	Geometric indeterminate	Pecked
3251	Q-New	44	Circles, concentric, 4 rings	Pecked
3252	A-New	2	Anthro. arms down (None 2)	Pecked
3253	A-New	55	Dot framing	Pecked
3254	A-New	70	Rake, double	Pecked
3255	A-New	37	Circle	Pecked
3256	A-New	22	Lizard without toes	Pecked
3257	A-New	2	Anthro. arms down (None 2)	Pecked
3260	C-New	2	Anthro. arms down (None 2)	Pecked
3261	C-New	1	Anthro. arms up (None 1)	Pecked
3262	C-New	12	Any stickperson holding material culture (NOT 14)	Pecked
3264	C-New	23	Quadruped with horns	Pecked

	Appendix IV. Prehistoric Rock Art Data from Tumamoc Hill			
Feature ID	Ferg ID	Element Code	Element Name	Primary Technique
3264	C-New	37	Circle	Pecked
3268	KK-New	63	Line, parallel	Scratched
3270	K-1, Map 9	72	Rectilinear abstract	Pecked
3271	K-2, Map 9	72	Rectilinear abstract	Pecked
3272	K-3, Map 9	22	Lizard without toes	Pecked
3273	K-4, Map 9	32	Bull's eye, 1 ring	Pecked
3273	K-4, Map 9	72	Rectilinear abstract	Pecked
3273	K-4, Map 9	83	Snake	Pecked
3274	K-5, Map 9	37	Circle	Pecked
3275	K-6, Map 9	32	Bull's eye, 1 ring	Pecked
3276	K-7, Map 9	26	Zoomorphic indeterminate	Pecked
3277	K-8, Map 9	53	Curvilinear abstract	Pecked
3277	K-8, Map 9	62	Line, straight	Pecked
3277	K-8, Map 9	72	Rectilinear abstract	Pecked
3278	K-9, Map 9	1	Anthro. arms up (None 1)	Pecked
3279	K-10, Map 9	37	Circle	Pecked
3280	K-11, Map 9	22	Lizard without toes	Pecked
3281	K-12, Map 9	1	Anthro. arms up (None 1)	Pecked
3282	K-13, Map 9	66	Pipette	Pecked
3283	K-14, Map 9	37	Circle	Pecked
3284	K-15, Map 9	24	Quadruped without horns	Pecked
3285	K-16, Map 9	12	Any stickperson holding material culture (NOT 14)	Pecked
3285	K-16, Map 9	64	Line, zigzag or wavy	Pecked
3286	K-17, Map 9	12	Any stickperson holding material culture (NOT 14)	Pecked
3287	K-18, Map 9	17	Anthropomorphic other	Pecked
3288	K-19, Map 9	17	Anthropomorphic other	Pecked
3288	K-19, Map 9	64	Line, zigzag or wavy	Pecked
3289	K-20, Map 9	64	Line, zigzag or wavy	Pecked
3290	K-21, Map 9	86	Sun disk	Pecked
3290	K-21, Map 9	90	Geometric indeterminate	Pecked
3291	K-22, Map 9	42	Circles, concentric, 2 rings	Pecked
3292	K-23, Map 9	47	Circles, sectioned	Pecked
3293	K-24, Map 9	37	Circle	Pecked
3294	K-25, Map 9	16	Anthropomorphic indeterminate	Pecked
3294	K-25, Map 9	42	Circles, concentric, 2 rings	Pecked
3294	K-25, Map 9	43	Circles, concentric, 3 rings	Pecked
3294	K-25, Map 9	90	Geometric indeterminate	Pecked
3296	K-26, Map 9	52	Cross hatch, grid	Pecked
3297	K-27, Map 9	52	Cross hatch, grid	Pecked
3298	K-28, Map 9	64	Line, zigzag or wavy	Pecked
3299	K-29, Map 9	2	Anthro. arms down (None 2)	Pecked

Feature ID	Ferg ID	Element Code	Element Name	Primary Technique
3300	K-30, Map 9	64	Line, zigzag or wavy	Pecked
3303	KK-New	37	Circle	Pecked
3303	KK-New	91	Geometric other	Pecked
3305	KK-New	23	Quadruped with horns	Pecked
3305	KK-New	32	Bull's eye, 1 ring	Pecked
3305	KK-New	37	Circle	Pecked
3305	KK-New	47	Circles, sectioned	Pecked
3305	KK-New	49	Cross	Pecked
3305	KK-New	74	Scroll, curvilinear clockwise	Pecked
3306	KK-New	23	Quadruped with horns	Pecked
3307	KK-New	4	Anthro. arms up with phallus (None 4)	Pecked
3308	KK-New	53	Curvilinear abstract	Pecked
3309	KK-New	46	Circles, line connected	Pecked
3310	KK-New	72	Rectilinear abstract	Scratched
3312	KK-New	90	Geometric indeterminate	Pecked
3314	KK-New	90	Geometric indeterminate	Pecked
3315	KK-New	90	Geometric indeterminate	Pecked
3316	KK-New	42	Circles, concentric, 2 rings	Pecked
3317	KK-New	1	Anthro. arms up (None 1)	Pecked
3317	KK-New	53	Curvilinear abstract	Pecked
3317	KK-New	72	Rectilinear abstract	Pecked
3317	KK-New	75	Scroll, curvilinear connected	Pecked
3317	KK-New	76	Scroll, curvilinear counterclockwise	Pecked
3317	KK-New	90	Geometric indeterminate	Pecked
3317	KK-New	90	Geometric indeterminate	Pecked
3318	KK-New	5	Anthro. arms down with phallus (None 5)	Pecked
3318	KK-New	53	Curvilinear abstract	Pecked
3318	KK-New	63	Line, parallel	Scratched
3320	KK-New	64	Line, zigzag or wavy	Pecked
3320	KK-New	64	Line, zigzag or wavy	Pecked
3321	N-5, Map 10	36	Chevron nested	Pecked
3321	N-5, Map 10	43	Circles, concentric, 3 rings	Pecked
3322	KK-New	33	Bull's eye, 2 rings	Pecked
3322	KK-New	90	Geometric indeterminate	Pecked
3323	KK-New	37	Circle	Pecked
3324	KK-New	62	Line, straight	Pecked
3325	KK-New	83	Snake	Pecked
3327	R-5, Map 13	8	Anthro. arms straight out with digits (None 8)	Pecked
3327	R-5, Map 13	37	Circle	Pecked
3330	R-New-Near	51	Cross hatch, diamond	Scratched

	Appendix IV. Prehistoric Rock Art Data from Tumamoc Hill			
Feature ID	Ferg ID	Element Code	Element Name	Primary Technique
3332	R-New	3	Anthro. arms straight out (None 3)	Pecked
3333	Q-9, Q-10, Map 12	13	Anthropomorphic other than a stick figure	Pecked
3333	Q-9, Q-10, Map 12	76	Scroll, curvilinear clockwise	Pecked
3335	T-2, Map 15	51	Cross hatch, diamond	Scratched
3335	T-2, Map 15	51	Cross hatch, diamond	Scratched
3335	T-2, Map 15	51	Cross hatch, diamond	Scratched
3335	T-2, Map 15	51	Cross hatch, diamond	Scratched
3335	T-2, Map 15	51	Cross hatch, diamond	Scratched
3335	T-2, Map 15	52	Cross hatch, grid	Scratched
3335	T-2, Map 15	52	Cross hatch, grid	Scratched
3335	T-2, Map 15	63	Line, parallel	Scratched
3339	T-New	7	Anthro. arms up with digits (None 7)	Pecked
3340	T-New	37	Circle	Pecked
3340	T-New	37	Circle	Pecked
3340	T-New	42	Circles, concentric, 2 rings	Pecked
3340	T-New	42	Circles, concentric, 2 rings	Pecked
3340	T-New	42	Circles, concentric, 2 rings	Pecked
3340	T-New	42	Circles, concentric, 2 rings	Pecked
3340	T-New	42	Circles, concentric, 2 rings	Pecked
3340	T-New	91	Geometric other	Pecked
3341	IS-5, Master Topo Map	7	Anthro. arms up with digits (None 7)	Pecked
3341	IS-5, Master Topo Map	42	Circles, concentric, 2 rings	Pecked
3345	R-New-Near	16	Anthropomorphic indeterminate	Pecked
3347	Q-New	53	Curvilinear abstract	Pecked
3348	R-New-Near	17	Anthropomorphic other	Pecked
3348	R-New-Near	17	Anthropomorphic other	Pecked
3348	R-New-Near	37	Circle	Pecked
3349	O-4, Map 11	66	Pipette	Pecked
3350	U-1, Map 16	63	Line, parallel	Scratched
3351	U-2, Map 16	17	Anthropomorphic other	Scratched
3351	U-2, Map 16	24	Quadruped without horns	Pecked
3351	U-2, Map 16	36	Chevron nested	Scratched
3351	U-2, Map 16	36	Chevron nested	Scratched
3351	U-2, Map 16	43	Circles, concentric, 3 rings	Pecked
3351	U-2, Map 16	50	Cross hatch, band	Scratched
3351	U-2, Map 16	50	Cross hatch, band	Scratched
3351	U-2, Map 16	50	Cross hatch, band	Scratched
3351	U-2, Map 16	52	Cross hatch, grid	Scratched
3351	U-2, Map 16	52	Cross hatch, grid	Scratched
3351	U-2, Map 16	58	Dot undefined pattern	Pecked
3351	U-2, Map 16	62	Line, straight	Scratched

	Appendix IV. Prehistoric Rock Art Data from Tumamoc Hill			
Feature ID	Ferg ID	Element Code	Element Name	Primary Technique
3351	U-2, Map 16	89	Triangle	Scratched
3351	U-2, Map 16	89	Triangle	Scratched
3352	U-3, Map 16	50	Cross hatch, band	Scratched
3352	U-3, Map 16	50	Cross hatch, band	Scratched
3352	U-3, Map 16	52	Cross hatch, grid	Scratched
3353	U-4, Map 16	50	Cross hatch, band	Scratched
3353	U-4, Map 16	89	Triangle	Scratched
3354	U-5, Map 16	52	Cross hatch, grid	Scratched
3355	U-6, Map 16	64	Line, zigzag or wavy	Scratched
3355	U-6, Map 16	64	Line, zigzag or wavy	Scratched
3355	U-6, Map 16	64	Line, zigzag or wavy	Scratched
3355	U-6, Map 16	64	Line, zigzag or wavy	Scratched
3355	U-6, Map 16	90	Geometric indeterminate	Pecked
3356	U-7, Map 16	36	Chevron nested	Scratched
3356	U-7, Map 16	52	Cross hatch, grid	Scratched
3357	U-8, Map 16	52	Cross hatch, grid	Scratched
3357	U-8, Map 16	52	Cross hatch, grid	Scratched
3357	U-8, Map 16	62	Line, straight	Scratched
3358	U-9, Map 16	36	Chevron nested	Scratched
4322	V-1, Map 17	34	Bull's eye, 3+ rings	Pecked
4323	V-2, Map 17	22	Lizard without toes	Pecked
4324	V-3, Map 17	2	Anthro. arms down (None 2)	Pecked
4324	V-3, Map 17	52	Cross hatch, grid	Scratched
4325	V-4, Map 17	12	Any stickperson holding material culture (NOT 14)	Pecked
4341	IS-3, Master Topo Map	1	Anthro. arms up (None 1)	Pecked
4341	IS-3, Master Topo Map	10	Anthro. arms and legs straight out w/digits (None 10)	Pecked
4341	IS-3, Master Topo Map	15	Foot	Pecked
4341	IS-3, Master Topo Map	15	Foot	Pecked
4341	IS-3, Master Topo Map	42	Circles, concentric, 2 rings	Pecked
4341	IS-3, Master Topo Map	42	Circles, concentric, 2 rings	Pecked
4341	IS-3, Master Topo Map	48	Circles with arc	Pecked
4341	IS-3, Master Topo Map	66	Pipette	Pecked
4341	IS-3, Master Topo Map	72	Rectilinear abstract	Pecked
4341	IS-3, Master Topo Map	90	Geometric indeterminate	Pecked
4342	S-1	84	Square	Pecked
4343	S-3	72	Rectilinear abstract	Pecked
4344	S-New	39	Circle cluster	Pecked
4345	S-9	90	Geometric indeterminate	Pecked
4348	S-New	62	Line, straight	Scratched
4349	S-New	53	Curvilinear abstract	Pecked

Feature ID	Ferg ID	Element Code	Element Name	Primary Technique
			Appendix IV. Prehistoric Rock Art Data from Tumamoc Hill	
4381	S-New	2	None2	Pecked
4381	S-New	26	Zoomorphic indeterminate	Pecked
4382	S-New	3	Anthro arms straight out (None 3)	Pecked
4383	U-New-Near	86	Sun disk	Pecked
4384	U-New	24	Quadruped without horns	Pecked
4384	U-New	62	Line, straight	Pecked
4386	IS-10-New-Near	64	Line, zigzag or wavy	Pecked
4388	IS-10 New-Near	43	Circles, concentric, 3 rings	Pecked
4388	IS-10 New-Near	53	Curvilinear abstract	Pecked
4388	IS-10 New-Near	90	Geometric indeterminate	Pecked
4389	IS-10-New-Near	23	Quadruped with horns	Pecked
4389	IS-10-New-Near	53	Curvilinear abstract	Pecked
4389	IS-10-New-Near	72	Rectilinear abstract	Pecked
4390	IS-10 New-Near	12	Any stickperson holding material culture (NOT 14)	Pecked
4391	IS-10-New-Near	62	Line, straight	Scratched
4392	IS-10-New-Near	63	Line, parallel	Scratched
4393	IS-10-New-Near	74	Scroll, curvilinear clockwise	Pecked
4393	IS-10-New-Near	74	Scroll, curvilinear clockwise	Pecked
4396	O-1, Map 11	2	Anthro. arms down (None 2)	Pecked
4396	O-1, Map 11	26	Zoomorphic indeterminate	Pecked
4397	P-5, Map 11	39	Circle cluster	Pecked
4398	R-6	51	Cross hatch, diamond	Scratched
4398	R-6	60	Ladder	Scratched
4398	R-6	90	Geometric indeterminate	Scratched
4399	R-New	51	Cross hatch, diamond	Scratched
4399	R-New	51	Cross hatch, diamond	Scratched
4399	R-New	51	Cross hatch, diamond	Scratched
4399	R-New	51	Cross hatch, diamond	Scratched
4404	R-New	51	Cross hatch, diamond	Scratched
4407	R-New	37	Circle	Pecked
4408	B-New	22	Lizard without toes	Pecked
4413	R-New	1	Anthro. arms up (None 1)	Pecked
4413	R-New	1	Anthro. arms up (None 1)	Pecked
4420	N-2	52	Cross hatch, grid	Scratched
4421	N-New	52	Cross hatch, grid	Scratched
4422	N-1	63	Line, parallel	Scratched
4423	N-7	86	Sun disk	Pecked
4425	N-New	52	Cross hatch, grid	Scratched
4425	N-New	60	Ladder	Scratched
4427	N-New	52	Cross hatch, grid	Scratched
4430	IS-2-New-Near	13	Anthropomorphic other than a stick figure	Pecked

	Appendix IV. Prehistoric Rock Art Data from Tumamoc Hill			
Feature ID	Ferg ID	Element Code	Element Name	Primary Technique
4430	IS-2-New-Near	24	Quadruped without horns	Pecked
4431	Q-New	1	Anthro. arms up (None 1)	Pecked
4432	Q-18	2	Anthro. arms down (None 2)	Pecked
4432	Q-18	2	Anthro. arms down (None 2)	Pecked
4432	Q-18	2	Anthro. arms down (None 2)	Pecked
4432	Q-18	6	Anthro. arms down with digits (None 6)	Pecked
4432	Q-18	72	Rectilinear abstract	Pecked
4437	Q-19	16	Anthropomorphic indeterminate	Pecked
4438	Q-New	90	Geometric indeterminate	Pecked
4439	Q-20	76	Scroll, curvilinear counterclockwise	Pecked
4444	K-New-Near	75	Scroll, curvilinear connected	Pecked
4445	IS-4	49	Cross	Pecked
4445	IS-4	72	Rectilinear abstract	Pecked
4447	IS-12	1	Anthro. arms up (None 1)	Pecked
4447	IS-12	23	Quadruped with horns	Pecked
4447	IS-12	42	Circles, concentric, 2 rings	Pecked
4447	IS-12	50	Cross hatch, band	Pecked
4447	IS-12	64	Line, zigzag or wavy	Pecked
4447	IS-12	73	Rectilinear meander	Pecked
4447	IS-12	73	Rectilinear meander	Pecked
4447	IS-12	73	Rectilinear meander	Pecked
4448	T-New	42	Circles, concentric, 2 rings	Abraded
4449	IS-11	68	Rain cloud	Pecked
4450	Pipeline-New	2	Anthro. arms down (None 2)	Pecked
4451	Pipeline-New	13	Anthropomorphic other than a stick figure	Pecked
4457	U-New	47	Circles, sectioned	Scratched
4457	U-New	63	Line, parallel	Scratched
4458	U-New	32	Bull's eye, 1 ring	Pecked
4458	U-New	63	Line, parallel	Scratched
4458	U-New	63	Line, parallel	Scratched
4459	U-New	52	Cross hatch, grid	Scratched
4461	IS-7	53	Curvilinear abstract	Pecked
4467	T-New	42	Circles, concentric, 2 rings	Pecked
4467	T-New	53	Curvilinear abstract	Pecked
4472	T-New	50	Cross hatch, band	Scratched
4472	T-New	62	Line, straight	Scratched
4474	So. Slope-New	41	Circle tailed	Pecked
4475	So. Slope-New	1	Anthro, arms up (None 1)	Pecked
4475	So. Slope-New	6	Anthro. arms down with digits (None 6)	Pecked
4478	So. Slope-New	1	Anthro arms up (None 1)	Pecked
4479	So. Slope-New	63	Line, parallel	Scratched

Appendix IV. Prehistoric Rock Art Data from Tumamoc Hill

Feature ID	Ferg ID	Element Code	Element Name	Primary Technique
4482	T-New	37	Circle	Pecked
4485	So. Slope-New	53	Curvilinear abstract	Pecked
4485	So. Slope-New	77	Scroll, curvilinear interlocking	Pecked
4486	T-New	37	Circle	Pecked
4487	Q-New	37	Circle	Pecked
4487	Q-New	62	Line, straight	Pecked
4488	Q-New	13	Anthropomorphic other than a stick figure	Pecked

Appendix V

Elements of Indeterminate Age from Tumamoc Hill

Appendix V. Elements of Indeterminate Age from Tumamoc Hill				
Feature ID	Ferg ID	Element Code	Element Name	Primary Technique
497	S-New	100	Not listed above indeterminate	Pecked
2988	F-6, Map 6	100	Not listed above indeterminate	Pecked
3001	J-3, Map 8	100	Not listed above indeterminate	Scratched
4401	R-New	100	Not listed above indeterminate	Scratched
4423	N-7	101	Not listed above other	Abraded
4470	V-New	101	Not listed above other	Scratched

Appendix VI

Graffiti Data from Tumamoc Hill

	Appendix VI. Graffiti Data from Tumamoc Hill			
Feature ID	Ferg ID	Element Code	Element name	Primary Technique
3	S-New	202	Letter and number	Scratched
16	N-New	200	Letter	Scratched
16	N-New	200	Letter	Scratched
16	N-New	202	Letter and number	Scratched
17	N-New	202	Letter and number	Scratched
17	N-New	202	Letter and number	scratched
17	N-New	202	Letter and number	Scratched
19	N-New	200	Letter	Pecked
20	N-6, Map 10	200	Letter	Abraded
20	N-6, Map 10	202	Letter and number	Scratched
20	N-6, Map 10	250	Modern other	Scratched
20	N-6, Map 10	250	Modern other	Scratched
21	N-New	250	Modern other	Scratched
23	N-New	200	Letter	Scratched
23	N-New	200	Letter	Scratched
23	N-New	202	Letter and number	Scratched
23	N-New	250	Modern other	Scratched
24	N-New	202	Letter and number	Scratched
102	R-1, Map 13	200	Letter	Scratched
102	R-1, Map 13	250	Modern other	Scratched
103	R-2, Map 13	200	Letter	Scratched
103	R-2, Map 13	250	Modern other	Scratched
108	S-New	200	Letter	Scratched
126	T-New	200	Letter	Scratched
126	T-New	202	Letter and number	Scratched
126	T-New	202	Letter and number	Scratched
126	T-New	202	Letter and number	Scratched
126	T-New	290	Modern indeterminate	Scratched
128	T-1, Map 15	200	Letter	Pecked
130	T-New	200	Letter	Abraded
130	T-New	200	Letter	Abraded
130	T-New	201	Number	Abraded
130	T-New	250	Modern other	Scratched
168	M-2, Master Topo Map	200	Letter	Scratched
168	M-2, Master Topo Map	200	Letter	Scratched
168	M-2, Master Topo Map	250	Modern other	Scratched
189	R-New-Near	202	Letter and number	Scratched
189	R-New-Near	202	Letter and number	Scratched
189	R-New-Near	202	Letter and number	Scratched
189	R-New-Near	202	Letter and number	Scratched
189	R-New-Near	202	Letter and number	Scratched

	Appendix VI. Graffiti Data from Tumamoc Hill			
Feature ID	Ferg ID	Element Code	Element name	Primary Technique
189	R-New-Near	202	Letter and number	Scratched
196	O-5, Map 11	250	Modern other	Pecked
196	O-5, Map 11	250	Modern other	Pecked
403	S-5, Map 14	200	Letter	Scratched
403	S-5, Map 14	250	Modern other	Pecked
409	Q-New	200	Letter	Scratched
411	Q-New	200	Letter	Other
412	Q-26, Map 12	200	Letter	Pecked
412	Q-26, Map 12	200	Letter	Pecked
412	Q-26, Map 12	250	Modern other	Scratched
413	Q-New	290	Modern indeterminate	Scratched
415	Q-New	200	Letter	Scratched
415	Q-New	200	Letter	Scratched
415	Q-New	201	Number	Scratched
415	Q-New	202	Letter and number	Scratched
415	Q-New	202	Letter and number	Scratched
415	Q-New	202	Letter and number	Scratched
416	Q-New	200	Letter	Incised
416	Q-New	202	Letter and number	Incised
417	Q-New	200	Letter	Scratched
417	Q-New	202	Letter and number	Other
417	Q-New	202	Letter and number	Scratched
418	Q-New	200	Letter	Scratched
418	Q-New	200	Letter	Pecked
418	Q-New	200	Letter	Pecked
418	Q-New	202	Letter and number	Scratched
418	Q-New	202	Letter and number	Scratched
418	Q-New	202	Letter and number	Scratched
420	Q-New	200	Letter	Abraded
420	Q-New	202	Letter and number	Scratched
422	Q-New	200	Letter	Abraded
422	Q-New	200	Letter	Scratched
422	Q-New	250	Modern other	Scratched
423	Q-New	201	Number	Scratched
423	Q-New	202	Letter and number	Pecked
425	Q-New	200	Letter	Scratched
425	Q-New	250	Modern other	Scratched
425	Q-New	250	Modern other	Scratched
426	Q-New	200	Letter	Pecked
426	Q-New	200	Letter	Pecked
426	Q-New	200	Letter	Pecked

Appendix VI. Graffiti Data from Tumamoc Hill				
Feature ID	Ferg ID	Element Code	Element name	Primary Technique
426	Q-New	200	Letter	Incised
426	Q-New	200	Letter	Incised
426	Q-New	202	Letter and number	Incised
429	Q-New	200	Letter	Scratched
429	Q-New	200	Letter	Scratched
429	Q-New	201	Number	Scratched
429	Q-New	201	Number	Blank
429	Q-New	290	Modern indeterminate	Scratched
430	Q-New	200	Letter	Scratched
430	Q-New	201	Number	Scratched
433	Q-New	200	Letter	Scratched
440	Q-New	200	Letter	Pecked
449	Q-New	200	Letter	Pecked
449	Q-New	200	Letter	Scratched
450	Q-New	200	Letter	Pecked
451	Q-New	200	Letter	Abraded
451	Q-New	200	Letter	Abraded
458	Q-New	202	Letter and number	Pecked
459	Q-11, Q-12, Q-13, Map 12	200	Letter	Scratched
460	Q-New	201	Number	Pecked
465	Q-New	200	Letter	Scratched
467	S-New	200	Letter	Incised
467	S-New	200	Letter	Pecked
467	S-New	200	Letter	Scratched
467	S-New	200	Letter	Incised
468	IS-10, Master Topo	200	Letter	Pecked
468	IS-10, Master Topo	200	Letter	Scratched
469	IS-10-New-Near	250	Modern other	Scratched
469	IS-10-New-Near	250	Modern other	Scratched
469	IS-10-New-Near	290	Modern indeterminate	Scratched
471	Q-New	200	Letter	Pecked
473	S-New	200	Letter	Incised
473	S-New	202	Letter and number	Incised
506	S-New	202	Letter and number	Scratched
514	S-New	250	Modern other	Abraded
518	P-New	202	Letter and number	Pecked
691	R-New-Near	202	Letter and number	Scratched
692	R-New-Near	200	Letter	Incised
694	Q-25, Map 12	200	Letter	Scratched
694	Q-25, Map 12	200	Letter	Scratched
694	Q-25, Map 12	200	Letter	Scratched

Feature ID	Ferg ID	Element Code	Element name	Primary Technique
		Appendix VI. Graffiti Data from Tumamoc Hill		
694	Q-25, Map 12	200	Letter	Pecked
694	Q-25, Map 12	200	Letter	Incised
694	Q-25, Map 12	200	Letter	Scratched
694	Q-25, Map 12	250	Modern other	Scratched
694	Q-25, Map 12	250	Modern other	Scratched
695	Q-1, Q-2, Map 12	200	Letter	Scratched
802	P-New	200	Letter	Abraded
802	P-New	200	Letter	Abraded
803	P-New	200	Letter	Scratched
804	IS-8, Master Topo	290	Modern indeterminate	Scratched
805	IS-10-New-Near	200	Letter	Incised
805	IS-10-New-Near	250	Modern other	Incised
2379	N-New	202	Letter and number	Incised
2379	N-New	202	Letter and number	Scratched
2380	N-New, Map 10	200	Letter	Scratched
2380	N-New, Map 10	250	Modern other	Scratched
2380	N-New, Map 10	250	Modern other	Scratched
2381	N-New	201	Number	Scratched
2383	N-New	200	Letter	Scratched
2383	N-New	200	Letter	Scratched
2383	N-New	200	Letter	Scratched
2383	N-New	250	Modern other	Abraded
2384	N-New	202	Letter and number	Scratched
2384	N-New	202	Letter and number	Scratched
2384	N-New	202	Letter and number	Scratched
2385	N-New	200	Letter	Scratched
2385	N-New	200	Letter	Scratched
2386	N-New	200	Letter	Scratched
2386	N-New	200	Letter	Scratched
2387	N-New	200	Letter	Scratched
2388	N-New	202	Letter and number	Scratched
2925	B-12, Map 2	250	Modern other	Scratched
2930	B-17, Map 2	200	Letter	Scratched
2933	C-3, Map 3	200	Letter	Scratched
2933	C-3, Map 3	200	Letter	Scratched
2941	D-6, Map 4	200	Letter	Other
2943	D-8, Map 4	290	Modern indeterminate	Scratched
2943	D-8, Map 4	290	Modern indeterminate	Scratched
2944	D-9, Map 4	200	Letter	Scratched
2944	D-9, Map 4	200	Letter	Scratched
2944	D-9, Map 4	250	Modern other	Scratched

	Appendix VI. Graffiti Data from Tumamoc Hill			
Feature ID	Ferg ID	Element Code	Element name	Primary Technique
2944	D-9, Map 4	250	Modern other	Scratched
2945	D-10, Map 4	250	Modern other	Scratched
2945	D-10, Map 4	250	Modern other	Scratched
2945	D-10, Map 4	250	Modern other	Scratched
2957	D-22, Map 4, Scratched Historic	290	Modern indeterminate	Scratched
2957	D-22, Map 4, Scratched Historic	290	Modern indeterminate	Scratched
2957	D-22, Map 4, Scratched Historic	290	Modern indeterminate	Scratched
2961	E-4, Map 5	200	Letter	Scratched
2961	E-4, Map 5	202	Letter and number	Scratched
2962	E-5, Map 5	201	Number	Scratched
2962	E-5, Map 5	250	Modern other	Scratched
2966	E-9, Map 5	200	Letter	Scratched
2966	E-9, Map 5	250	Modern other	Scratched
2970	E-13, Map 5	202	Letter and number	Scratched
2975	E-18, Map 5	250	Modern other	Scratched
2979	E-22, Map 5	250	Modern other	Scratched
2983	F-1, Map 6	250	Modern other	Scratched
3001	J-3, Map 8	200	Letter	Abraded
3001	J-3, Map 8	201	Number	Abraded
3007	J-New	200	Letter	Abraded
3008	J-New	200	Letter	Abraded
3009	J-New	250	Modern other	Scratched
3009	J-New	250	Modern other	Scratched
3009	J-New	250	Modern other	Scratched
3009	J-New	290	Modern indeterminate	Scratched
3011	J-New	200	Letter	Abraded
3014	F-New	200	Letter	Pecked
3014	F-New	250	Modern other	Scratched
3015	F-New	200	Letter	Scratched
3017	E-New	200	Letter	Scratched
3017	E-New	200	Letter	Scratched
3017	E-New	250	Modern other	Scratched
3017	E-New	250	Modern other	Scratched
3017	E-New	290	Modern indeterminate	Scratched
3018	E-New	200	Letter	Scratched
3020	E-New	200	Letter	Pecked
3020	E-New	200	Letter	Pecked
3020	E-New	200	Letter	Pecked
3020	E-New	200	Letter	Pecked
3020	E-New	200	Letter	Scratched
3023	E-New	250	Modern other	Scratched

Feature ID	Ferg ID	Element Code	Element name	Primary Technique
3027	D-New	250	Modern other	Scratched
3243	D-New	202	Letter and number	Scratched
3243	D-New	250	Modern other	Scratched
3243	D-New	250	Modern other	Scratched
3244	D-New	200	Letter	Scratched
3250	IS-13	200	Letter	Scratched
3250	IS-13	200	Letter	Scratched
3250	IS-13	200	Letter	Scratched
3250	IS-13	200	Letter	Scratched
3250	IS-13	202	Letter and number	Scratched
3250	IS-13	202	Letter and number	Scratched
3250	IS-13	202	Letter and number	Other
3250	IS-13	250	Modern other	Scratched
3250	IS-13	290	Modern indeterminate	Scratched
3256	A-New	250	Modern other	Scratched
3256	A-New	290	Modern indeterminate	Scratched
3256	A-New	290	Modern indeterminate	Scratched
3258	A-New	202	Letter and number	Scratched
3258	A-New	202	Letter and number	Scratched
3259	A-New	202	Letter and number	Scratched
3259	A-New	202	Letter and number	Scratched
3263	C-New	200	Letter	Pecked
3265	C-New	202	Letter and number	Scratched
3266	K-New	200	Letter	Scratched
3267	K-New	200	Letter	Scratched
3267	K-New	290	Modern indeterminate	Scratched
3267	K-New	290	Modern indeterminate	Scratched
3267	K-New	290	Modern indeterminate	Scratched
3269	KK-New	202	Letter and number	Scratched
3294	K-25, Map 9	200	Letter	Scratched
3294	K-25, Map 9	200	Letter	Scratched
3295	K-Historic, Map 9	250	Modern other	Pecked
3301	KK-New	202	Letter and number	Scratched
3302	KK-New	202	Letter and number	Scratched
3304	KK-New	200	Letter	Pecked
3311	KK-New	202	Letter and number	Scratched
3313	KK-New	200	Letter	Scratched
3317	KK-New	200	Letter	Scratched
3318	KK-New	200	Letter	Scratched
3319	KK-New	200	Letter	Scratched
3319	KK-New	202	Letter and number	Scratched

Appendix VI. Graffiti Data from Tumamoc Hill

Appendix VI. Graffiti Data from Tumamoc Hill				
Feature ID	Ferg ID	Element Code	Element name	Primary Technique
3319	KK-New	290	Modern indeterminate	Scratched
3321	N-5, Map 10	200	Letter	Scratched
3321	N-5, Map 10	290	Modern indeterminate	Scratched
3326	KK-New	200	Letter	Scratched
3328	R-New-Near	200	Letter	Scratched
3329	R-New-Near	250	Modern other	Scratched
3333	Q-9, Q-10, Map 12	200	Letter	Scratched
3334	T-New	202	Letter and number	Incised
3335	T-2, Map 15	200	Letter	Scratched
3335	T-2, Map 15	200	Letter	Scratched
3335	T-2, Map 15	200	Letter	Scratched
3335	T-2, Map 15	201	Number	Scratched
3335	T-2, Map 15	202	Letter and number	Scratched
3335	T-2, Map 15	202	Letter and number	Scratched
3335	T-2, Map 15	202	Letter and number	Scratched
3335	T-2, Map 15	202	Letter and number	Scratched
3335	T-2, Map 15	202	Letter and number	Scratched
3335	T-2, Map 15	250	Modern other	Scratched
3335	T-2, Map 15	250	Modern other	Pecked
3336	T-New	202	Letter and number	Scratched
3338	T-New	201	Number	Scratched
3338	T-New	250	Modern other	Scratched
3342	N-New-Near	200	Letter	Scratched
3342	N-New-Near	200	Letter	Scratched
3342	N-New-Near	200	Letter	Incised
3342	N-New-Near	200	Letter	Scratched
3342	N-New-Near	200	Letter	Scratched
3342	N-New-Near	200	Letter	Scratched
3342	N-New-Near	200	Letter	Scratched
3342	N-New-Near	200	Letter	Scratched
3342	N-New-Near	200	Letter	Scratched
3342	N-New-Near	200	Letter	Scratched
3342	N-New-Near	202	Letter and number	Scratched
3342	N-New-Near	202	Letter and number	Scratched
3342	N-New-Near	202	Letter and number	Scratched
3342	N-New-Near	202	Letter and number	Scratched
3342	N-New-Near	202	Letter and number	Scratched
3342	N-New-Near	202	Letter and number	Scratched
3342	N-New-Near	202	Letter and number	Scratched
3342	N-New-Near	202	Letter and number	Scratched

Feature ID	Ferg ID	Element Code	Element name	Primary Technique
3342	N-New-Near	202	Letter and number	Scratched
3342	N-New-Near	202	Letter and number	Scratched
3342	N-New-Near	202	Letter and number	Scratched
3343	T-New	202	Letter and number	Scratched
3357	U-8, Map 16	200	Letter	Scratched
3359	U-New	200	Letter	Scratched
3359	U-New	250	Modern other	Scratched
3360	U-New	202	Letter and number	Incised
4321	IS-10-New-Near	202	Letter and number	Other
4322	V-1, Map 17	200	Letter	Scratched
4322	V-1, Map 17	200	Letter	Scratched
4323	V-2, Map 17	200	Letter	Scratched
4323	V-2, Map 17	202	Letter and number	Scratched
4323	V-2, Map 17	202	Letter and number	Scratched
4326	V-New	200	Letter	Scratched
4326	V-New	201	Number	Scratched
4326	V-New	202	Letter and number	Scratched
4327	V-New	200	Letter	Scratched
4327	V-New	202	Letter and number	Scratched
4328	V-New	200	Letter	Scratched
4329	V-New	200	Letter	Scratched
4330	V-New	200	Letter	Scratched
4331	V-New	200	Letter	Scratched
4331	V-New	200	Letter	Scratched
4331	V-New	200	Letter	Scratched
4331	V-New	250	Modern other	Scratched
4332	V-New	200	Letter	Scratched
4333	V-New	200	Letter	Scratched
4334	V-New	290	Modern indeterminate	Scratched
4334	V-New	290	Modern indeterminate	Scratched
4335	V-New	200	Letter	Scratched
4336	V-New	200	Letter	Scratched
4336	V-New	200	Letter	Scratched
4337	V-New	202	Letter and number	Incised
4338	R-New-Near	202	Letter and number	Scratched
4338	R-New-Near	290	Modern indeterminate	Scratched
4341	L-Near, IS-3, Master Topo Map	250	Modern other	Scratched
4341	L-Near, IS-3, Master Topo Map	250	Modern other	Scratched
4348	S-New	200	Letter	Scratched
4350	S-New	290	Modern indeterminate	Incised
4385	U-New-Near	200	Letter	Scratched

Appendix VI. Graffiti Data from Tumamoc Hill				
Feature ID	Ferg ID	Element Code	Element name	Primary Technique
4385	U-New-Near	202	Letter and number	Scratched
4386	IS-10-New_Near	200	Letter	Pecked
4386	IS-10-New_Near	200	Letter	Scratched
4394	Q-New	202	Letter and number	Incised
4394	Q-New	202	Letter and number	Incised
4395	Q-New	200	Letter	Scratched
4400	R-New	200	Letter	Scratched
4400	R-New	290	Modern indeterminate	Scratched
4401	R-New	290	Modern indeterminate	Scratched
4402	R-New	200	Letter	Scratched
4403	R-New	200	Letter	Abraded
4405	R-New	200	Letter	Scratched
4405	R-New	202	Letter and number	Scratched
4405	R-New	202	Letter and number	Scratched
4405	R-New	202	Letter and number	Scratched
4406	R-New	202	Letter and number	Scratched
4407	R-New	200	Letter	Scratched
4407	R-New	200	Letter	Scratched
4407	R-New	250	Modern other	Scratched
4407	R-New	290	Modern indeterminate	Scratched
4409	R-New	200	Letter	Scratched
4409	R-New	200	Letter	Scratched
4409	R-New	202	Letter and number	Scratched
4409	R-New	202	Letter and number	Scratched
4409	R-New	290	Modern indeterminate	Scratched
4409	R-New	290	Modern indeterminate	Scratched
4410	R-New	200	Letter	Abraded
4410	R-New	200	Letter	Scratched
4410	R-New	200	Letter	Abraded
4410	R-New	200	Letter	Abraded
4410	R-New	200	Letter	Abraded
4410	R-New	201	Number	Scratched
4410	R-New	201	Number	Scratched
4410	R-New	202	Letter and number	Scratched
4411	R-New	202	Letter and number	Scratched
4411	R-New	202	Letter and number	Scratched
4412	R-New	200	Letter	Incised
4412	R-New	200	Letter	Incised
4412	R-New	202	Letter and number	Scratched
4412	R-New	202	Letter and number	Scratched
4412	R-New	202	Letter and number	Scratched

		Appendix VI. Graffiti Data from Tumamoc Hill		
Feature ID	Ferg ID	Element Code	Element name	Primary Technique
4413	R-New	200	Letter	Abraded
4413	R-New	202	Letter and number	Scratched
4414	R-New	202	Letter and number	Scratched
4414	R-New	202	Letter and number	Scratched
4414	R-New	250	Modern other	Scratched
4414	R-New	290	Modern indeterminate	Scratched
4415	R-New	202	Letter and number	Scratched
4416	R-New	200	Letter	Scratched
4416	R-New	290	Modern indeterminate	Pecked
4417	R-New	202	Letter and number	Scratched
4418	R-New	202	Letter and number	Scratched
4419	R-New	200	Letter	Scratched
4424	N-New	200	Letter	Scratched
4424	N-New	200	Letter	Scratched
4424	N-New	250	Modern other	Scratched
4424	N-New	250	Modern other	Scratched
4424	N-New	250	Modern other	Scratched
4424	N-New	250	Modern other	Scratched
4424	N-New	250	Modern other	Scratched
4424	N-New	250	Modern other	Scratched
4426	N-New	250	Modern other	Scratched
4428	N-New	200	Letter	Scratched
4433	Q-New	200	Letter	Incised
4433	Q-New	200	Letter	Incised
4434	Q-New	200	Letter	Pecked
4434	Q-New	200	Letter	Scratched
4434	Q-New	200	Letter	Scratched
4434	Q-New	202	Letter and number	Scratched
4434	Q-New	250	Modern other	Scratched
4435	Q-New	201	Number	Scratched
4435	Q-New	201	Number	Scratched
4436	Q-New	200	Letter	Pecked
4436	Q-New	200	Letter	Pecked
4436	Q-New	200	Letter	Pecked
4440	Q-New	200	Letter	Scratched
4440	Q-New	201	Number	Abraded
4441	Q-New	200	Letter	Scratched
4442	Q-New	250	Modern other	Scratched
4442	Q-New	250	Modern other	Scratched
4443	Q-New	201	Number	Incised
4446	Q-New	200	Letter	Incised

Appendix VI. Graffiti Data from Tumamoc Hill

Feature ID	Ferg ID	Element Code	Element name	Primary Technique
4446	Q-New	200	Letter	Other
4452	U-New	202	Letter and number	Scratched
4453	U-New	202	Letter and number	Scratched
4453	U-New	202	Letter and number	Scratched
4453	U-New	250	Modern other	Scratched
4454	U-New	202	Letter and number	Scratched
4455	U-New	250	Modern other	Scratched
4455	U-New	250	Modern other	Scratched
4456	U-New	200	Letter	Scratched
4456	U-New	202	Letter and number	Scratched
4457	U-New	200	Letter	Scratched
4460	U-New	200	Letter	Scratched
4462	T-New	200	Letter	Pecked
4463	T-New	202	Letter and number	Pecked
4464	T-New	200	Letter	Scratched
4464	T-New	200	Letter	Scratched
4465	T-New	200	Letter	Scratched
4466	T-New	202	Letter and number	Pecked
4468	T-New	200	Letter	Abraded
4468	T-New	200	Letter	Scratched
4468	T-New	201	Number	Pecked
4468	T-New	250	Modern other	Scratched
4469	T-New	200	Letter	Pecked
4470	V-New	200	Letter	Scratched
4471	T-New	200	Letter	Scratched
4471	T-New	200	Letter	Scratched
4471	T-New	200	Letter	Scratched
4471	T-New	200	Letter	Scratched
4471	T-New	250	Modern other	Scratched
4471	T-New	250	Modern other	Scratched
4473	So. Slope-New	200	Letter	Pecked
4476	So. Slope-New	200	Letter	Scratched
4477	So. Slope-New	200	Letter	Pecked
4480	So. Slope-New	200	Letter	Pecked
4481	So. Slope-New	200	Letter	Scratched
4483	So. Slope-New	200	Letter	Scratched
4483	So. Slope-New	200	Letter	Scratched
4484	So. Slope-New	200	Letter	Scratched
4488	Q-New	202	Letter and number	Scratched
4489	R-New	202	Letter and number	Scratched

Appendix VII

Datable Graffiti on Tumamoc Hill

Feature ID	Recorded Date	Interpreted Date	Additional Data
		Appendix VII. Datable Graffiti on Tumamoc Hill	
4452	NA [a]	1867-1868	Co.C32 US II
189	April 14, 1880	1880	Jene Harley
2961	Nov 22, 1885	1885	M.L. Sy.E. Sr.A.
4338	1890	1890	Stephen McKenna [b]
458	1891	1891	WD FH
4394	1891	1891	TM
4394	1891	1891	RP
4410	1891	1891	"Georgia Hazel Scott" & "Hugh McAnally" adjacent [c]
4410	1891	1891	"Georgia Hazel Scott" & "Hugh McAnally" adjacent
4412	1891	1891	GHS
4413	1891	1891	Georgia Hazel Scott
4414	1891	1891	Hazel
4414	1891	1891	ZAR
417	1892	1892	RAP?
418	1896	1896	T. Mounier [d]
418	1896	1896	RA Powers [e]
3258	1903	1903	Albert Urbina
518	2 · 1905	1905	JRV; EWW
4415	1905	1905	WBP
426	1906	1906	VHM-OKLA
4414	1906	1906	WTM
126	4' 1910	1910	WAE
126	1911	1911	FK
4435	1913	1913	
4435	1913	1913	
4434	1913	1913	GM AA
189	1913	1913	EW Hobbs Toledo Ohio
3335	1915	1915	JH
4489	1917	1917	Rock H
3342	1918	1918	FM
3342	1919	1919	
2384	1921	1921	GC; CKR
4417	1921	1921	RA
17	23	1923	CGS
17	12-29-23	1923	THS; Gary
24	12/27/23	1923	THS; B. Jackson
3342	12/29/23	1923	BJ
4409	1923	1923	Art McAnally [f]
429	1927	1927	
126	1930	1930	FC
2384	1931	1931	Sam

	Appendix VII. Datable Graffiti on Tumamoc Hill		
Feature ID	Recorded Date	Interpreted Date	Additional Data
4410	1931	1931	My boy friend f.. me here
4411	1932	1932	EA
4412	1935	1935	Wagner
4412	1935	1935	Wagner
3269	12/29/36	1936	LF
3301	12/29/36	1936	Geo Dudley
418	38	1938	BJS
4466	38	1938	EM
417	Sep 5 1939	1939	Second World War Starts
423	1939	1939	L Lamberton
3342	1940	1940	RA?
130	194x	1940	
3319	1941	1941	RALP
4409	1941	1941	Filberto Pintor [g]
691	1941	1941	WM
3335	4-5-42	1942	
429	1944	1944	
4440	1945	1945	
4443	1945	1945	
506	1945	1945	AB
189	1949	1949	Skip Bernard ?? Ohio
4456	May 1949	1949	DUKIT CAMA?HO
189	1950	1950	Arnold
17	12-29-51	1951	THS; JR
189	1951	1951	Harold N. Huffman
4453	March 10 1952	1952	Alex C
4385	1952	1952	Alex
3342	1955	1955	Ronnie Hill
3336	1955	1955	Paul
3335	8/16/56	1956	WH
3335	1956	1956	Rob B
3259	1957	1957	Albert Urbina
3259	March 2 1957	1957	
2384	1957	1957	RP
4326	60	1960	CE
16	12/30/61	1961	GR
4323	2/24/61	1961	Fernando Lopez
3001	65	1965	Mendoza
3335	1965	1965	
4468	1965	1965	
4463	65	1965	EU

	Appendix VII. Datable Graffiti on Tumamoc Hill		
Feature ID	Recorded Date	Interpreted Date	Additional Data
23	67	1967	Joan; Lillian
2388	1967	1967	??
3342	1/21/67	1967	FY
3343	1969	1969	ACOST
189	Mar 8, 1970	1970	Harry Silvers Kokomo, Indiana
2381	74	1974	
20	Dec 1977	1977	GH
4326	77	1977	
3335	1978	1978	LEY
3335	78	1978	WH
4489	1981	1981	None
3338	1984	1984	
4337	1984	1984	Pete Slipp
415	89	1989	??
420	89	1989	JK
4488	90	1990	U
3360	2/10/91	1991	Steve
415	92	1992	VHZ
416	92	1992	RCF
473	1992	1992	Matt Wolf
3334	93	1993	RN
3	3-23-96	1996	Frank
4327	Mar 98	1998	Doug
3342	4/30 2000	2000	B
3342	2000	2000	Frank Wood, Jr.
3342	200 [6?]	2000	Jokne
4418	4/30 2000	2000	Frank Wood, Jr.
3342	12/21/00	2000	Bonnie, My Love, Danny
4405	03	2003	ROU NAPO
3265	2/12/04	2004	Frank Wood
3342	2004	2004	I love you Jeffrey
3342	3/4 2005	2005	TD y BT
4321	05	2005	Cholla High
3342	2005	2005	JR?
2970	12/7 2007	2007	Frank Wood
4321	07	2007	Cholla High
4405	07	2007	Amber Alex
4405	07	2007	Alex + Amber KicK [?]
4405	08	2008	WCD DK
4321	08	2008	Cholla High
3258	19xx	??	Frank Wood

Feature ID	Recorded Date	Interpreted Date	Additional Data
3243	x8	??	C
2962	19	??	
3250		??	Not in photo
3250	4	??	A
3250	2	??	Heath
3302	21	??	`
3311	2x	??	PJ AM
2379	Feb 19xx	??	Bob Loves Anqrlogue
423	x7xx	??	
430	19	??	
415	9	??	RCF
415	100	??	G
4406	750 (or 7SJ)	??	
4411	#2	??	R England Fontana
4453	Nov 24 1800	1800 [bogus?]	RH
4454	1879	1879 [bogus?]	Zorro
4323	Feb 09	1909 [bogus?]	RD F [recorded in May 2008]
2379	Apr 1832	1932 [bogus?]	Frank Loves Yvonne
465			Yunt [h]

Appendix VII. Datable Graffiti on Tumamoc Hill

[a.] Company C, 32nd U.S. Infantry, was stationed at Camp Lowell in downtown Tucson from June 1867 until May 1868.

[b.] Stephen McKenna was born on 9 November 1881, the son of Michael McKenna and Manuela Sosa. Thus, he was nine years old when he scratched his name on Tumamoc. Manuela Sosa's father, Jose Sosa, purchased a Sonoran rowhouse on South Main Ave. in 1858 that is now called the Sosa-Carrillo-Fremont House; in 1878 the family sold it to Leopoldo Carrillo (Arizona Daily Star 1907; Castillo n.d.; Cuming, Harry, and Mary Cuming 1996; Tucson Citizen 1907).

[c.] Hugh McAnally was born about 1918; thus, although his name appears to be assciated with Georgia Hazel Scott and the date 1891, it was apparently written at a later date. We could find no additional information about him (Pima County census 1930).

[d.] Thomas A. Mounier was born in Montana in 1881and lived in Tucson as a child. As an adult he lived in Bisbee where he worked as a mechanic in the copper mine. He would have been 10 years old and 15 years old when he wrote his name on Tumamoc (his name is inscribed twice with different dates) (Cochise County census 1930; Tucson City Directory 1897-1898).

[e.] Robert Powers' inscription appears twice, both times in association with Thomas Mounier; his identity is somewhat problematic. A Robert A. Powers appears in the Cochise County directory about the same time as Mounier. Powers was apparently born in California in 1878, thus making him 13 years old and 18 years old when he inscribed his name. In the 1920 and 1930 censuses he is listed as living in Douglas with his wife Clara; he and Mounier were both the sons of Irish immigrants. He and Mounier were apparently friends over a number of years (Cochise County census 1920, 1930; Tucson City Directory 1897-1898).

[f.] Art McAnally was born about 1911 so he was about 13 when he wrote his name on Tumamoc. The family was from Arkansas. In the 1930 census, Art, then 19, is listed as a salesman in an ice cream plant (Pima County census 1930).

[g.] Filberto C. Pintor was the son of Geronimo and Manuela Pintor. In the 1930 census he is listed as being two years old, so he would have been 13 when he wrote his name on the hill. Army records show that he enlisted as a private in 1945 and that he had two years of high school education (Pima County census 1930).

[h.] A John Yunt owned the Arizona Tourist Court at 1749 South. 6th Ave. in 1935 (Tucson City Directory 1935).

Part III
Solar Interactions with Tumamoc Hill Petroglyphs

John Fountain and Janine Hernbrode

Petroglyphs on and near the summit of Tumamoc Hill were examined for solar interactions. Seven separate solar markers were observed. Interactions were observed at equinox and both solstices. Despite having searched, no interactions were found on cross-quarter days, though such interactions have been observed elsewhere in the Tucson Mountains. Marking equinoxes and solstices may be an effort to show reverence for the sun and aid in setting dates for ceremonies. They also could provide additional data to guide agricultural efforts.

INTRODUCTION

In the course of the Arizona Archaeological and Historical Society's project to re-survey the petroglyphs on Tumamoc Hill, the second author noticed an unusual play of light over one glyph on the southeast corner of the summit. She wondered if this phenomenon was unique or repeated elsewhere on the site. Since the first author had investigated solar interactions at a several other sites, he was invited to join the effort to search for solar interactions on the hill.

SOLAR MARKERS

In 1976, Ken Hedges (1986) noticed that at winter solstice, a thin wedge of light passed through the head of an anthropomorphic pictograph in a cave near La Rumarosa, Baja California. This and the announcement by Anna Sofaer (1979) of daggers of light interacting with spiral petroglyphs at Fajada Butte in Chaco Canyon on equinox and the solstices spurred many rock art researchers to search for similar interactions elsewhere. These efforts proved surprisingly successful. Fountain (2004) summarized these efforts. Not only were interactions found on the quarter days of equinox and solstices, many were also found at cross-quarter days: those days that are halfway in time between equinoxes and solstices. These distinctive interactions are called *indirect solar markers* and have been found throughout the Southwestern United States. While solar markers are found at major rock art sites, they may also be found in isolation. They may be found on canyon walls and in open terrain. Some are easily observed by many, while others are found in tight quarters where only a couple of observers may be accommodated. *Direct solar markers* are structures, rock art, or other man-made indicators from which the rising or setting of the sun may be seen at a distinctive feature on the horizon on important seasonal days.

Solar markers may be formed by the shadow of a nearby stone or a rock aperture creating a patch of light or shadow. These are called *gnomon* interactions. They may also occur by light and shadow formed by grazing illumination that we call *self-shadowing*. The latter class is difficult to predict since they depend critically on small undulations of the rock on which the petroglyph is made.

It has been suggested (Williamson 1984), that solar markers were needed to determine planting and harvest times. While calendar dates may have provided a useful guide, farmers would have probably relied more heavily on local indicators such as recent rainfall, budding of native plants, and insect activity. Calendars are also important for religious, social and political purposes. Since some sites have far more solar markers on a given date than are needed for identifying a particular calendar date (e.g. Hardscrabble Wash, see Fountain 1998), Fountain believes it more likely that they were primarily created to commemorate or revere the sun. It is well documented (McCluskey 1977), that direct horizon observation of the sun was widely practiced throughout the American Southwest.

TUMAMOC HILL INTERACTIONS

Several years ago avocational archaeologist Cherie Freeman described to Fountain some interesting light interactions with a petroglyph on the southeast corner of the summit of Tumamoc Hill. This along with Hernbrode's observation gave us encouragement that a search for other interactions might prove productive. We examined the petroglyphs on and near the summit of Tumamoc Hill to identify those with possible interactions. Fountain prepared graphs of altitude and azimuth of the sun on quarter and cross-quarter days. A clinometer and compass then allowed us to predict times for possible interactions and to exclude many glyphs. Because of irregularities in the rock surfaces, self-shadowing interactions are particularly difficult to predict accurately. During observations we moved around the area to look for suggestive sunlight patterns

that may lead to interactions. While sunlight patterns appeared on glyphs as predicted, only about half yielded distinctive interactions.

Between March 2007 and June 2008 we visited the site on quarter days, cross-quarter days, and control days to observe and photograph possible interactions. While the duration of interactions varied from very brief to an hour, we found that taking a picture once a minute was usually satisfactory. We took care to minimize shadows caused by nearby vegetation. We also visited the site on control dates—days well separated from quarter and cross-quarter days. No distinctive interactions were found with one important exception discussed below. Most of the rocks with candidate petroglyphs were so firmly embedded in the soil that it is unlikely that they would have shifted by seismic or human activity. One stone that was part of a pithouse wall had a faint petroglyph, and it underwent a solar interaction of sorts. It was rejected both because the solar interaction was noticeably off and because it could have easily been moved.

Interestingly most potential solar markers were found in a cluster of petroglyphs roughly 5 by 10 m on the southeast corner of the summit, which included the locations where Freeman and Hernbrode had made their observations. All of the interactions occurred between sunrise and noon. We found no interactions beginning after local noon. Interactions were found at both solstices and equinox. No interactions were found on cross-quarter days. Descriptions of the most convincing interactions follow.

Winter Solstice

Three significant interactions were observed at winter solstice. The first occurred at first light of sunrise. The shadow of an adjacent, pointed rock fell in a natural hole in a rock around which a circular, rayed glyph had been made (Figure III.1). The edges of the shadow-casting rock had been abraded or weathered. It

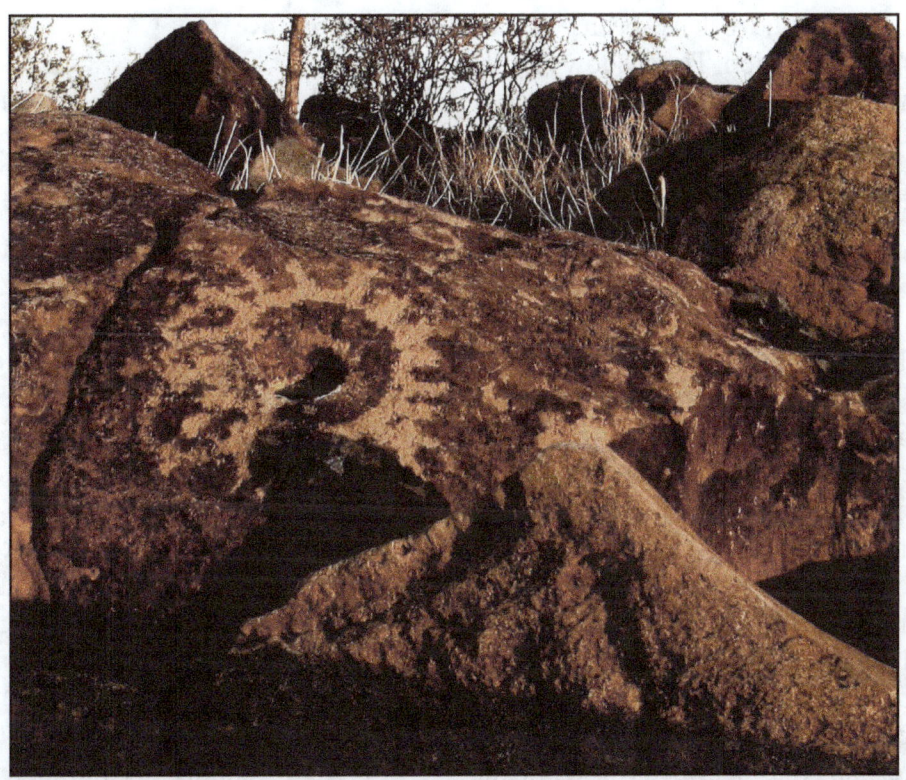

Figure III.1. At sunrise a shadow appears extending downward from a glyph surrounding a natural hole in the rock (TH-F436).

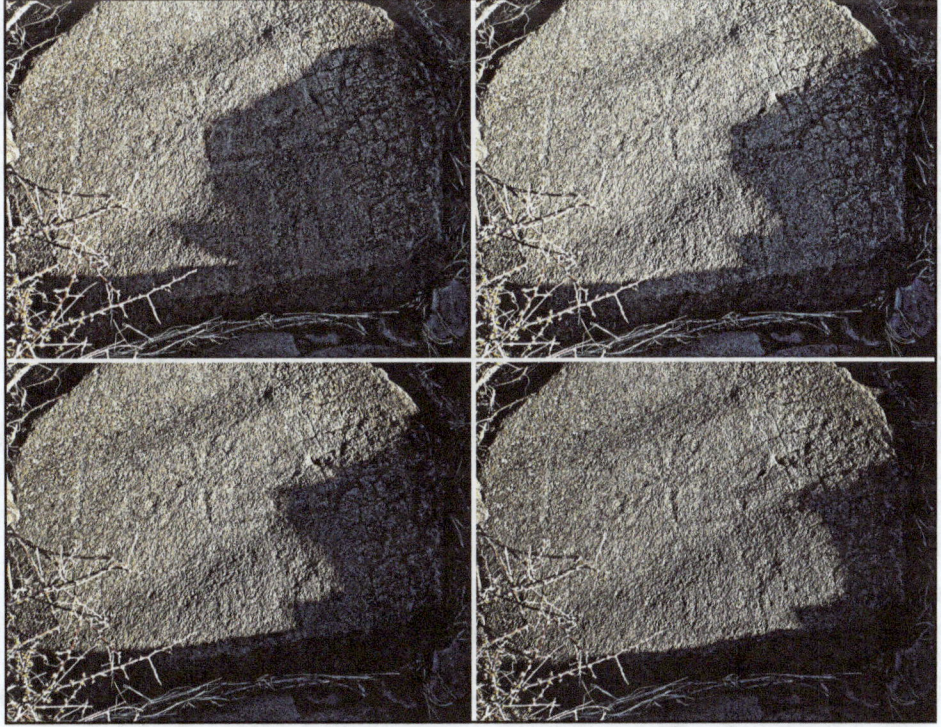

Figure III.2. Shadow pointers cross hand, head, and elbow of a horizontal anthropomorphic glyph at winter solstice. The fainter, linear shadows are from vegetation (TH-F453).

is uncertain whether the rock had been modified to produce the interaction. The shadow rapidly moved down the rock as the sun rose.

A horizontal anthropomorphic glyph is situated near the center of a cluster of glyphs that showed interactions. A corner of shadow moved across the center of an uplifted hand. The shadow then moved to the body, conforming to the shape of the body. It is not unreasonable to suppose that the shadow line suggested the shape of the anthropomorphic figure to the glyph maker. The shadow moved on to point to the elbow of the other arm before moving off the rock (Figure III.2).

On the west face of an upright rock there is a three-ring concentric circle glyph, shown in Figure III.3. It interacted near local noon. Indeed, it underwent an interesting interaction at about this time on every day that we observed, including days well away from quarter and cross-quarter days. While the interactions were of a similar character, they differed in detail throughout the year. The head, hand, and foot of an anthropomorphic glyph just to the left of the concentric circles were sometimes highlighted. While an interesting and probably intentional interaction, it cannot be considered a solar marker since it does not specifically mark a seasonal day. Elsewhere interactions that vary little with time have been observed (Fountain 1998).

Equinox

In Figure III.4, a narrow wedge of light appears tangent to the upper part of the inner of two concentric circles. It broadens to fill out the circle before widening to illuminate the entire rock face.

At equinox a line of light extends across the two hands of an anthropomorphic glyph in Figure III.5a. The figure appears to be holding a bow. A line of light was observed to pass through the head at winter solstice.

Summer Solstice

The glyph in Figure III.4 also interacts at summer solstice, but in an entirely different way. As seen in Figure III.6, a thin line first appears at the lower right of the inner circle. It broadens outward until it contacts the outer circle. The point of the light pattern then moves upward and leftward along the circumference of the outer circle before broadening and filling the entire rock. A glyph interacting on two different seasonal days strongly indicates that the glyph was intentionally made to mark those days.

A glyph of three concentric circles with a central dot is shown in Figure III.7. The circles are distorted outward in the upper right. A patch of light appears at this upper right point. The light forms a wedge moving downward until tangent to the circle surrounding the central dot before expanding to illuminate the entire glyph. It is interesting to note that the point of the wedge of light follows a natural crack in the rock.

In addition to the equinox interaction of Figure III.5a, at summer solstice a thin line appears through the crotch of an anthropomorphic glyph (Figure III.5b) before broadening to illuminate the entire glyph. This is yet another instance of interactions with a glyph on multiple significant seasonal days.

OTHER MARKERS

Other suggestive interactions were observed. In Figures III.1 through III.7 we have illustrated those interactions for which there is little doubt that glyphs were intentionally placed to mark seasonal days.

The slopes of Tumamoc Hill also have clusters of rock art, and Hernbrode has identified several glyphs with interaction potential. Fountain's limited search for direct solar markers was not fruitful.

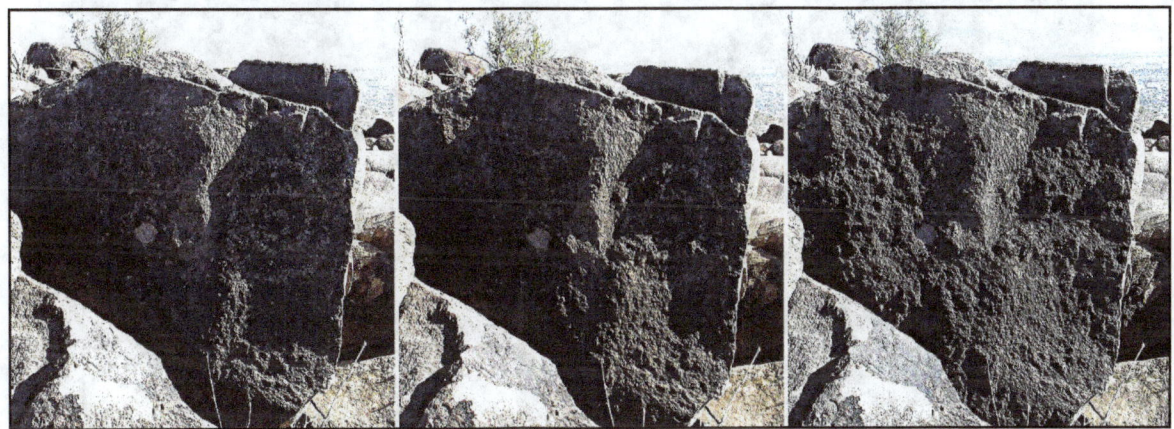

Figure III.3. Interactions with this three-ring concentric circle glyph occur throughout the year. The winter solstice interaction is shown here (TH-F437).

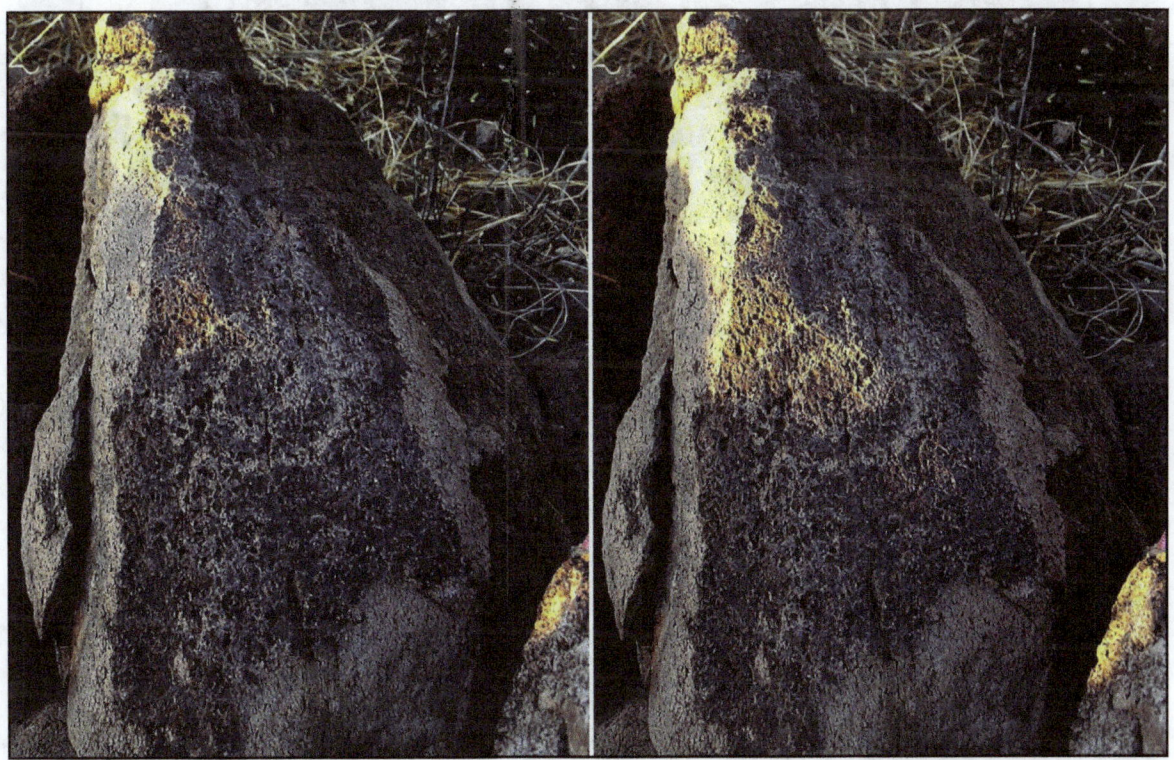

Figure III.4. A wedge of light tangent to the inner of two circles expands to fill that circle at equinox (TH-F455).

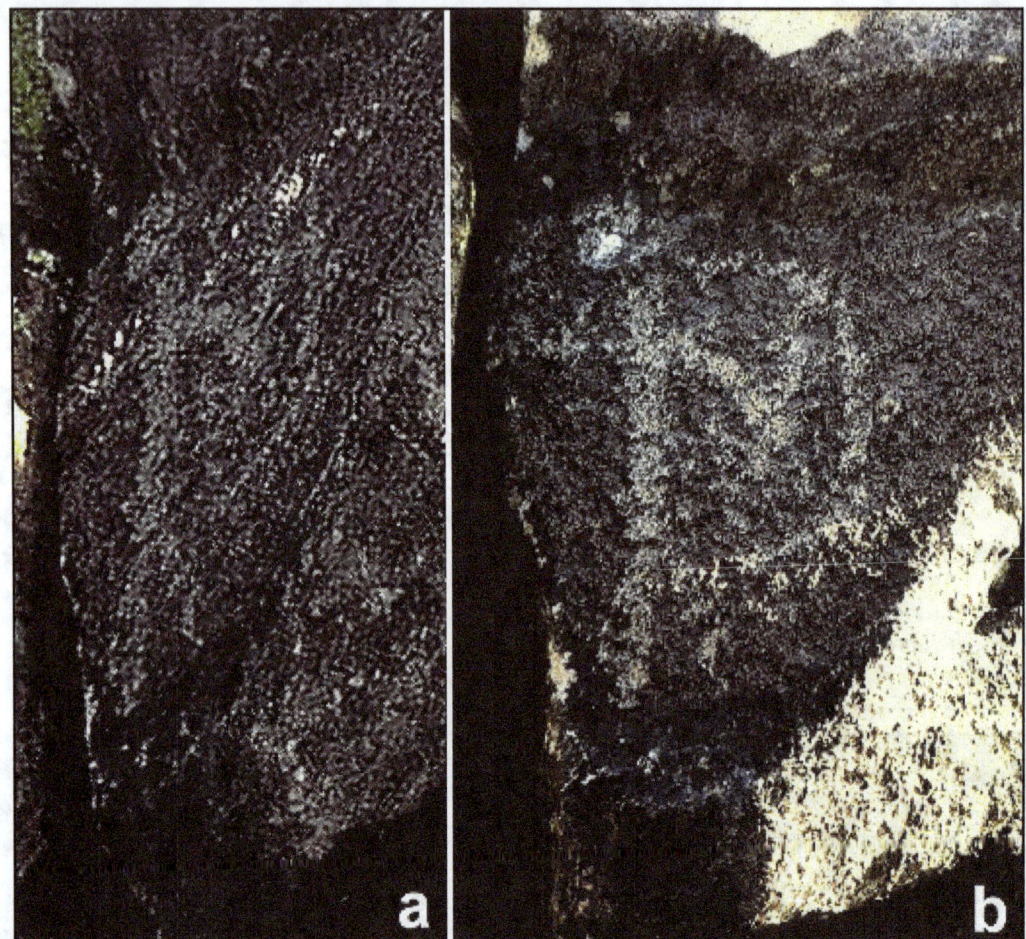

Figure III.5. A line of light extends from one hand of the anthropomorphic glyph to another at equinox (a) (TH-F695). The line of light extends to the crotch at summer solstice (b).

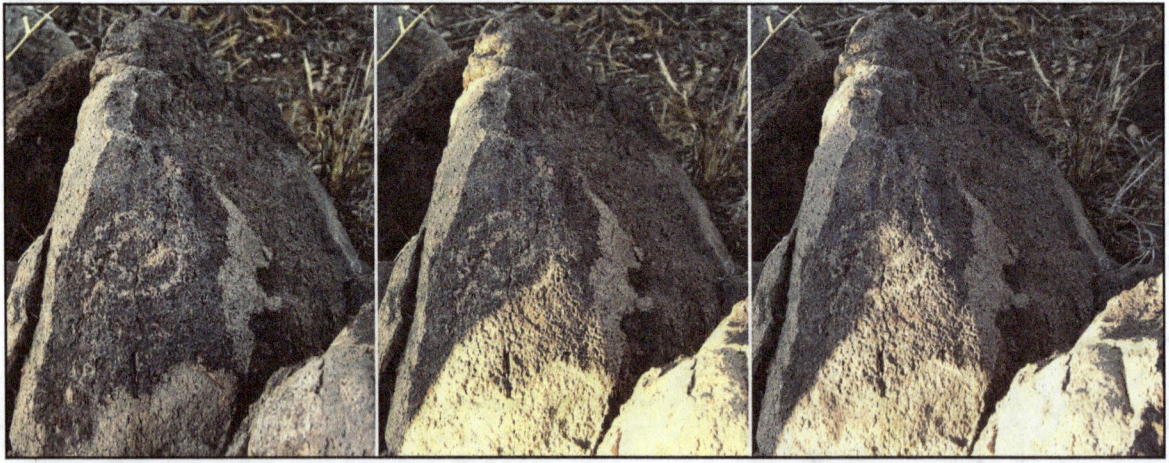

Figure III.6. At summer solstice, the same glyph as in Figure III.4 undergoes a different and more complex interaction (TH-F455).

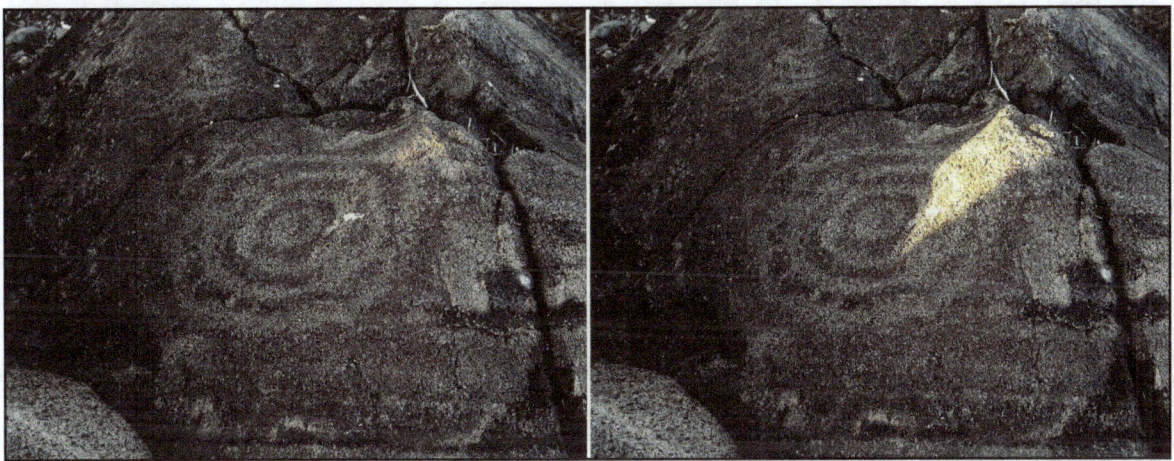

Figure III.7. Light forms at the distorted end of concentric circles and moves along a natural crack to become tangent to the inner circle at summer solstice (TH-F434).

CONCLUSIONS

While an occasional coincidental interaction may be expected, several interactions on more than one seasonal day strongly strengthen the hypothesis that the glyphs were intentionally placed to mark those days. Distinctly different interactions with a glyph on two different seasonal days are also indicative of intentional placement of the glyph as a solar marker. We conclude that the interactions described here were probably the result of petroglyphs intentionally placed to mark seasonal days.

The absence of significant interactions on cross-quarter days at this site (except for the glyph in Figure III.3, which interacts throughout the year) is probably significant. Either the practice of marking these days had not yet been established at the time the glyphs were made or they held significance inappropriate for this site. We have observed cross-quarter day solar markers elsewhere in the Tucson Mountains though the style, quality of execution, and degree of repatination of the petroglyphs in other locations suggest younger ages.

Acknowledgments. We thank Cherie Freeman for information about her original observations and for her participation in observational efforts. The following also participated in the observations: Peter Boyle, Danica Davison, Valerie Davison, Gayle Hartmann, Joy Hernbrode, Robert Hernbrode, Albert Lannon, Kaitlin Meadows, Dwight Riggs, and Donna Tang. Loans of camera equipment from Cynthia McDaniel, Patrice Davison, and Nancy Coleman helped the observations go smoothly.

REFERENCES CITED

Fountain, John

1998　Solar Interactions at Hardscrabble Wash. *Rock Art Papers* 13:127-133, edited by Ken Hedges. San Diego Museum Papers 36.

2004　A Database of Rock Art Solar Markers. In *Current Studies in Archaeoastronomy: Conversations across Time and Space*, edited by John W. Fountain and Rolf M. Sinclair, pp 101-108. Carolina Academic Press, Durham.

Hedges, Ken
  1986   The Sunwatcher of La Rumarosa. *Rock Art Papers* 4:17-23, edited by Ken Hedges. San Diego Museum of Man Papers 21.

McCluskey, Stephen C.
  1977   The Astronomy of the Hopi Indians. *Journal for the History of Astronomy* 8:174-195.

Sofaer, Anna, Volker Zinser, and Rolf M. Sinclair
  1979   A Unique Solar Marking Construct. *Science* 206(4416):283-291.

Williamson, Ray A.
  1984   *Living the Sky*. University of Oklahoma Press, Norman.

www.ingramcontent.com/pod-product-compliance
Lightning Source LLC
Chambersburg PA
CBHW081559220526

45468CB00010B/2691